Cribbage

Boards

1863-1998

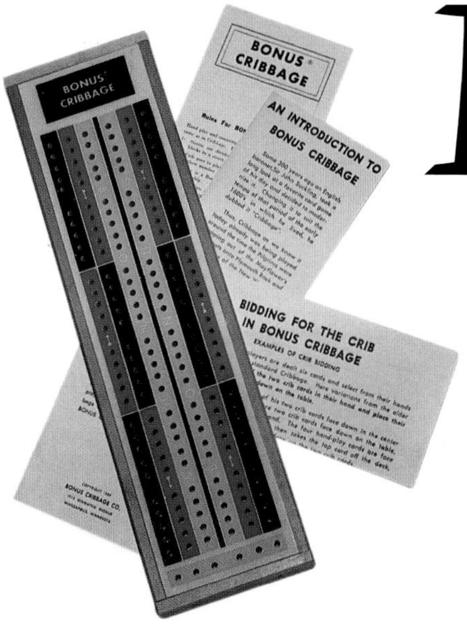

Bette L. Bemis

Schiffer Publishing Ltd

4880 Lower Valley Road, Atglen, PA 19310 USA

Dedication

First of all, I dedicate this book to my husband Fred, who has supported all my efforts in spite of the fact that he doesn't even play cribbage! He has recognized the far-reaching effects of my projects and has spent much time assisting me in my search for answers to the many puzzles that have surfaced. I am deeply indebted to him for all of his assistance.

This book is also dedicated to Thomas F. O' Gara, a member of the Cribbage Board Collectors Society, who has earned the reputation as the Super Collector of cribbage boards. Tom has assiduously pursued the mysteries surrounding boards and their manufacturers, preventing much data from becoming extinct. The world of cribbage board collectors owes a debt of gratitude to his perseverance and the solid evidence that he has developed.

Copyright © 2000 by Bette L. Bemis
Library of Congress Catalog Card Number: 99-64711

All rights reserved. No part of this work may be reproduced or used in any form or by any means—graphic, electronic, or mechanical, including photocopying or information storage and retrieval systems—without written permission from the copyright holder.

"Schiffer," "Schiffer Publishing Ltd. & Design," and the "Design of pen and ink well" are registered trademarks of Schiffer Publishing Ltd.

Book Design by Anne Davidsen
Type set in Zapf Chancery /Souvenir

ISBN: 0-7643-0977-3

Printed in China
1 2 3 4

Author Photo courtesy of *The Westerly Sun*, Westerly, RI

Published by Schiffer Publishing Ltd.
4880 Lower Valley Road
Atglen, PA 19310
Phone: (610) 593-1777; Fax: (610) 593-2002
E-mail: Schifferbk@aol.com
Please visit our web site catalog at
www.schifferbooks.com
or write for a free catalog.
This book may be purchased from the publisher.
Please include $3.95 for shipping.

In Europe, Schiffer books are distributed by
Bushwood Books
6 Marksbury Rd.
Kew Gardens
Surrey TW9 4JF England
Phone: 44 (0)181 392-8585; Fax: 44 (0)181 392-9876
E-mail: Bushwd@aol.com

Please try your bookstore first.

We are interested in hearing from authors
with book ideas on related subjects.

Contents

Chapter III. American Manufacturers and Distributors

Chapter IV. Getting Started Collecting

Resources

Compendia

Glossary of Cribbage Board Terminology   141

Bibliography   143

Acknowledgments

I would like to acknowledge many of the collectors who have taken the time to provide answers to the questions that I have asked in the Cribbage Board Collectors Society newsletters and correspondence. It has amazed me that some of them continue to take pen in hand, knowing that I usually respond by asking even more questions! Jeffrey Renno, David Zipkin, Woody Ward, Al Tenenbaum, Arnold Gordon, Dave Schroeder, Charlie Douthit, Ethel Frost and her late husband David, the late Milton Wasby, Matt Nakaya, the late John Adler, Robert Massicotte, Richard Massicotte, Frank Wurman, Mike Platt, Bernard Reising, John B. MacDonald, Susan Stevens, Ray Lemeir, Frank LaBue, Connie and Woodie Ward, H.J. Macone, Wilson Gartner, Roy Boyles, Joseph Petrus Wergin, DeLynn Colvert, Gerard Caruso of Crisloid, Inc., just to mention a few, deserve special mention for their contributions to the CBCS archives.

A special thanks is given to Paul Ellinwood, John B. MacDonald, Thomas O' Gara, David Schroeder, Frank Wurman, and the Estate of Margaret M. Campbell of Baltimore, Maryland — Michael Campbell for the Estate, all of whom have permitted photos of their boards to be included in this book.

Introduction

In the prolific world of collecting, cribbage boards are a relatively new discovery. Cribbage boards, however, have existed for over 350 years, and hundreds, possibly thousands of variations have been hand crafted or manufactured over the years. In spite of the fact that cribbage boards have been around for that long, very little has been written about them. Documentation about manufacturers and their board styles is rather sketchy, and there are many pieces of the puzzle that will probably never be retrieved.

Until recently, old boards were not in high demand, and they could be bought for next to nothing. Anyone who has been monitoring the antiques and collectibles market over the past few years, however, has noted a gradual rise in the prices of almost anything old, including cribbage boards. A side benefit of these increased values is that people now are less apt to throw their "junk" away. The yard sales take on new meaning as the collector hurries from one site to another, ever in pursuit of that lucky find. Imagine the "high" that I got the day that I found 17 old boards at one sale! They were not in pristine condition, but several of them had not been previously identified, and my archives were really enhanced by the information found on those boards. My cost for the boards? Ten dollars well spent!

Several years ago, I founded a small mail order business for the sale of cribbage novelties. Its goal was to provide a resource for various items related to the game of cribbage and to provide an outlet through which craftsmen could sell their products. That is what happened for a very short period of time. Soon I was receiving letters of inquiry about old cribbage boards that people owned, the inquirers assuming that I was an expert of sorts on the subject ! Needless to say, I wasn't, and the only old board that I owned at the time was one that my grandfather had crafted in England long before I was born.

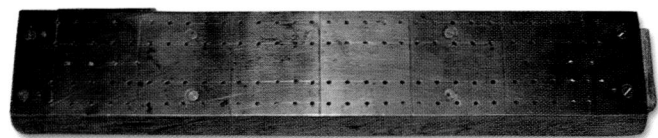

The years passed, and the pile of letters inquiring about old boards grew. I tried to ignore them, but eventually my curiosity got the better of me. My trips to yard sales, flea markets and antique stores took on new meaning as I began to focus on looking for old boards. To my astonishment, many of the ones that I found were quite inexpensive, and I soon had a collection. By handling my *new*, old boards, I soon found myself in a better position

to answer the letters that constantly arrived. My mail order business, in which I carry a variety of boards, also became a resource for me.

Although I had handled many cribbage boards in my mail order business, I had never really *looked* at them — the number of holes, how the holes were arranged in the make-up of the streets, how the sides were constructed, where the peg slot cover was located, and other features too numerous to list at this time. The first time that the differences in these features became apparent, it was like having a light turned on in the brain. I am sure that it is pretty much like that for most collectors in the early stages, no matter what they are collecting. I found myself obsessed with learning more about the boards in my collection, boards that friends owned, ones that I saw in shops, and those about which strangers had written to me. The need to know more has not waned since my collection was started.

Every once in awhile, I will come across someone who has just thrown some boards away, as "they weren't worth anything." My nerves jangle, and I wonder why the conversation couldn't have taken place sooner. What potentially important piece of evidence has just been lost forever? One of my goals in writing this reference book is to help non-collectors understand that we ARE interested in preserving as many cribbage boards as possible. That board which is full of cigarette burns, looks as though it has been beaten with a hammer (probably by a sore loser), has nails for pegs and looks like it is ready for use as kindling, may well be another piece to the puzzle which board collectors are trying to solve. In other words, a board doesn't have to be beautiful, rare, or expensive for the dedicated collector to be interested in preserving it. We'll give you a quarter for it — you'll be 25 cents richer — and we will be excited at our find. I once paid 25 cents for TWO boards in terrible condition, but a twin to one of them, which was manufactured, hasn't surfaced yet.

In my search for historical information about the manufacturing of cribbage boards, many companies that still exist have been contacted. Unfortunately, the responses have provided little information of historical significance. It seems as though the age of the computer, which is certainly an exciting new era, has some negative sides to it. When manufacturers were converting their handwritten or typed data to computers, apparently only the most relevant and current information was saved by most of them. Much of the historical information, which was considered non-essential, was discarded by many companies. That graveyard of information is now the location of rich histories lost forever. This sad discovery has slowed down the process of reconstructing information about cribbage boards, and it will affect historians who are compiling information on a multitude of other collectibles as well. We will have to concentrate on collecting the remaining available data, or it will also be lost. As long as the boards, their boxes and instruction sheets still exist, however, it has been possible to reconstruct much of the history of cribbage boards and their manufactur-ers. Books which focus on specific collectibles will become more and more important to future generations of collectors as less and less data is saved by manufacturers.

When I first began this project, my son Eric suggested that I purchase a new computer (my old one was nearly 10 years old) so that I could get on the Internet and talk

high evaluation so that the profit will be greater. While I personally feel that price guides are a distraction when dealing with new subject matter, they are a necessary inclusion in reference books in order to establish standards. My philosophy about this matter has slowly mellowed, for the increasing values of my boards gives me a greater sense of pride in my collection. When a board is purchased for one or two dollars at a yard sale and I eventually discover that it is worth many times that, then I am anxious to get back on the road to find more.

New collectors should be cautioned that there are many factors which will create a wide range of pricing for any one

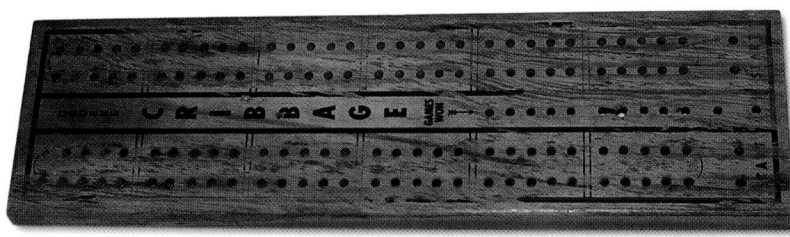

to experts on cribbage boards. Imagine his shock when I informed him that I WAS one of the experts! Much information has been entrusted to me for safekeeping, and all that I write reflects the accumulated knowledge of many devoted collectors.

This book will focus primarily on American manufacturers of cribbage boards, although there are some references to boards manufactured elsewhere. Inlays, ivories, and other hand-crafted boards will receive only cursory attention as well, for there is already enough information on them to fill a second book.

In summary, let me open your eyes to a new and exciting collectible subject. If the information found in this book is interesting enough, you may develop an urge to drag out that old board that you have tucked away, go to a few yard sales so that you can add a few more boards to it, and — voila ! — another collection has been born! At the very least, after reading this you will be a little more informed about a relatively new and exciting field of collecting, for it provides a general overview of data, as well as pointers needed for searching out the unusual find. When asked by someone why I was putting so much effort into writing this book, I replied that there were no reference books in print about cribbage boards. Now there is, thanks to the many people who have generously contributed their bits and pieces of cribbage board information to my archives.

Cribbage Board Values

Naturally, a reference book about cribbage boards must include a guide to pricing. The collector hopes that any prices listed will be on the low end so that new purchases won't cost an arm or a leg. The seller hopes for a

style of cribbage board. One example would be the location where the board is sold. If it is purchased in the area where it was manufactured, there is usually a good supply of the boards selling for a reasonable price. If the boards have traveled with families moving to distant locations, the scarcity of the style in that area will most likely command a higher price. The key, then, is to try to purchase the boards as close to the original source as possible.

Another factor which determines the value of a board is its condition. Naturally, if the board is in excellent condition, it will command a good price. If it was originally boxed, and the box *with* instructions (MBI) are intact, then it will be worth even more. Full of nicks and cigarette burns, it will be turned down by most collectors no matter how little its price tag. Of course, if I happen on the scene and my collection doesn't include that particular style, I will probably purchase it so that I can document its characteristics!

The values listed in this book are based on information that has been received from collectors, over the Internet, in antique stores and flea markets, on cribbage boards that are in good condition and in the box (if one was used for packaging). In some instances, the prices listed reflect the higher prices that have been paid and aren't necessarily a true reflection of the value. Prices have a tendency to fluctuate, so the values listed in this book should be limited to use as a general guideline. Many of the boards listed are still being produced, and their values are listed at CMP (current market price).

In summary, pricing is a variable which depends on several factors. In my opinion, if a person likes a board and can afford the price, negotiate for the lowest price the seller is willing to take, then buy it!

Chapter I:
History of Cribbage and the Board

Sir John Suckling, Inventor of Cribbage

The card game called *CRIBBIDGE* was invented in the early 1600s by an Englishman called Sir John Suckling. Sir John was born in 1609, the son of a wealthy nobleman who was the Secretary of State to King James I. During his early years, Sir John developed a reputation as a poet, gambler, and a lover of women, not necessarily in that order. His skill at cards was undeniable, and he was a very lucky player. Eventually, he invented a new game, which was modeled after an ancient game called *Noddy.* He called it *Cribbidge,* and because he had made up the rules, he was usually the winner. The game soon became the most popular card game in England.

Sir John eventually was forced to flee to France after an unsuccessful attempt to free a friend, the Earl of Strafford, who was imprisoned in the Tower of London. He took very few funds with him and was forced into a life of near poverty. As legend has it, Sir John Suckling, nearly broke and far from his old friends, committed suicide by taking poison in 1642. His legacy, the invention of the game of cribbage, has continued to be popular to this day, for which cribbage board collectors are eternally grateful!

The Game of Cribbage

When Sir John Suckling invented the game of *Cribbidge,* he used a count of 61 points as the "Win." The game itself is played little differently today than when he invented it in the 1630s. It is, however, now more commonly played to 121 points rather than the original 61 points, and all cribbage tournaments played in the United States use 121 points as game win.

Cribbage, by the way, may be the only early game whose inventor is known. Few changes have been made in the way that the game has been played over the years, which is a great tribute to Suckling's skill.

Since this is a reference book about cribbage boards and not a book designed to explain cribbage, I recommend any of the many sources of information that are available about the game itself. Most boards for sale in the marketplace contain simple sets of instruction, as well.

Earlier Games with Similar Characteristics

Game of Hounds and Jackals (Also known as the Game of Fifty Eight Holes or Dogs and Jackals)

The Game of Hounds and Jackals apparently was popular among the early Egyptians, for the contents of several tombs, including one belonging to

Amenemhet IV (1801-1792 BC) have included a board identified as such.

The game board consisted of a wooden box and had a palm tree design carved in the top, which was usually ivory. Although the tops varied somewhat on the various boards that have been uncovered, most of them con-

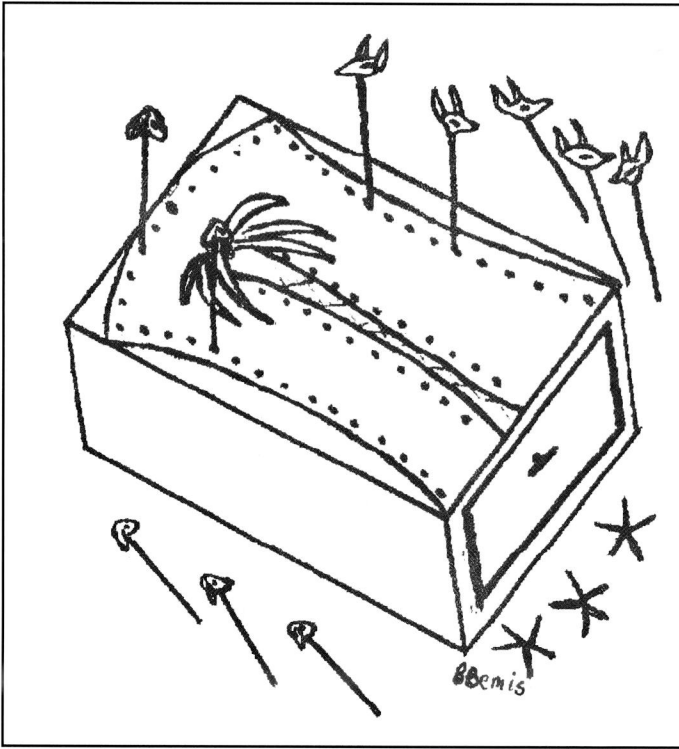

tained fifty-eight holes grouped in sets of five. There were 29 holes located around the outer edge of the box for each player, with the last 10 holes going up the side of the palm tree. The game was played with long pegs which fit into the holes. Some pegs were headed with carvings of white dogs which bear a resemblance to the god Anubis, while others had carvings of black jackals at the top. Each player had five pegs, and the object of the game was for a player to get the pegs into his last five game holes before his opponent. Included with the boards were convex disks or five-pointed stars, which bear a strong resemblance to the jacks used in game play today. It is presumed that these were used as dice and that the game was played for gambling purposes. The cribbage board also contains sets of five holes and uses pegs for scoring, leading experts to believe that Sir John Suckling had access to information about this ancient game when inventing Cribbidge and its board.

Samples of Hounds and Jackals game boards can be found at the Metropolitan Museum of Art in New York and in the Louvre Museum in Paris. The game was also played in the movie *The Ten Commandments*, making it fairly easy to view the game pieces.

Noddy

Noddy is an early game which probably was invented in England sometime around the sixteenth century. The players each received 3 cards, and the next card was turned up. If it was a Jack, then the dealer received 2 points for "Knave Noddy." In early cribbage, if the cut card was a Jack, it was also referred to as "Knave Noddy," providing further reinforcement that the game of cribbage evolved from *Noddy*. Cards were played to a count of 31, or as near as the players could come to it. After the cards were played out, the hands were counted, with the turn-up card being used as the fourth card for the count in each player's hand. Two of a kind, three of a kind and four of a kind as well as certain individual cards were used for the final count of the hands. A book written in 1688 by Randall Holmes called *Academy of Armory* is one of the few sources of information on the game.

Information which is available about Noddy does not indicate that a board was used in scoring, but the characteristics of the game are very similar to the game of Cribbidge. It is quite possible that Sir John Suckling combined the use of the board from the ancient game of Dogs and Jackals with the basic rules of Noddy in order to create his new game.

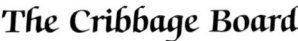

The Cribbage Board

The question arises as to why so many cribbage boards are designed with 60 holes, or 2 streets of 30 holes each, per player. Since the game was played for a long time with the win being at 61 points, there was no need for boards to have 120 holes. In fact, there is no documentation of a 120 hole board prior to the 20th century, so we must conclude that the use of 121 points for the Win came into popular practice sometime in the 20th century. The use of 2 streets with 30 holes each, remains popular to this day among manufacturers and crafters of cribbage boards. When playing on a board with 60 holes per player, the players merely circle their streets twice, thus accomplishing a sweep of 120 holes. As a result of this method of play, the board has become commonly known as a "two player, twice around" (2P,T.A.) board.

The earliest known board — the one used by Sir John Suckling — supposedly looked like a ship's course char-

ter (traverse board). Apparently it didn't take inventive minds long to replace the style by creating a true Cribbidge board, for early reports of the game indicate that they existed in forms not unlike the twice around boards that are still in use today.

The cribbage board is not actually a necessary component for the game of cribbage. Cribbage scoring can be achieved on paper or by using other sorts of markers such as poker chips, match sticks, or nails. Most of the alternatives, however, can make for a rather messy field, so use of the board is preferred. One must not forget this bit of information, however, for it is possible to become stranded in a remote setting where only a deck of cards

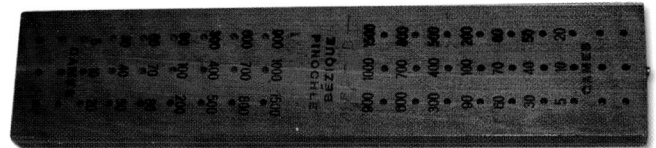

and a bucket of nails are available. The game CAN go on in spite of the lack of a cribbage board!

Cribbage boards have been used for scoring in games other than cribbage. Many old books on card games make reference to cribbage boards being used for scoring games such as Bezique, Whist, Pinochle, Gin Rummy, and Dominoes. In fact, some of the old cribbage boards had a set of "wheels" containing 10 holes, or multiples, on the bottom or top. Other cribbage boards have been found which have a series of holes on the bottom, and are marked *Bezique* or *Pinochle*. In some cases, these old boards were called Game Counters or Game Scoring Devices, according to many of the patents from the 1800s. Many of the old cribbage board boxes had two slots for storing playing cards, one for a standard deck, the other for a deck of Pinochle playing cards. In modern times, the board has seen broader uses, even being cited as a means of keeping track of the rows completed by knitters!

Identifying Cribbage Boards and Their Manufacturers

When trying to identify an unmarked cribbage board, there are several clues that can help with the process. The mystery surrounding a supposedly unmarked board can be dramatically reduced by taking a closer look at its design. By applying a few simple observations which are explained in this section, the board will take on new meaning, and the identity of the manufacturer will probably surface. There are few manufactured boards in collections that remain unidentified, and with the progress being made, most of them will eventually be placed on the "found" list. Even the hand-crafted board will often produce clues as to its origin, but the process of identification is usually quite tedious. Unless the collector is resolutely determined to place a name to it, then it is not worth the time spent. Only in cases where the board's value will increase dramatically by being identified, will the average collector spend the time doing so.

The following section lists the various methods used to identify manufacturers of cribbage boards, and if close attention is given to the process, then most boards can be identified.

Markings and Logos

Some cribbage board manufacturers placed their name or Logo (Trademark) on their products, making the process of identifying and cataloging them fairly easy. For instance, most W. C. Horn, Bros. & Co. boards were marked plainly with the company name and model number with an indented stamp on the underside. The name McCrillis was added to the stamp, possibly if or when Horn purchased the company. If the stamp has a KC model number, then the board was manufac-

tured sometime in the early 1960s after C. R. Gibson bought out Horn. Horn's method of identification is the most meticulous system that has been used by cribbage board manufacturers.

Other companies, such as Wm. F. Drueke & Sons, Inc., used a variety of methods to identify their boards. Some Drueke boards had an indented company name on the underside, some had their name on the face of the board, and some

boards had a label with the model number and company name. Unfortunately, if the label has been removed, then identifying the manufacturer is a slower process.

The E.S. Lowe Co., Inc. usually identified their boards with the name Lowe enclosed by a diamond. When the company was taken over by Milton Bradley in 1974, "E.S." was added to Lowe, and "A Milton Bradley Company" stamped below. Once again, the design of the Logo will assist with identifying the approximate age of the board.

Some manufacturers, such as the Pacific Game Company, used stenciled designs on the face of many of their boards. The model number and company name or Logo (Pleasantime) was usually incorporated nicely into the design, leaving no question as to who the manufacturer was. When the model number is included, the information is complete.

One historical company, C. W. Le Count, inscribed its name on the side of the nickel-faced plate of some of their boards. The company also inscribed its name on many of the metal peg slot covers. Since many of the boards in collections have neither of these identifications, it appears that this wasn't always standard practice.

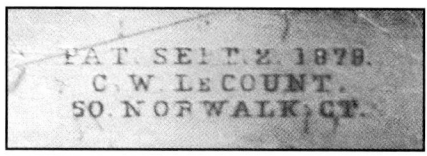

Board Structure — Sides and Ends

Not until a collector accumulates several "identical" boards from one company do the subtle differences, such as the variations in the style of the edges, become apparent. Milton Bradley, for instance, used a distinctive double groove on the sides of many of their boards, and when they took over Lowe, at least one of the newer Lowe boards, style 1503, assumed the double grooves. Prior to the take-over, Lowe's No. 1503 had straight sides with a step-down on the upper edge. The Coca-Cola advertising boards, which were manufactured by Milton Bradley in the 1930s and 1940s, also have the double grooved sides, although less prominent.

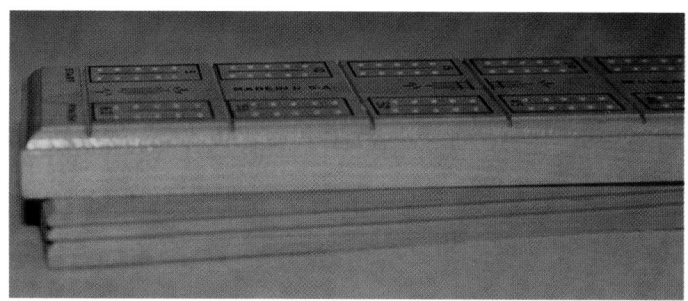

Horn used several different side styles during their manufacturing years, and in the late 1930s they introduced boards with "streamlined" ends. The sides of the board were straight but the ends were rounded off, thus the name. The C3 style was the first model introduced with the streamlined ends, followed by C33. It appears that Horn was the first manufacturer to introduce the streamlined ends, but it wasn't long before others were following suit.

The Drueke Company used a variety of side styles, but the most common style found on their older boards has a straight edge at the top, with a rounded ridge just below. Although other companies used similar techniques, the Drueke ridge is distinctive and will aid in the identifi-

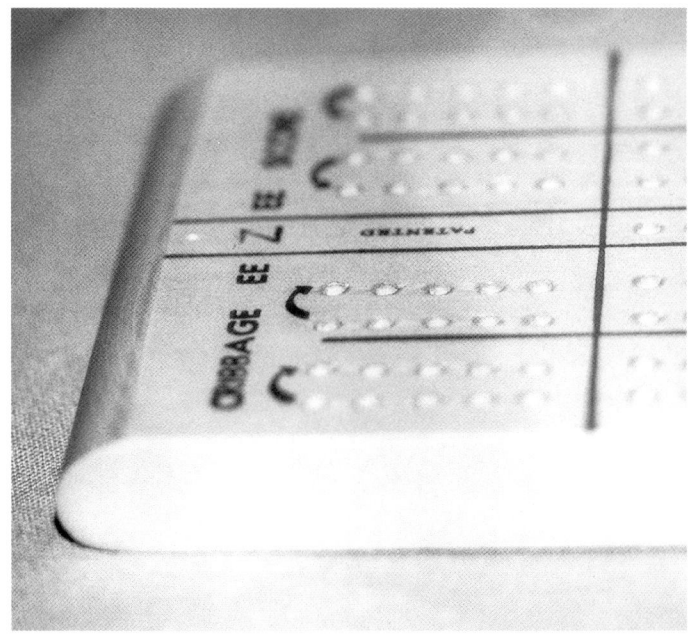

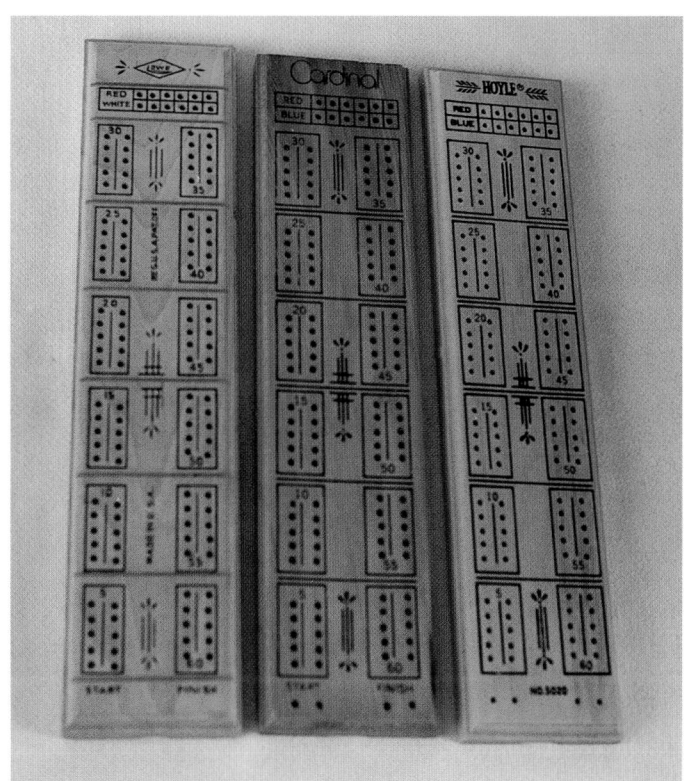

cation of an otherwise unmarked board. Most other companies used flat or concave sides on their boards, precluding this method of identification.

Decals and Stenciling

This form of identification can be tricky, for the same design was sometimes used by several companies. One example of duplication can be illustrated with boards from three different companies: Cardinal No. 61, Hoyle No. 5020, and Lowe No. 1503. The Lowe board boxes are marked "Made in U.S.A." The Cardinal and Hoyle peg slot covers are marked "Made in Taiwan". Fortunately, each company included their name in the stencil on the face of their boards, and judging by the various methods used to identify the era of manufacture, Lowe was probably the first to use the design.

A variety of stenciled designs were used by different manufacturers. H. Baron Co. used a distinctive rectangular checkerboard design down the center of some of their boards, some broken by space, others going from one

end to the other. At both ends of the stencil, there are two separate graduated lines which make the design distinctively Baron. There are other companies which used the rectangular checkerboard design, but the end lines are not present on those boards. Boards having the rectangular checkerboard center stencils without the graduated end lines are not Baron boards.

Starter Holes and Games Won Holes

Most cribbage board manufacturers used standard designs for their starter holes and Games Won (GW) holes, or none at all. Some manufacturers, however, used a specific pattern for the hole designs, which has facilitated the identification process. Horn, for instance, used a distinctive starter hole pattern on many of their boards. Horn boards, of course, had many distinctive markings, including the company name indented on the underside, making this form of identification secondary. If other manufacturers had used a permanent form such as this, then research would be so much easier!

Games Won (GW) holes are considered an optional addition, added at the discretion of the manufacturer or craftsman. When they are used, the most common combination is in multiples of 5 GW holes. The boards which have a unique GW hole setup, are usually identified by other means. Worthy of mention, however, is a triangular set of 6 holes used by Lowe on their No. 1505 board. When used in such unique patterns, GW holes give the boards a nice sense of balance, and collectors are always on the look-out for new designs.

Peg Slot Covers

There are many kinds of peg slot cover styles found on the various cribbage boards that have been manufactured, so this method of identifying board manufacturers is rarely used. One unique style, however, a cover with a flange at one end, has been found only on Stancraft boards (Standard Packaging Corp.) and has become a primary means of determining if the board was manufactured under the Hoyle, Kent, or Stancraft name.

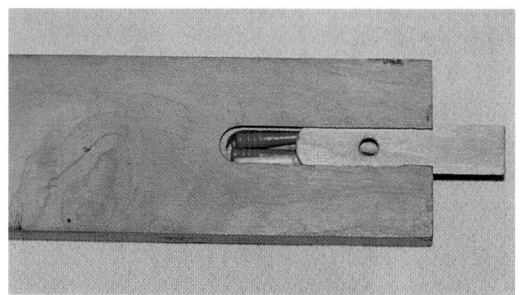

Occasionally, World War II era cribbage boards are located that have manufactured wooden peg slot covers. Many of the same board styles are more frequently found with metal covers and were manufactured over a period of time which would have included that era. Collectors surmise, therefore, that the manufacturers of these boards probably converted to wood for their peg slot covers during World War II in order to preserve the metal for more important projects related to the war effort!

Boxes

Many manufactured boards were sold packaged in boxes. If the model number cannot be found on the board and the box is still available, then it is probable that the number will be on the box. Let's examine, for instance, the E. S. Lowe Crib-Derby board. The board itself is stamped with the familiar Lowe diamond-shaped logo, but the model number of the board, No. 1502, can be found only on the box.

Sometimes, the design of the box will also reveal the approximate date of manufacture. W. C. Horn used about four different styles of boxes during their years of manufacture, and when C. R. Gibson took over the firm, a new box style was introduced. In addition to the Horn

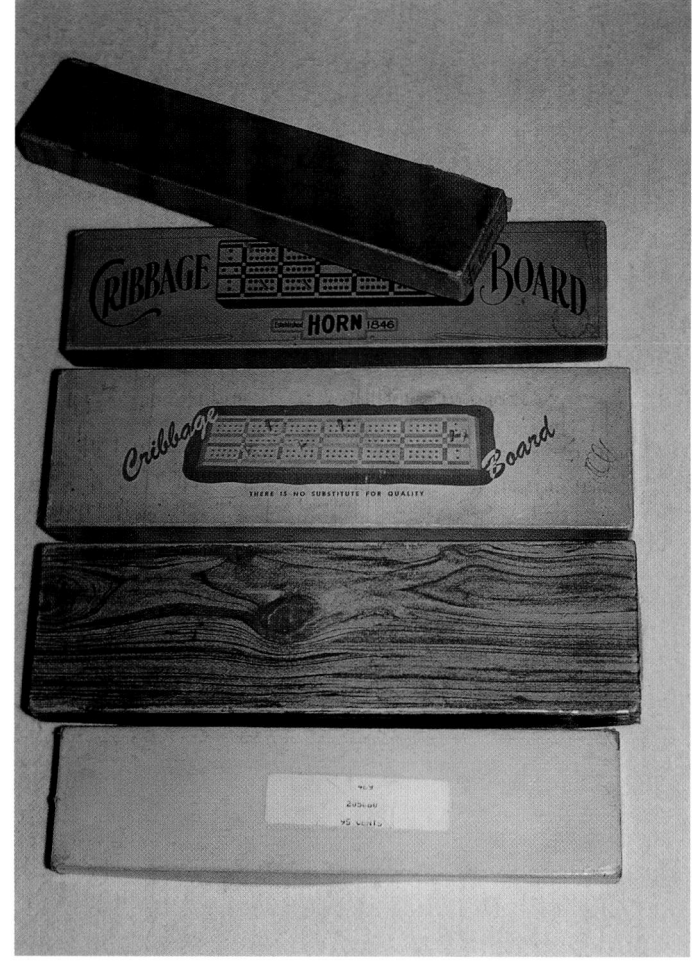

boards being stamped with the company name and model number, the box itself is marked with all of the necessary information needed for identification. This is just one of the many attributes of the Horn boards that has made them a favorite among collectors.

Instruction Sheets

When trying to ascertain the date that a cribbage board style was first manufactured, the instruction or rules sheet is frequently utilized in the research. Some instruction sheets, such as ones found with the Horn boards, have photos of boards on them. As the years passed, the evolution of new styles can be tracked by the minor changes made in the instruction sheet and the boards illustrated. One of the earliest Horn instruction sheets has three boards illustrated on the back page, no numbers

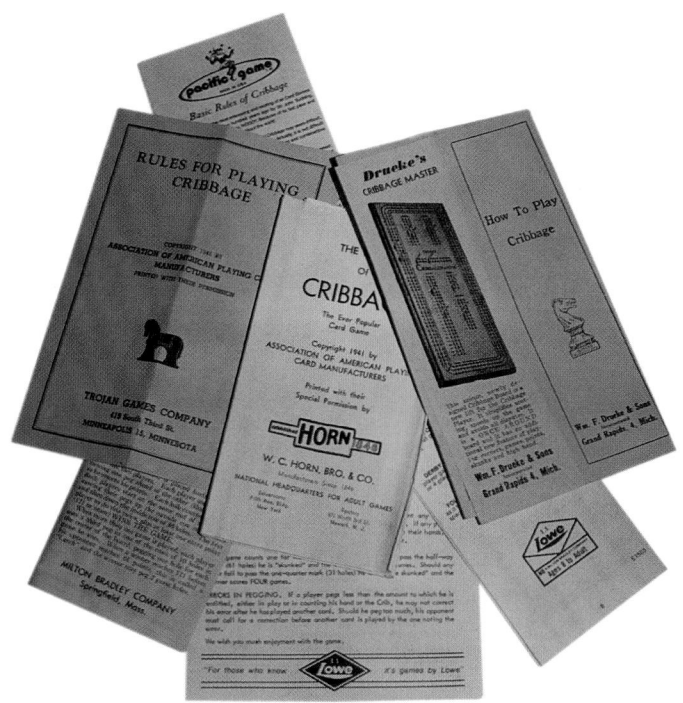

listed. The boards pictured are Models C 230, C 2, and 61 (no C). Instruction sheets published at a later date have different board styles illustrated, and the model numbers are included. Still later, subtle changes with the boards which are illustrated provide a clue as to when new styles were introduced. For instance, the instruction sheets with rules copyrighted in 1941 have an illustration of the "new streamline board" (C 33), and the statement *"We make over 30 different styles of Cribbage Score Boards."*

Although most of them aren't dated, the format of addresses on instruction sheets will reveal some clues as to era of manufacture. Some companies, like Cardinal Industries, Inc., which have a long history in the market-

ing of cribbage boards, show several address changes on their instruction sheets. When we have information as to when the company moved, then we can establish the approximate date that a particular board style was introduced.

Postal codes also provide clues as to the approximate age of the instruction sheets. Two digit area codes were introduced in New York on May 6, 1943. Five digit Zip Codes were introduced July 1, 1963 and the plus 4 code was added in October, 1984.

Patents and Design Registry Numbers

Some cribbage boards have a patent number, patent date or *Patent Pending* stamped on them. If the patent number is included, then the board was probably manufactured in 1927 or later, as patent numbers weren't required on items manufactured prior to that time. Most boards manufactured prior to 1927 usually had only the date that the board was patented stamped on them. The U.S. Patent and Trademark Office (PTO), which is located in Washington, DC, will issue a copy of a patent for a small fee, if the patent number is submitted. Without the number, the only way to obtain a copy is to personally search the files at the PTO or to hire someone to do it, and not everyone can hop on a plane to Washington and visit the PTO to do research! *Patent Pending* isn't proof that a patent was actually issued, so it is best to look for more solid evidence that the board was patented.

Sometimes puzzles regarding patents are solved quite by chance, as is the case involving a Hedgehog-style game board manufactured by John Gill. The board is stamped with the date that it was patented (December 22, 1863) and the name of the company. Several years after obtaining the original data, I received a letter from the great-great-great grandson of John Gill, requesting any information that I might have about the board. He had a copy of the patent, but had never seen a board! Needless to say, he was provided with photos and other information about "Hedgehogs," and I was provided with a copy of the patent. A happy ending to a puzzle that took several years to resolve.

U.S. Design Patents were first issued in 1843, and they usually show up on a newly designed style such as the Crib-Derby racetrack style board (Pat. Design No. 149863). When a Design Patent number is included with a board, one can be reasonably certain that it is the first of its kind (unless the original designer neglected to patent the design).

Patents really finalize the identification process of a board. About the only thing lacking, after obtaining a copy of the patent, is usually the name of the manufacturer. The patent gives all the statistics about the board, names the inventor and his/her address, tells the date that the patent was applied for as well as the date that it was issued.

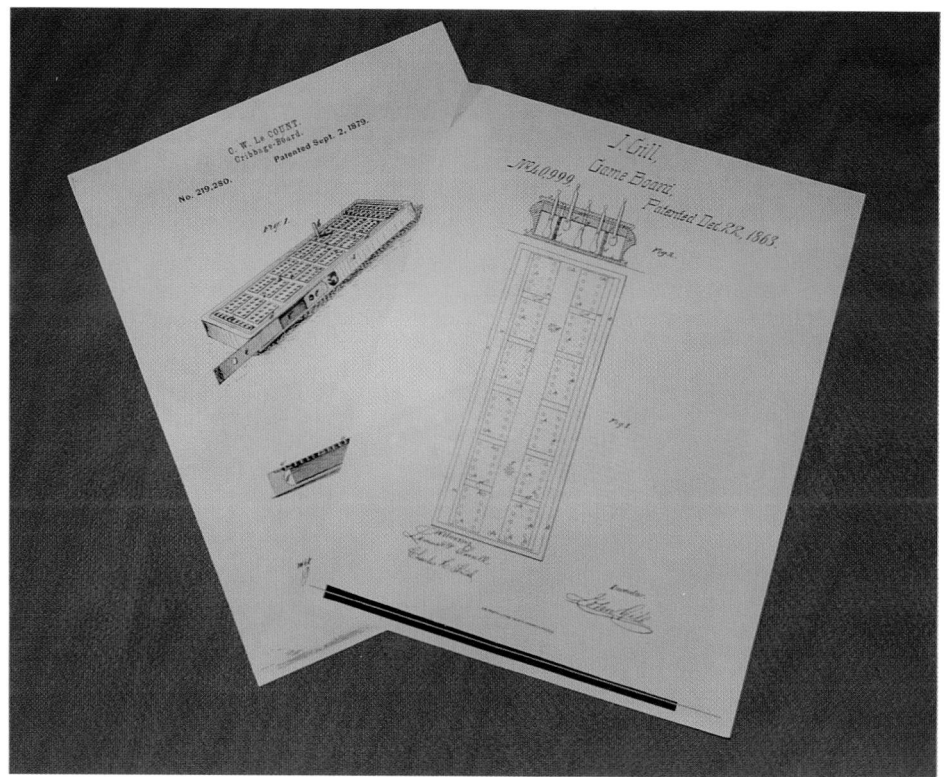

Street Designs

History of the Number of Peg Holes

At one point in my research, I began to question why some cribbage boards had 60 holes and others had 120 holes per player. After reviewing many photos of boards from the early 1900s and before, I found none that were set up with 120 holes. Determined to find an old board with 120 holes, I contacted collectors who had extensive collections, and the same response was received from everyone — they didn't have any boards with 120 hole streets from that era in their collections. Then the pieces fell into place. The old game of cribbage was played to 61 points for the win, so WHY would a 120 hole board have been needed ?!!

In order, then, to determine when the 120 hole boards were originally introduced, the first puzzle which needed to be solved was to determine when the rules on points needed for game win changed. Instruction sheets from the 19th century cite 61 as being game win. For example, the instruction sheets found with the C. W. Le Count boards from the late 19th century state *"...playing until sixty-one is reached, which wins the game."*

A Horn instruction sheet, containing Hoyle rules which were copyrighted in 1915, states that the sixty-first, or Game Hole, is the objective point, and whoever reaches this first wins the game. By 1940, the Horn rules were indicating a choice of 61 or 121 points for Game. Horn also included a sample Bicycle Playing Card with some of their boards (copyright 1937) which was called *Cribbage Scoring Condensed*. The card noted that Game was 121 points.

Old books on games, such as the Hoyle texts, also show that the transition from Game at 61 points to 121 points was in process by the mid-1930s.

Since its inception in 1979, the American Cribbage Congress has used the 121 point system for game win. The International Cribbage Association, an organization which was founded in 1977, also used the 121 point system for game win. Present day rules for cribbage generally cite the standard game win being at 121 holes. To this day, however, many new cribbage boards still contain 60 holes per player. Hence comes the expression "twice around play," meaning that each player cruises his streets two times in order to reach the 121st hole (or the Win).

Game rules included with many English boards show a slightly different story. A board manufactured by Waddington Playing Card Co. Ltd. in the 1980s contains a rules sheet which records the object of the game as *"...to score 61 points..."*. The custom of game win at 61 points in England has prevailed, even into the 1990s, according to players from many parts of that country. Newer rules sheets, such as one found in a board manufactured by House of Marbles in the 1990s give the choice of *"...normal length of the game is either 61 OR 121 holes..."*. This would indicate that the British are probably in a transition period in this area, much as was experienced in the United States and Canada several decades ago.

Research shows that many of the boards manufactured in Canada in the 1950s contained 120 holes per player. For example, the first "29" cribbage board, which was designed in 1953 and patented in 1956 by Edward M. Hirst of Burnaby, British Columbia., demonstrates the popularity of game win at 121 points in that decade. The

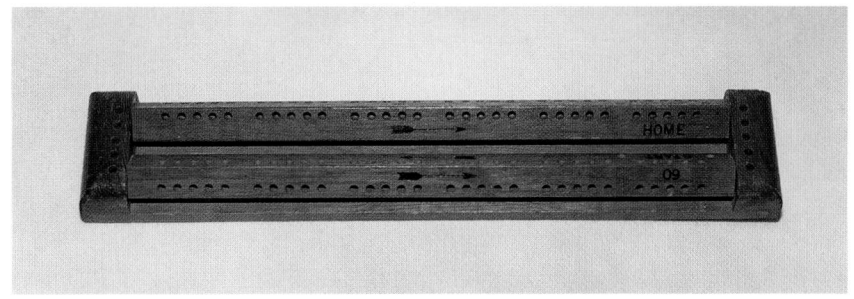

popular Canadian Brooks-style board from the 1950s also had 120 holes per player.

Several early examples of boards with 120 holes per player in American-made styles are known, of which two models were patented. The boards which qualify as early once-around models with 121 game points for the win are as follow:

     1. Saves Argument: patent filed 2/06/39 by S. C. Eddy

     2. Crib-Derby: Crib-Derby Company: The first race track-style board known. Patent filed 6/08/48 by R. O. Evans.

     3. EEZEE Cribbage Score Board: W. C. Horn, Bro. & Co. Original date of manufacture unknown.

     4. Model 1505: E. S. Lowe Co. Possibly the earliest S- shaped track board. Original date of manufacture unknown.

     5. Model 28-250: H. Baron Co. Original date of manufacture unknown.

Unless additional information is found, the Saves Argument cribbage board appears to be the oldest manufactured and patented once-around board of record in the United States.

As to the question of when and where game play to 121 points for the win was first introduced, there is still no clear-cut answer. I believe, however, that the original boards with 121 holes were designed and manufactured in Canada, quite possibly by the Acme Ruler and Advertising Co., Ltd. of Toronto.

Street Design Variations

The design of the streets on various boards takes on new meaning if you care to review them as a whole form of art. While some companies may have stuck to the simple twice-around (T.A.) straight up and down style, many companies offered variations in their street designs. On some boards, the streets were painted a different color for each player. Other companies enclosed their double 5 holes in rectangular boxes, arrows, fancy decals or some other means. In other words, the street design could provide a diversion to a sometimes otherwise dull game! Let us examine some of the designs of the pegging holes and to identify the companies that produced them.

Brooks Style: Acme Ruler and Advertising Co., Ltd., formerly of Toronto, manufactured the Brooks-style cribbage board for many years. When Glanson Company of New York took over the distributorship, then the manufacture of the boards, they continued to produce the board and to stencil "Brooks Cribbage Board" on the face. One of the more common terms for this street design is "once-around continuous track." This term, however, is a catch-all phrase for several variations of once-around street designs. The design, which continues to be extremely popular, is now manufactured in massive quantities in Taiwan and Japan and sold to American distributors of games. The only American company known to have manufactured boards with this style street in recent years is Crisloid, Inc. It is cost prohibitive to manufacture boards in America when many foreign firms have much lower production costs.

Continuous Track: This is the most common term for all boards on which the player needs only to circle the streets once in order to peg 120 holes. It can be applied to the wide rectangular boards which have the peg holes along the outer edge, with pegging starting and ending at the same corner, and it applies to all of the designs listed in this section.

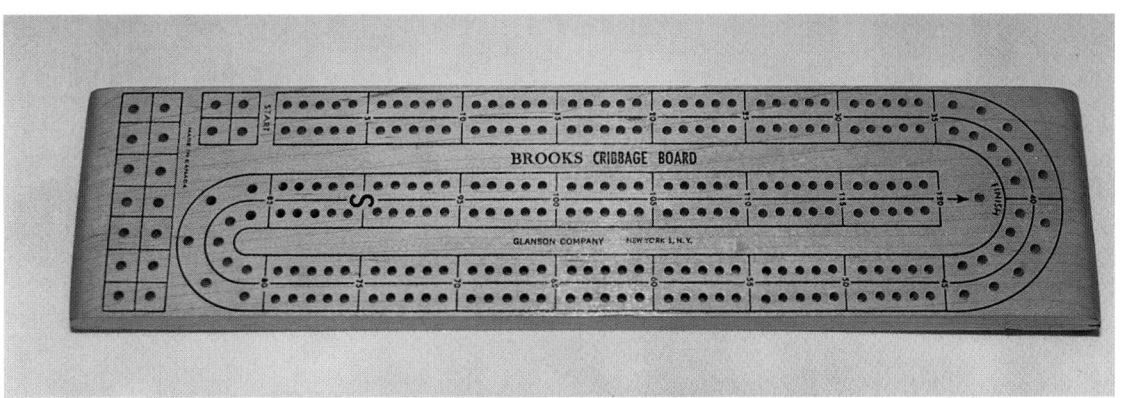

At one time, The Drueke Company included an insert with their wide rectangular boards explaining how to use the center pegging holes, which were added to make the game more interesting. It included:

Corners - first person to pass a Corner, wins it and pegs in the center

Games - scoring for Games Won

Points - tally for Total Points received for each player

Skunks - tally for Skunks given by each player

Double Skunk - tally for Double Skunks given by each player

High Hand - used to mark the amount of the High Hand, allowing the
players to determine who held the largest hand of the evening.

Race Track: Boards with this street design are usually wider than most others. The oval Crib-Derby board, manufactured by the Crib-Derby Co., was the first Race Track style board that was manufactured and had a design patent for it. Other companies eventually began manufacturing boards which were rectangular in shape, with the tracks running around the outer edge. The streets on these boards are usually called continuous track, but on occasion the term "Race Track" surfaces in reference to the style.

29 Board: Perhaps no cribbage board design has ever generated more interest among people, young and old alike, than the "29" board. Featuring a once-around 120 hole track, the board is easy to play on, with little chance for error.

The history of the board and the progressive sequence of its manufacture from Canada to the United States, and finally to the Asian countries is quite interesting. In the field of cribbage board collecting, we have tracked this progressive sequence not only with the "29" board but also with all of the most popular and inexpensive boards in use today (with the exception of the tournament long board).

Many variations to the "29" board have been manufactured all over the world, but most people are not aware of how or by whom the design was first created. Once upon a time, a man called Edward M. Hirst lived in Burnaby, British Columbia. Mr. Hirst was overcome by polio when he was 28 years old and spent the rest of his life in a wheelchair. He was an avid woodworker, and in 1953 he designed the first "29" board. From that point on until his death in 1960, he was kept busy trying to keep up with the demand for this very popular and uniquely designed board. It has been said that folks would wait months for their order to be filled, because he hand-crafted every board by himself. Mr. Hirst had the foresight to register his "29" board design, and Patent No.20554/141 was issued for the design on June 4, 1956.

A firm located in Vancouver called Ryco Sales Ltd. began mass producing the board in 1962, two years af-

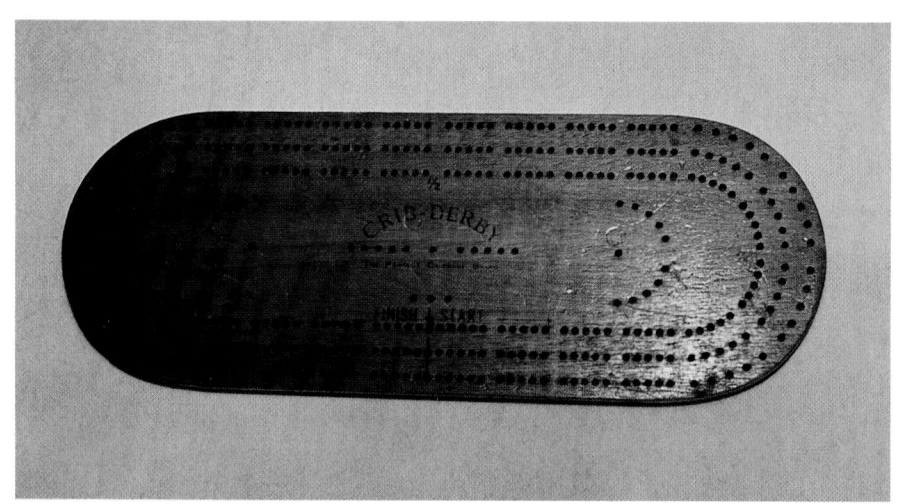

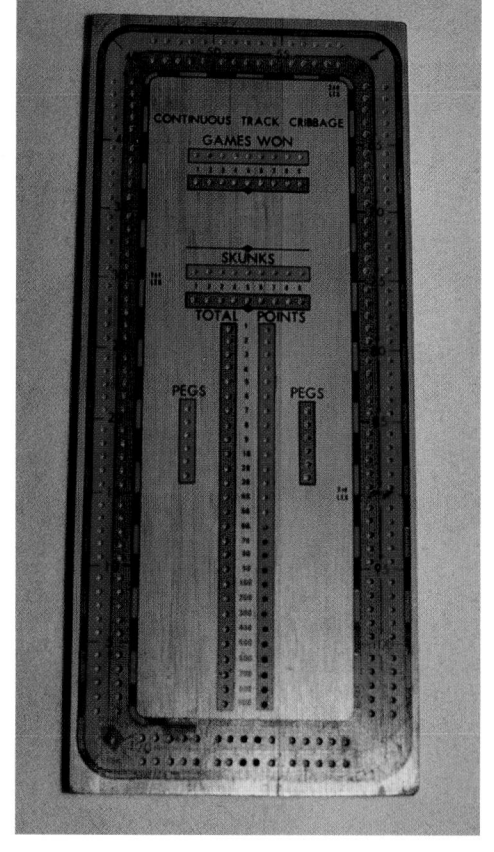

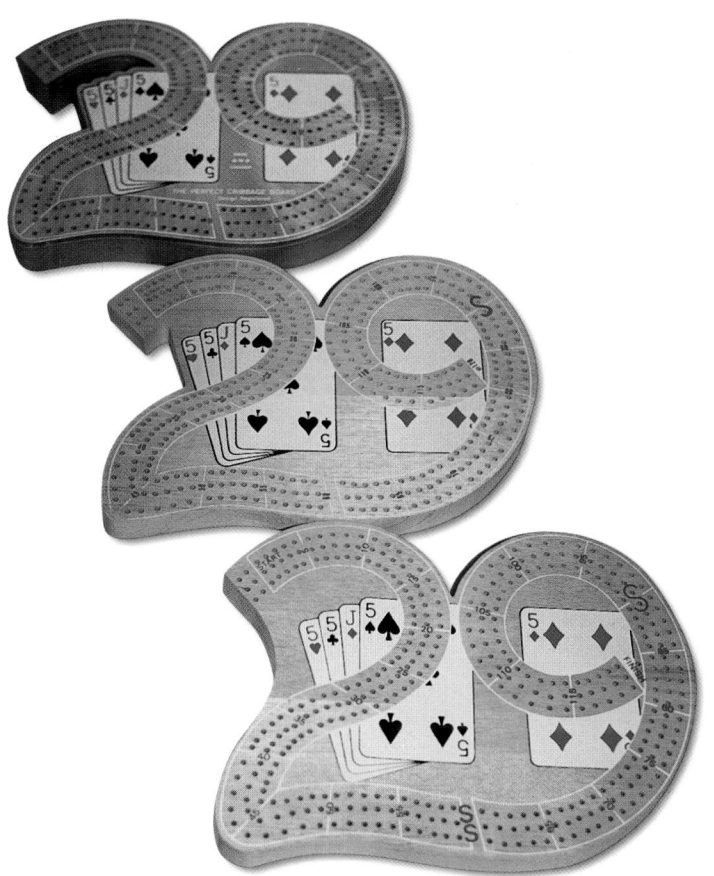

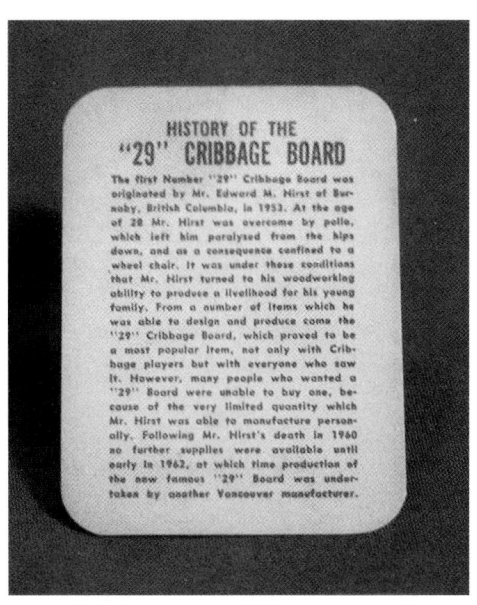

ter Mr. Hirst's death. The history of the "29" board might have been lost forever but for the fact that Ryco attached a card with its history to their board. Somerville Industries, Ltd. also manufactured a "29" board, which they called *The Perfect Cribbage Board*. Their subsidiary, Paulite Plastics Co. Ltd., also produced a plastic version. Somerville and Paulite produced the board from 1962 to 1964, when the company was purchased by Milton Bradley Co. of Springfield, Massachusetts. Milton Bradley did not continue the production of the board. Somerville, Paulite and Ryco are the only known Canadian manufacturers of the "29" board, and all three companies featured the 5 of diamonds as the cut card.

In the progressive steps of manufacture, the United States became home to the next generation in the manufacturing process, with three firms known to have manufactured the "29" board. Pacific Game Co. manufactured a plastic version in the early 1970s which had a compartment on the bottom for a deck of cards, and featured a 5 of

hearts as the cut card. Crisloid, Inc. manufactured a wooden version with a 5 of diamonds, which they labeled *Official Mister Cribbage Board*. The Drueke Co. supposedly manufactured the board as well, but little is known about it.

The final stage of manufacture naturally moves to the Asian countries, most frequently in Taiwan. American manufacturers such as Crisloid eventually found that they could not mass produce the board as cheaply as it could be done in Taiwan, even when the import tariffs were included in the price. When production stopped here, the sale of the boards generally moved to American venders rather than manufacturers.

All "29" boards are basically identical in size and feature the 29 hand on the face. There are three styles — the classic board, the board with card storage (the same size as the classic), and the mini board which is ideal for use as a travel board. The variations, which are minor, include the suit of the cut card used by the various companies. The diamond, heart and spade have been used,

but not the 5 of clubs. The face of the 2 was fully open on the Canadian boards, but is only partially open or is fully closed on the Taiwan boards.

Z Shape: While this street design is sometimes called *S*- shape, it really is an "*S*" in reverse. For the sake of clarity, this book will identify such street designs as a "*Z*." Crisloid, Inc. manufactures model 1012, which features this style track.

S Shape: There are several styles of *S* shaped streets. They can be elongated, squat or wide, and some even have extended arms which curve back almost to the center end of the board. E. S. Lowe Co., Inc. model 1505 features this style, and the board is marked Reg. U.S.A. Pat. Off., indicating that the company was the originator of the design.

M Shape: Drueke designed several boards with an *M*-shaped street which featured the tops of the "*M*" rounded off. These boards continue to be manufactured by them.

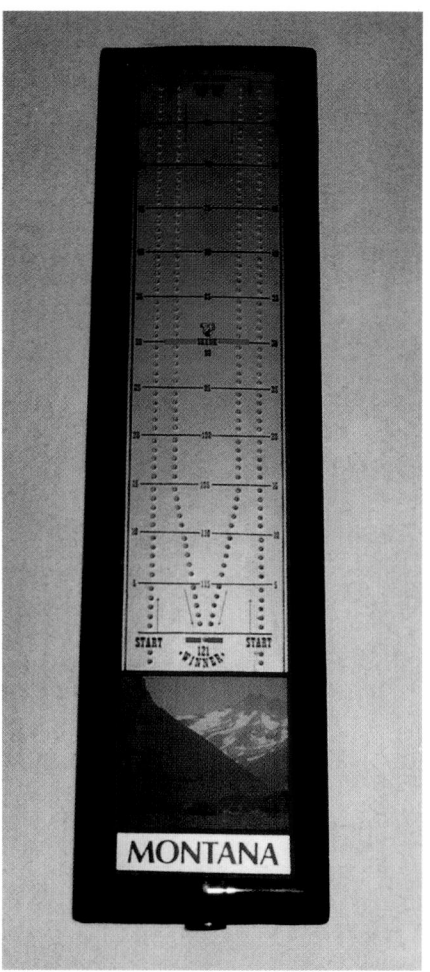

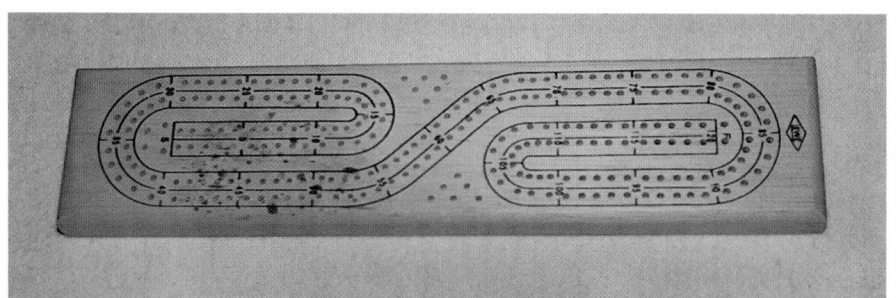

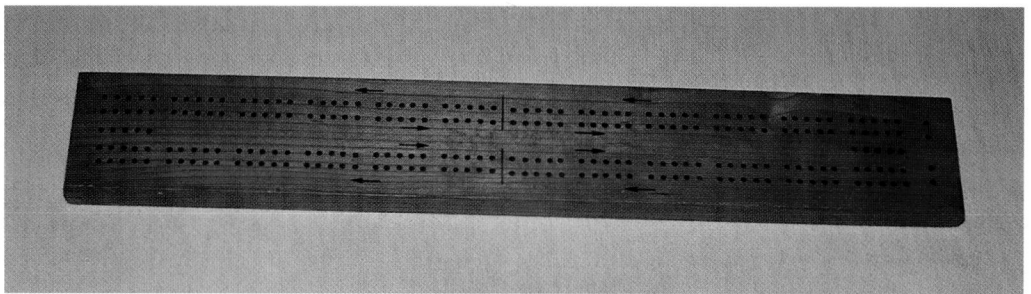

Another *M*-shape design features streets which are asymmetrical, the inside tracks of the "*M*" gradually coming together at the bottom, with a single peg-out hole. The board was originally introduced in 1983 at the Montana Championship Tournament and was designed by DeLynn Colvert, who is a nationally acclaimed cribbage player and author of books on the game of cribbage.

The Tournament Long Board: This section would not be complete without including this "no frills" once-around 120 hole cribbage board. The board was copyrighted in 1979 by Joseph Petrus Wergin, who was one of the Founders and the first president of the American Cribbage Congress (ACC). Imprinted on the face of the original boards was "THE LONG BOARD - Official for THE MASTERS CLASSICS." The board made its official debut in the early 1980s at the Madison Masters Classic, an ACC sanctioned tournament, and it continues to be the primary board used in ACC tournaments to this day. Its popularity is based primarily on the theory that it is difficult to peg in any direction other than toward the finish, although many avid contenders, including me, will dispute that statement! Mr. Wergin, who was the president of the ACC for nearly 13 years, never stopped campaigning for higher visibility of the game. He authored many books on cribbage as well as other card games.

Chapter II.
Special Cribbage Board Categories

Some categories in this section include information on boards manufactured in other countries as well as hand-crafted boards. This is done in order to provide collectors with an overview of the various styles and designs which can be established in their collections. To the novice, a cribbage board is a cribbage board — period. For the advanced collector, the challenge is often derived from grouping the cribbage boards into new and adventuresome categories which often include a mix of manufactured and hand-crafted boards.

Advertising Boards

Advertising products have been manufactured for well over 100 years, and at one time they were important give-aways, promoting the manufacturer's name by including highly visible and colorful logos and trademarks on them. All that changed, however, with the advent Advertising products are still in popular use today, but there are many more powerful ways to advertise, so most of them are now sold rather than given away by the companies. During the era when using products to advertise was common, many colorful logos and trademarks were used on items such as yardsticks, pencils, playing cards, buttons, and almost every product imaginable, including cribbage boards.

Among the most famous of all giveaway cribbage boards are the Coca-Cola advertising boards, which were manufactured primarily in the 1930s. Two styles were produced by the Milton Bradley Company of Springfield, Massachusetts. Some of the Coca-Cola boards came boxed with a score pad, pencil, instructions and playing cards. There are many good specimens still in existence, and they can be purchased at reasonable prices in most areas.

Tobacco advertising boards are found in fairly abundant numbers to this day, which leads one to believe that the early tobacco industry recognized that cribbage and smoking went hand-in-hand. A collection of advertising boards is likely to have five or six different companies represented, most of which were based in England. Many of the tobacco advertising boards found in the United States came from the early 20th Century manufacturers of the English tobacco products, and it is presumed that they came here with the immigrants. Since the boards were promotional giveaways, it would stand to reason that even the poorest of families could own one. Cribbage was a popular game there, and when the Englishmen began to emigrate to the United States in the late 1800s, many of them brought their favorite cribbage board with them. It stored easily in their valise, and it was to be a source of security and comfort in the new world. A cheap means of entertainment, it would also provide them with a familiar activity for their spare moments.

One English tobacco products manufacturer whose boards are still readily available, some of which are of recent vintage, is the Wills's brand. Advertising boards for the following tobacco products, Wills's Gold Flakes, Wills's Woodbines, Wills's and Sons Fine Shag, and Wills's Star Cigarettes, are also fairly reasonable in price. Wills's tobacco products, by the way, are still produced in England.

Examples of other English companies who advertised on cribbage boards are Capstan, Players, and Weights tobacco products. Although most American tobacco companies chose to use their decorated product containers as primary advertising giveaways, there is a cribbage board that was manufactured with the Marlboro logo.

A classic example of the importance which was placed on the use of advertising giveaways can be exemplified

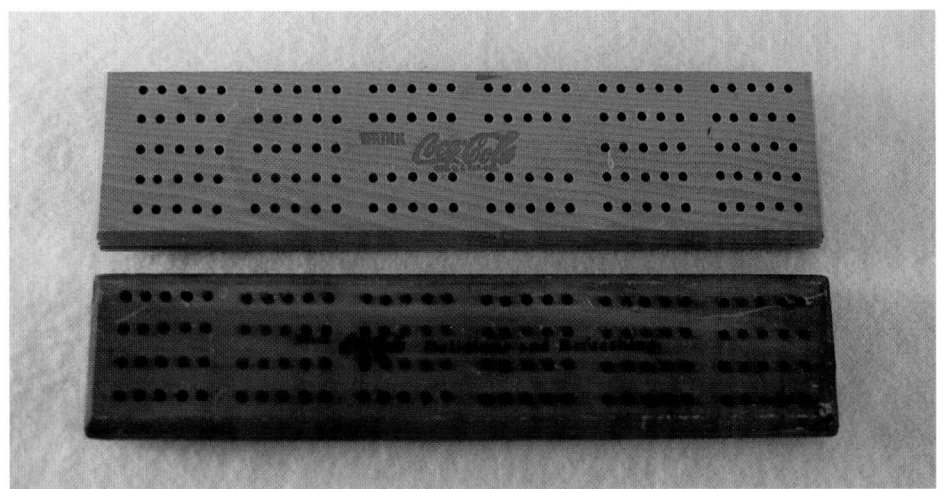

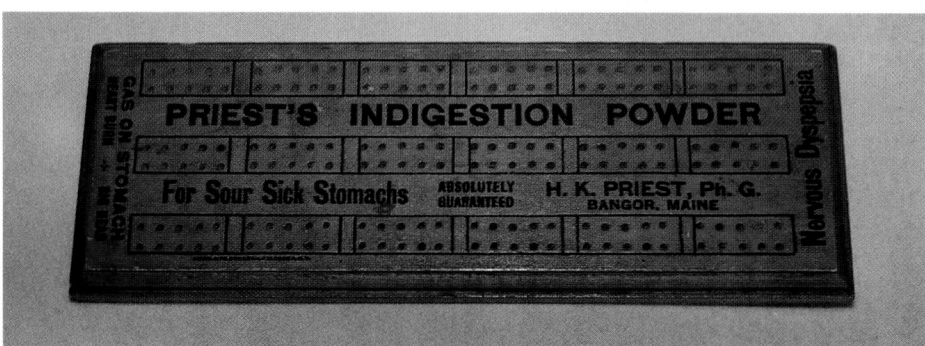

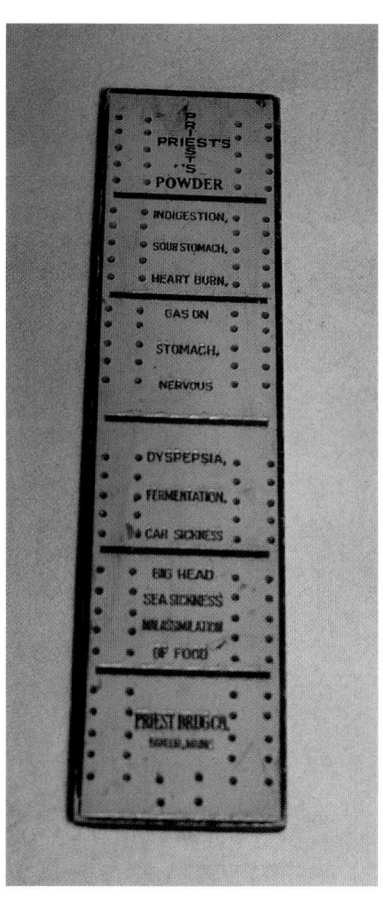

by the cribbage boards which were mailed out to customers by the Priest Drug Company of Bangor, Maine. My collection contains two styles, one of which was mailed to the Union Hotel of Groveton, New Hampshire. Although the postage stamps are no longer on one of the boards, their outline remains. The face of the board is a three player, twice around design, and it advertises Priest's Indigestion Powder in detail. On the underside, the area opposite the mailing address has a printed sheet of information about the indigestion powder. The board was manufactured by the American Manufacturing Concern of Falconer, New York.

The second Priest's cribbage board was mailed to the "Shetucket Coal and Lumber Company, 203 Mn., Norwich, Conn." and a three cent Lincoln stamp dating to the 1922-1925 era remains on the board. The face of the board is two player, twice around, and it also contains information about the Priest's products.

Acme Ruler and Advertising Co., Ltd., formerly of Toronto, Canada, was another manufacturer of advertising boards, perhaps the largest outside the United States. Acme's basic boards had a Brooks-style track, but other styles were also used by them.

There are many other types of advertising boards available, and collectors are always excited when a new product listing is discovered.

Souvenir Boards

Of the earliest forms of souvenir boards known, Mauchline-ware (Scottish Souvenir) — an early form of souvenir and advertising art — was frequently distributed in the late 19th Century by both Great Britain and New England landmarks. Pictured here is an example containing two scenes, one of Mt. Kineo and one of Mt. Kineo House which was located on Moosehead Lake in Maine.

Tartanware and Tunbridge Ware are other examples of English boards which were manufactured as souvenir boards.

American-made souvenir boards first became popular in the early 20th Century, and the most commonly used style was a slice of wood, usually Redwood, with the bark attached. They were crafted in two basic shapes — a round board and a diagonal-cut board. In spite of the advanced age of some of these boards, many are still found with the bark intact. New England landmarks such as the Mohawk Trail in Massachusetts and the mountain resorts of New Hampshire and Maine were popular sources of this style.

Souvenir boards can still be found in abundance wherever there are tourist attractions, and they are currently found in two basic styles. One is a folding board

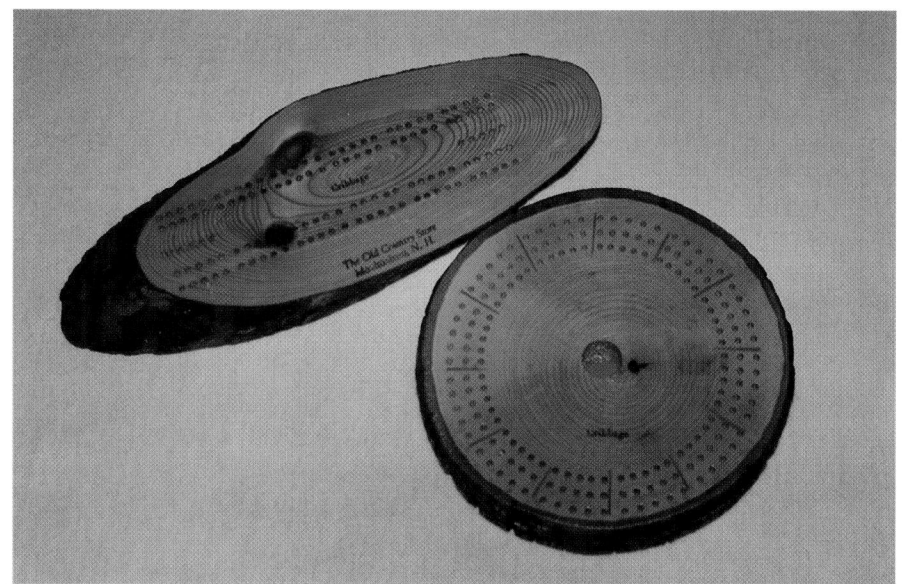

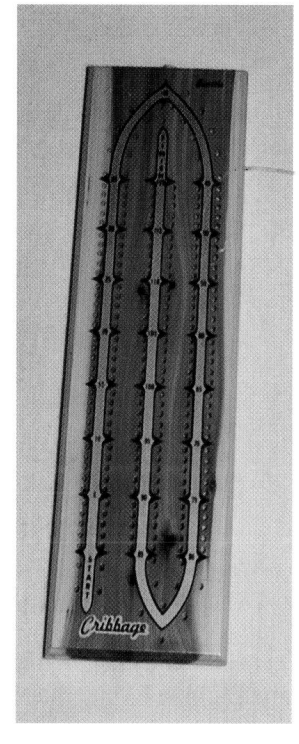

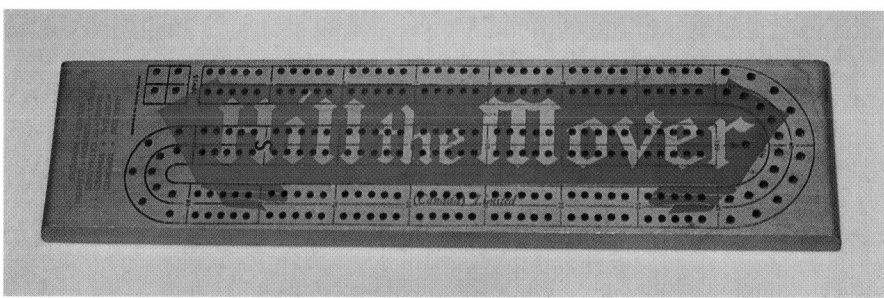

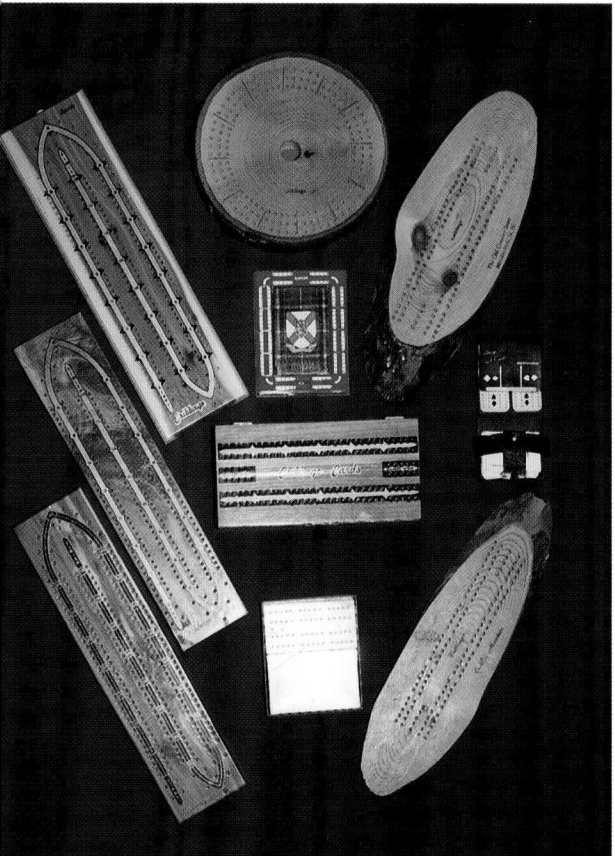

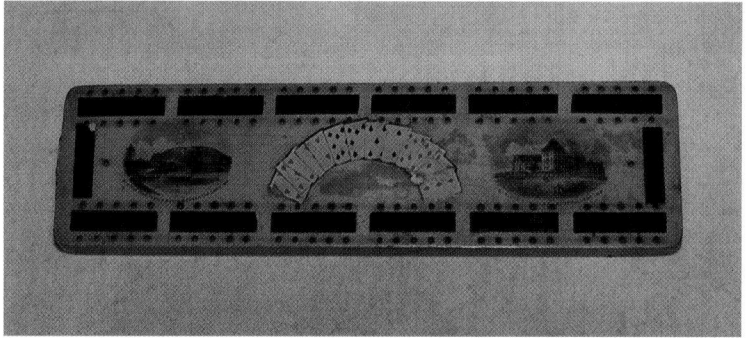

which comes packed with a deck of cards, and the other features once-around play on a Brooks-style track. Each board is stamped with the name of the place where it was bought and has a few other decorative features. Most are made in the Far East and are inexpensively priced.

War Boards

Little has been published about the history of cribbage boards and our servicemen, but they were, in fact, a most important focus of recreation with our troops down through the various wars. The boards traveled well, taking up little space, and were easily replaced if lost. Most servicemen, from veterans of World War I all the way to Desert Storm, recall at least minimal exposure to the game, and some veterans recount stories of how a board stored in their pocket spared their life by taking a bullet intended for them. Many of the World War II boards which are housed in collections are so badly worn from use that it is a wonder that they were not discarded when the servicemen were discharged. Evidently, the boards were a comfort measure during times of great stress, and they were treasured to a point where the owners couldn't bear to discard them.

The Civil War

Evidence of the game's popularity during wartime really surfaces during the Civil War era, when the soldiers would intricately carve cribbage boards as they rested between battles. Folklore has it that when the soldiers went to battle, they would leave their cribbage boards and cards behind with a trusted friend. If they were killed in battle, they did not want these "gambling" items sent home to their families with their personal effects, for gambling was frowned upon by the "good people of the day." Since the soldiers were constantly on the road, and even when taken as prisoners, there was usually a supply of wood for them to carve. Many fine examples of these highly prized boards can be found in museums.

World War I

During World War I, cribbage boards were not made specifically for use in the war effort, although some small folding boards were being produced that were carried by

servicemen. One such board is a small folding leather model, dark green on the cover and yellow on the playing surface. The manufacturer is unknown, but many of the boards have survived with at least a partial history of their use by soldiers of that era.

World War II

World War II is a different story. The popularity of the war effort, and the need to keep the servicemen entertained during their leisure hours, produced an abundance of traveling games that families could buy and send to their loved ones. Four major manufacturers, The E. S. Lowe Co., The Drueke Co., Metro Mfg. Co., and the Spartan Co. produced libraries of games which were packed in small, ready to mail boxes. These sets were all produced from 1942 on, and they frequently included patriotic playing cards as well as inserts which promoted the sale of war savings bonds and stamps.

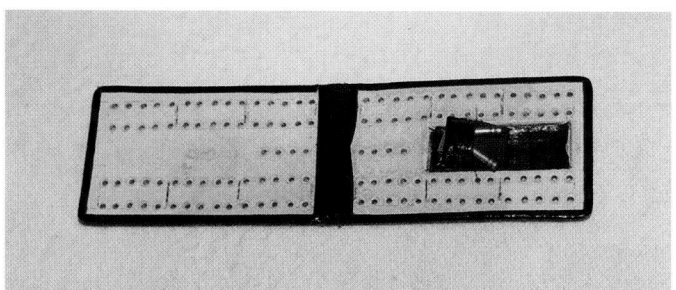

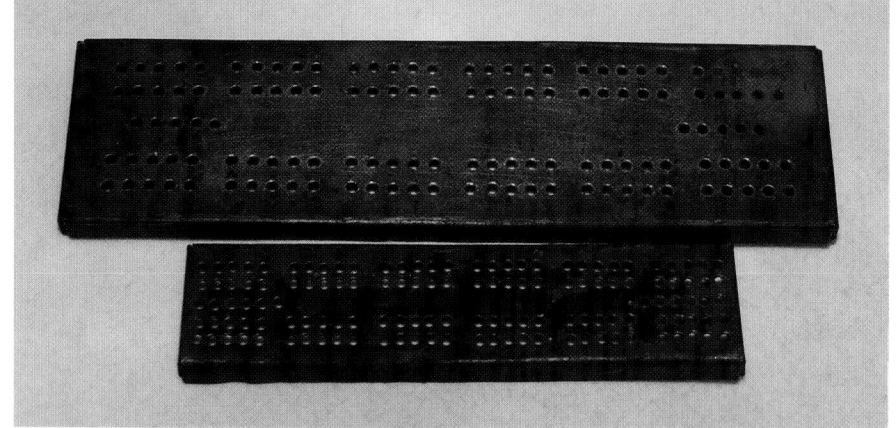

Small folding or straight leather boards which fit in the pocket were also popular, and they were manufactured by E. S. Lowe Co., J. S. Co., W.C. Horn, Bros. & Co., and several other manufacturers.

Individual craftsmen, especially those who were too old to serve in active duty, frequently banded together to hand-craft batches of boards to be sent overseas. They made them in both large and small sizes, working together to produce a quality product in which they took great pride.

Korean and Viet Nam Wars

No cribbage boards were manufactured specifically for the Korean or Viet Nam Wars, although the game continued to provide a source of rest and recreation for the many servicemen who participated in these conflicts. By this time, however, small folding travel boards had become popular, and families would frequently pack a board and deck of cards when sending "Care" packages to their loved ones. The CBCS archives contain many letters from men who served in both wars, recounting their experiences playing cribbage during their rest periods.

Persian Gulf War (Desert Storm)

Now along comes warfare of the 1990s and the Desert Storm War, and we all know how our patriotism was sparked by the thoughts of troops once again going into war. The members of the American Cribbage Congress (ACC) rallied together to donate money for the manufacture of a special Desert Storm cribbage board, and under the direction of Mickey Griffin of Lincoln, Nebraska, well over 1000 boards were donated by the members for use in Saudi Arabia by our troops. The boards were imprinted with the ACC logo and were manufactured by Vandercraft, Inc. of Prineville, Oregon. The project was called the "Operation Desert Shield Cribbage Board Drive."

The Air War With Yugoslavia — 1999

Up to the time of the release of this book, there have been no plans to offer any commemorative cribbage boards relative to the air war in Yugoslavia. History seems to dictate that intensive military activity needs to occur before patriotism erupts into supportive action on the home front.

Ivory

Although most boards in this category are hand-crafted, there are so many reproductions on the market today that the category commands recognition, if only to alert collectors of the hazards of blindly assuming that an "ivory" board is authentic!

Eskimo Ivory

The wonderful art of carving and scrimshawing walrus tusks, teeth and other ivory or bone artifacts by the Eskimos of Alaska as well as the natives from the northern areas of Canada is legendary, to say the least. Much information is documented about their carvings, especially those from Nunivak Island, the Yupik carvers from St. Lawrence Island, as well as the individual artists of the early 20th Century such as Happy Jack (Angokwazhuk) from Cape Nome. Local libraries and book stores can provide books and articles on the history of the Alaskan and Eskimo ivories, such as those written by Dorothy Jean Ray. Many of these books and articles will also provide information about the regulations regarding the sale of ivory, which were established in the early 1970s by the Convention on the International Trade in Endangered Species (sponsored by the United Nations).

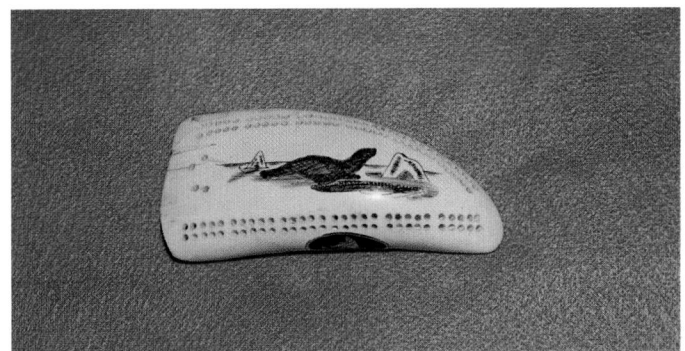

Whaling Ship Ivories

The whalers of the late 19th Century are renowned for their exquisitely carved walrus bones, teeth, and tusks. History has it that the whalers, who spent long, lonely months and years away from their families, took to carving and scrimshawing the bones and ivories of the whales to help pass the time. Examples of these whale bone and ivory cribbage boards are on display in various whaling museums, including the New Bedford (Massachusetts) Whaling Museum and the Peabody Museum of Salem, Massachusetts. Many of these museum boards have been reproduced, and some of them are so realistic that they often fool even the experts! Bette's Cribb, my little mail

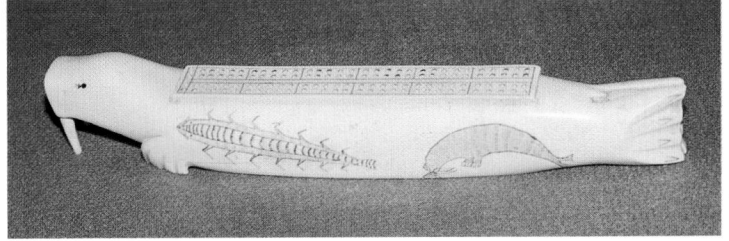

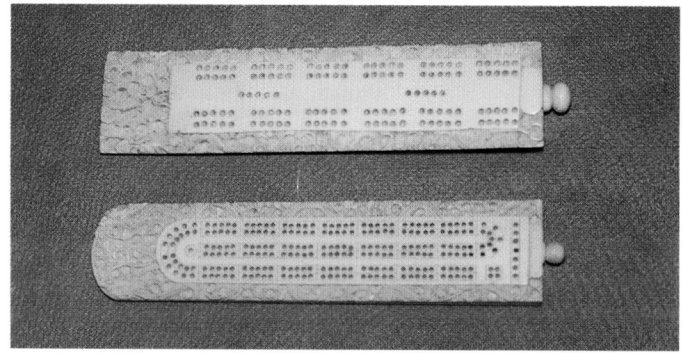

order catalog for cribbage novelties, has offered several of the "Save the Whale" and other artists' scrimshawed cribbage board reproductions.

Far East Ivories

Carved elephant ivory from Japan and Hong Kong became very popular right after WWII, as tradesmen rushed to recover from the losses of the war. With American servicemen and officials highly visible and anxious to take home souvenirs, the market for these ivory products flourished. Many of the photos that I have received are of carved cribbage boards that servicemen purchased NEW during that time period. The carvings are usually of dragons or floral designs, and the boards are usually approximately seven inches in length, graduating in thickness from one end to the other. Most have a screw-in cover at one end to hold the pegs. These boards were often sold in satin or velvet-lined boxes, which enhanced the rich patina of the elephant ivory when displayed. Most, if not all, contained labels identifying the pieces as made from elephant ivory, as well as the origin of the product. Several of the boxes that I have seen are stamped with the name and address of the distributors, such as Hang On Factory (Hong Kong), Haiwa Trading Co., Ltd. (Tokyo), Kwong On Ivory Factory (Hong Kong), and HaKusui Ivory Co. (Yokohama).

The ivories make for a wonderful and eclectic collection, whether they be carved, scrimshawed, or plain. The expert will know whether the board is authentic or not. The novice will need to seek assistance in that determination, or (s)he might well become the victim of misjudgment!

American Prison Craft Boards

Down through the years, it has been traditional for prisoners to craft products, including games, in order to help them learn new trades and to provide them with an income. The art of crafting cribbage boards by French prisoners of the English was first recorded in the early 1800s, during the Napoleonic wars. By the mid-1800s, "prisoner of war" boards were hand-crafted in great numbers in English military prisons. Prisoners would carve various items from the animal bones left over from their food supply. Once carved, they would then use fire ash or dyes from local vegetation to give color to the carvings.

Dating back to the 1800s, American prisons have been a source of some rather unique boards, done by their often famous creators. One such example is an inlaid cribbage board which was made by Dr. Samuel A. Mudd, the physician who treated John Wilkes Booth after he assassinated President Abraham Lincoln. After his trial, Dr. Mudd was incarcerated at Dry Tortugas, and during that period he kept himself busy by crafting various objects, including cribbage boards. At least one of these boards still exists, and its authenticity has been verified by the present owners.

In recent years, many American prisons have offered their inmates an opportunity to create crafts, and the outcome in some cases has been exquisite. The Maine State Prison has a Showroom Outlet where the general public can visit and purchase a variety of products, including cribbage boards, which have been crafted by the inmates.

My collection also contains a board, crafted years ago at the Middlesex County House of Correction, on which is printed *"Compliments of the Inmates at the Middlesex County House of Correction Joseph M. McElroy, Sheriff."*

As a final cap to the topic of prison-created boards, I would like to tell of a letter that I once received from a prisoner who wanted to tell me about the games of cribbage that he and his colleagues played. In the course of

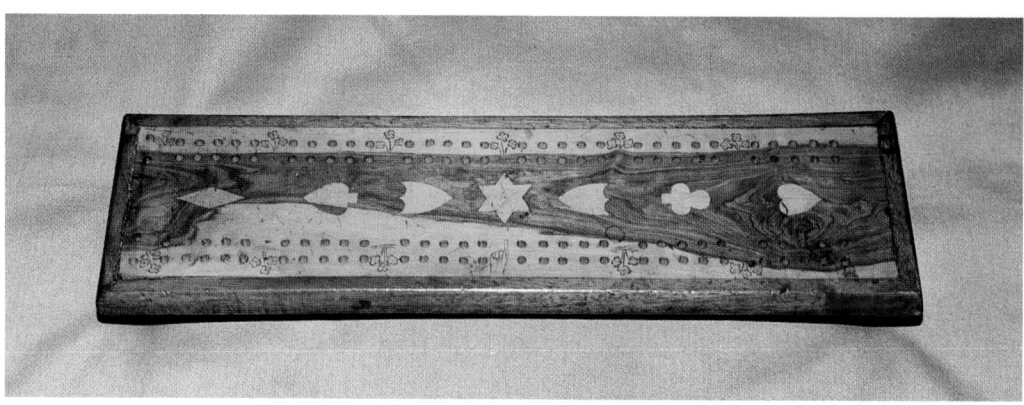

Courtesy of the Estate of Margaret M. Campbell of Baltimore, Maryland.

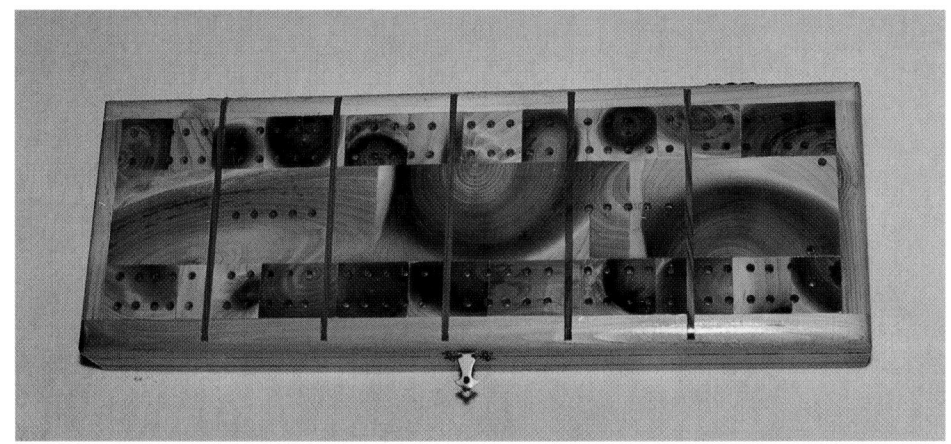

the letter, he described the cribbage board that they were using — an inverted tissue box into which he had poked holes, using twigs for pegs. This man's inventiveness is a reminder to me that you really don't need a fancy board in order to play a good game of cribbage!

Unique and Patented Favorites

Many variations to the cribbage board have been manufactured down through the years. Some have a magnetic face and use small magnetized disks for the count. Other boards have been designed which have an abacus-like feature, with beads that slide along a channel. There are electronic boards as well as multi-layer boards which rotate as the score is counted. The following listing contains some of my favorite styles.

"Hedgehog" or "Pull-Up" Boards

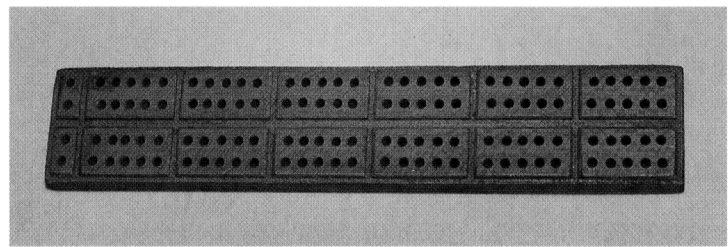

The Hedgehog (or pull-up)-style boards have a unique history all their own. Presumed to have originally been designed in England, their popularity in the United States led to the design and manufacture of at least five different models over a period of time that went from the mid-1800s all the way to the early 1960s.

The Hedgehog-style board was designed with stationary pegs instead of holes for pegs, all the boards having 60 pegs per player. On most boards, the pegs pulled up, but there is at least one style on which the pegs pushed down. Most boards featured a form of spring-load, which

when triggered, would return the pegs to their original position, making the style easy to manipulate.

The earliest known "Hedgehog" board to be manufactured in the U.S. was one patented by John Gill of New York City, whose advertisements quoted *"Manufacturer of Piano-Forte Hardware - also manufacturer of Improved Patent Cribbage Boards"*. The board was patented December 22, 1863, and the company was still advertising its availability in their 1875 advertisements.

As recently as the 1960s, Peg O' Matic, Inc. of Minneapolis manufactured a modern version of the "Hedgehog," which was made of wood and had plastic pegs which pushed down. Due to the popularity of the revived style, this board was even sold through the former W.T. Grant Co. for the conservative price of $4.95.

The Hedgehog-style board continued to be popular throughout the years, and rules on game play in cribbage which were copyrighted by the USPCC in 1915 state-*"..Points are scored as they are made on a 'pull-up' board .."*. Other rules for cribbage indicate the use of the "pull-up" boards as well.

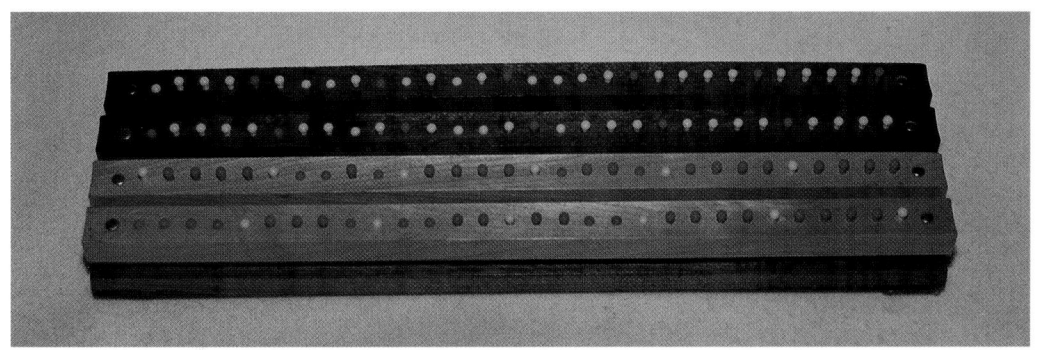

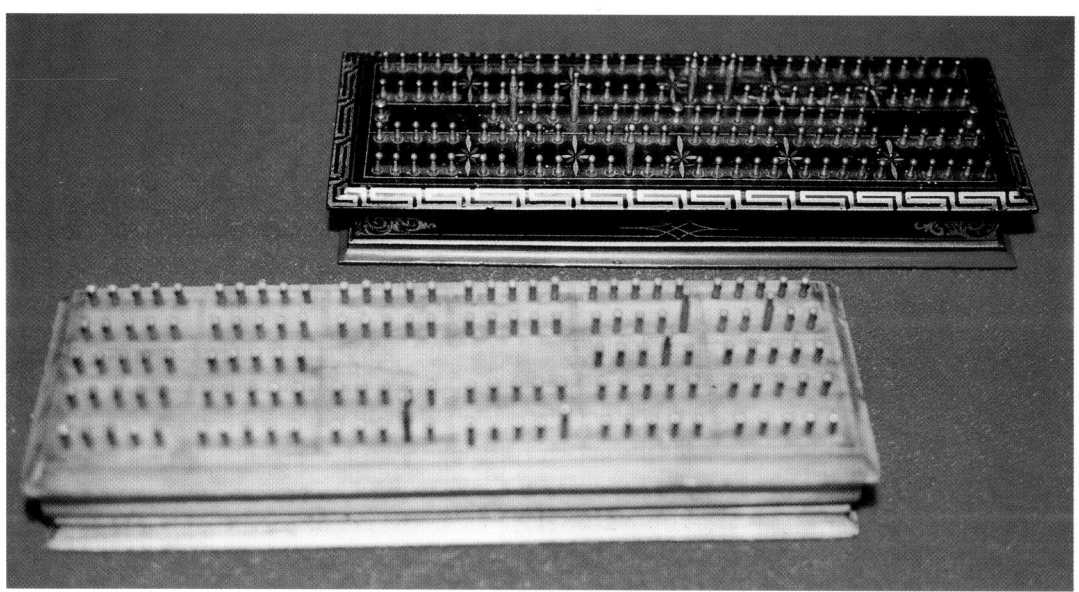

As to why the idea of permanent pegs originated, one can only imagine that the original designer got tired of replacing lost pegs, or handling little pegs, and decided to eliminate the problem!

Paper Boards (disposable)

The first paper board about which there is any information was copyrighted by W. C. Stevens, Jr. of Canoga Park, California, in 1983. Cribbage players gave a cool reception to the idea, and Mr. Stevens never received proper recognition for it.

Several years later, a New England firm began producing pads of disposable boards that had various designs on them, and the products achieved a certain success. Actually, Mr. Stevens' idea made sense, when one considers how many cribbage boards have been lost in travel. Just tear off a sheet, stick it in your pocket, and throw it away when done with the game. How many times have we wanted to throw away our boards after a really rotten game? What a great opportunity to fulfill that urge!

Punchboard

Punchboards were a popular means of simple gambling in the early 1900s, fading out of popularity in the 1950s when the government began to frown on them as a form of unauthorized lottery. They were displayed primarily in grocery and candy stores, and children were frequently the purchasers of the "punches." The boards were made of heavy cardboard and contained many small holes which were enclosed in foil. When a special key was used to punch the foil through to the back-side, a small piece of paper was also removed which had winning (or losing) information on it. Two companies manufactured the cribbage board punchboard, Harlich Mfg. Co. of Chicago and Hamilton Mfg. Co. of Minneapolis. Since both boards were identical in style, it is presumed that one company bought out the other and continued to manufacture the style.

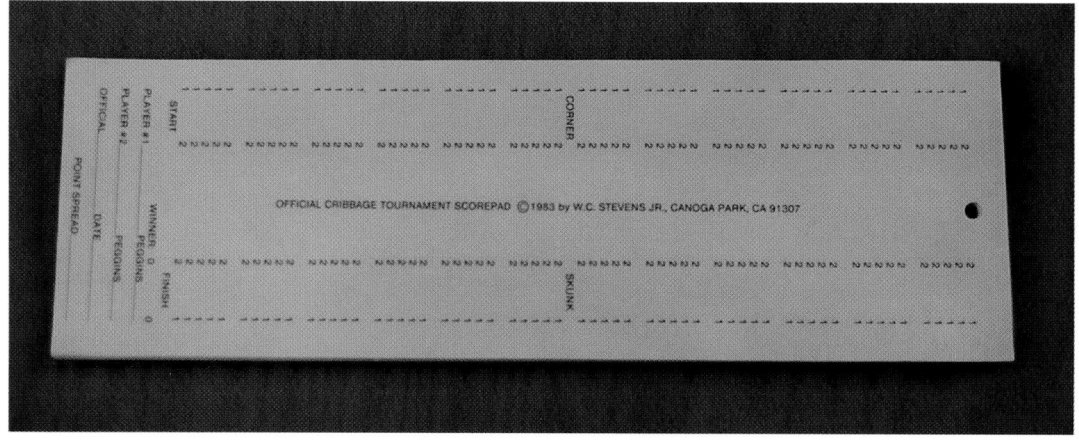

Saves Argument

"Saves Argument" is by far the most intriguing of modern-day patented boards, because it may well have been the first 121 hole board patented in the United States. The board was patented by S. C. Eddy of Kalamazoo, Michigan, in 1940, and indications are that he personally saw to the manufacture of his product. The board consisted of two rotating blocks affixed to a base, each block having 30 peg holes on all 4 sides. The blocks also had arrows on them, indicating the direction of play.

Slip Gear

The slip gear board was manufactured in two styles. Style No. 1 was "geared" for use in cribbage, and was graduated in 60 points to one revolution of the dial. Style No.2 was used primarily for play of the games "Kitchen" and "Honeymoon" Bridge, Pinochle, Five Hundred, Bezique, and other games that had large totals for scores.

The boards had geared rotating wheels and dials for game score and were made with metal tops and a wooden base. There are two symbols on the face of the board, a horseshoe and a whirling three part circle. The instruction sheet bears no manufacturer's name.

Board Game Variations of Cribbage

There are many variations to the game of cribbage, dating back to at least 1875 when McLoughlin Bros. published Cribbage Authors. In addition to the games listed here, there must be others that have not been recorded by the Cribbage Board Collectors Society. There are also game variations which are electronic and computerized, but they are not included in the list. The games listed here use either a cribbage board or a worksheet which is accepted as one.

BONUS CRIBBAGE® was copyrighted by Blaine G. Danielson in 1959 and was manufactured by the Bonus Cribbage Company of Minneapolis. The board contains 3 sets of black and 3 sets of red streets (total of 60 holes) on either side of center streets of solid yellow. The end of the board pivots for peg storage.

CRIBBAGE AUTHORS was entered into the Act of Congress in 1875 and was manufactured by McLoughlin Bros. of New York City. It consisted of a deck of 72 cards and appears to have been played very much like the original game of Authors. The authors used were Wm. F.

Adams, Charlotte Bronte, William Collins, George W. Curtis, James De Mille, Charles Dickens, Nathaniel Hawthorne, J. G. Holland, Washington Irving, Henry W. Longfellow, J. Russel Lowell, Louise Muhlbach, Miss Muloch, Charles Reade, Sir Walter Scott, Bayard Taylor, Alfred Tennyson, and John G. Whittier.

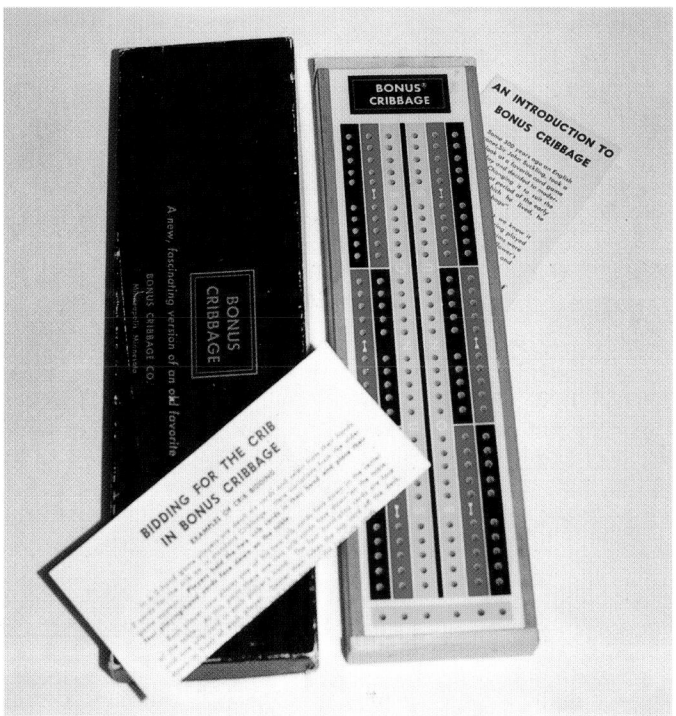

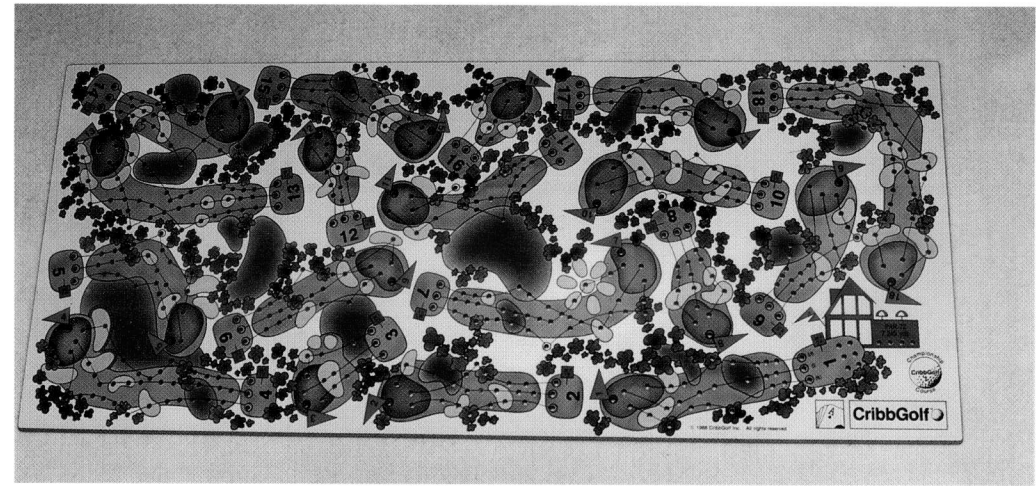

CRIBBGOLF® was copyrighted in 1991 and manufactured by JK Games Inc. It combines golf and the game of cribbage for a challenging and interesting form of entertainment.

CRIBBLE® was developed by Sandy Beck in 1989 and copyrighted in 1991. It was developed by Beck when he discovered that many of his cribbage hands would make better poker hands! The game combines poker and the game of cribbage, and was manufactured by Becton Enterprises, Inc.

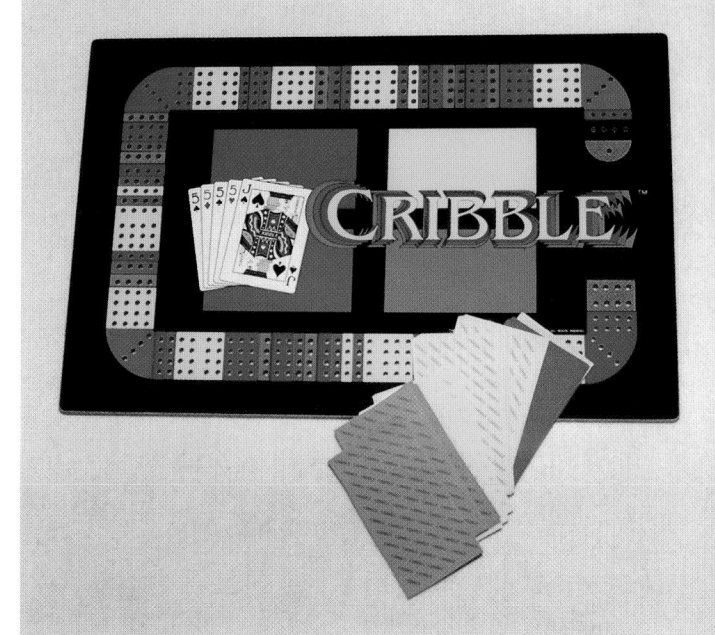

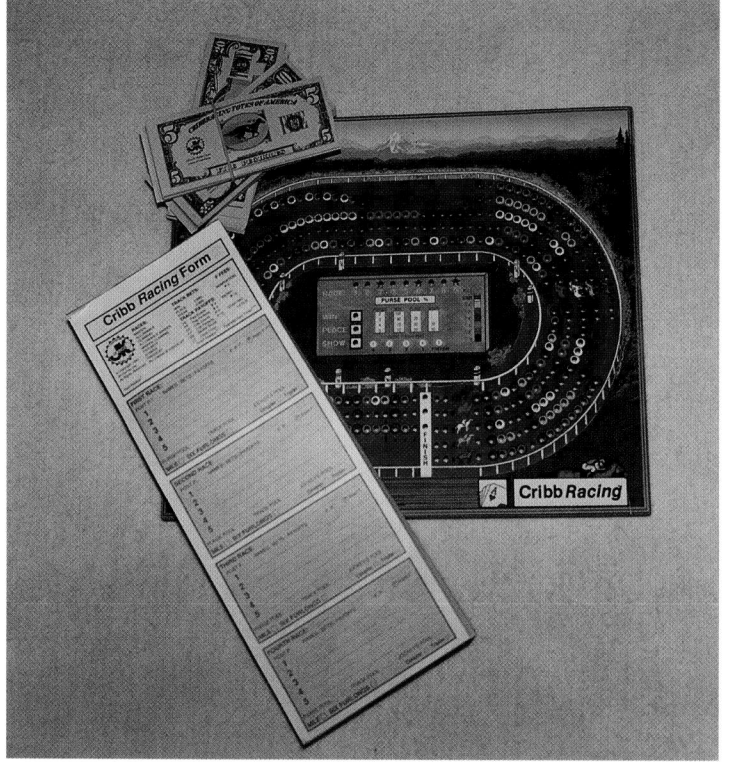

CRIBBRACING™ was copyrighted in 1991 and was produced by JK Games, Inc. The board is in the form of a race track, and the game combines racing and cribbage.

CRIBBAGE FOOTBALL® was copyrighted in 1977 by William D. Goodwin, and combines the game of football with cribbage.

CROSS CRIBB™ was designed by Tony Nelson and copyrighted in 1996. It was published by Maynards.

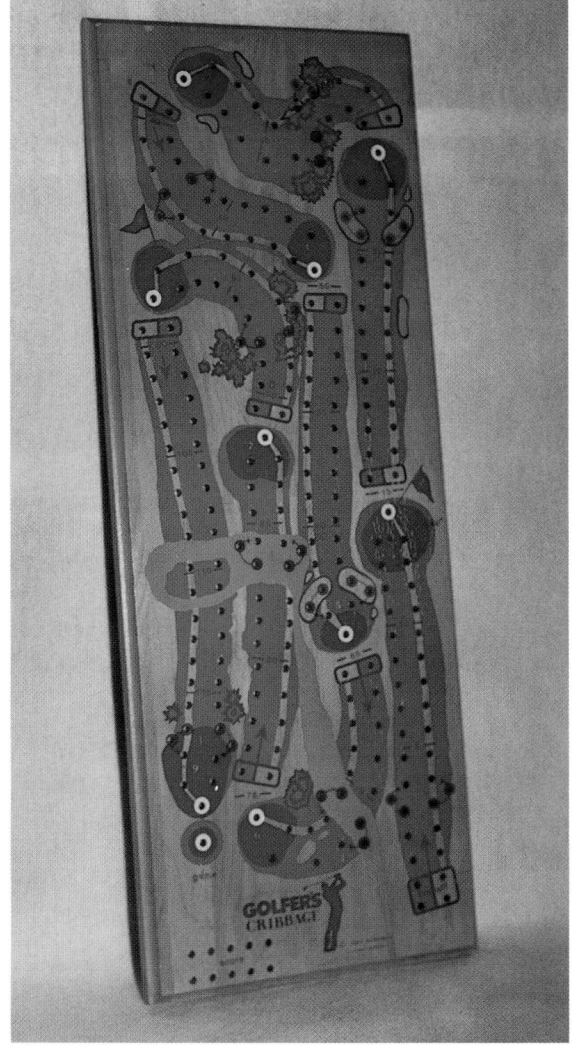

GOLFER'S CRIBBAGE was invented by Marjorie A. and William M. Kendrick and patented by them in 1986. This is the earliest known combination of a golf and cribbage game.

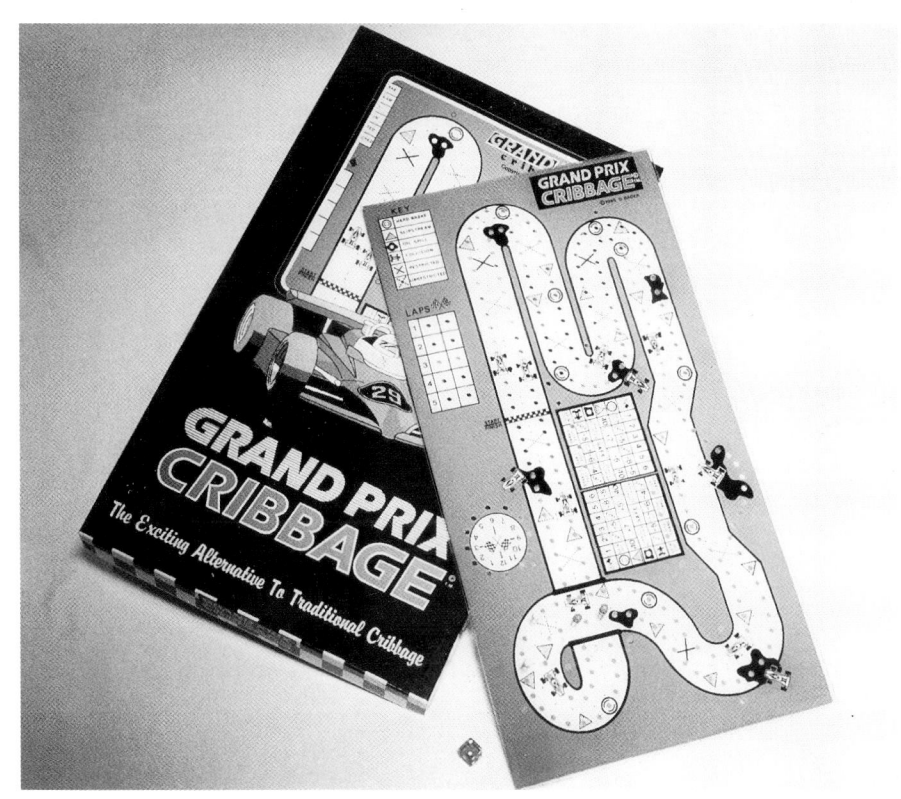

GRAND PRIX CRIBBAGE was manufactured in the 1980s and featured a clear plastic race track. It combined car racing and cribbage.

OPEN CRIBBAGE®(Not Shown) was copyrighted in 1996 and offered a slight variation to the traditional game of cribbage.

PEGOSAURUS™ was copyrighted in 1991 and produced by Allan Ltd. Although this game never became popular, it was a wonderful beginner for young cribbage players. The graphics on the board and playing cards were of dinosaurs, creating a stimulating setting for old and young alike.

PENTAKRIBB® was copyrighted in 1983 and manufactured by D. Higgins Enterprises. A score sheet was used instead of a board.

PENTAKRIBB® **with TUFACE** was manufactured by DalJon, Inc. and was a variation of PentaKribb.

PHILADELPHIA LAWYER
or CRACKER BARREL CRIBBAGE

"An Old Country Store Game Formerly Played on the Top of a Cracker Barrel" "Patent Pending" was printed on the board as well as the title of the game. Although several of these boards have been located, the instructions are still missing. The game was manufactured by Recreational Games, Inc. Northbrook, Illinois.

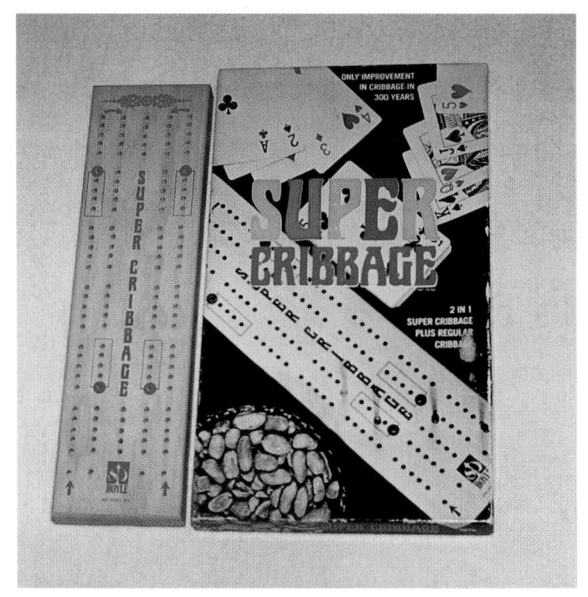

RACE TRACK CRIBBAGE (Not shown), model No. 1949, was produced by Drueke. It consisted of a dual purpose board on which a regulation game of cribbage could be played or a variation called "Race Track Cribbage."

STRATEGY CRIBBAGE (Not shown) was created in the late 1980s and was sold through catalogs. It consisted of a 3 player board with Brooks-style tracks of red-white and blue, divided unevenly by solid white blocks. The number of pegging holes located between the solid white blocks varies from 3 to 6, with total holes on each player's street being 120. Bonus and penalty holes enliven an otherwise traditional game of cribbage.

SUPER CRIBBAGE ,model No. 5070, was produced by Hoyle. The rules offered minor variations to the standard game, and the face of the board was stenciled with rectangles and certain designated holes to identify the variations.

WESTERN CRIBBAGE® was copyrighted in 1986 by W. G. McSpadden, founder of the Western Cribbage Association. This game was never formally manufactured, but many hand-crafted sets were distributed. Each person who purchased the game was awarded a Charter Player Certificate.

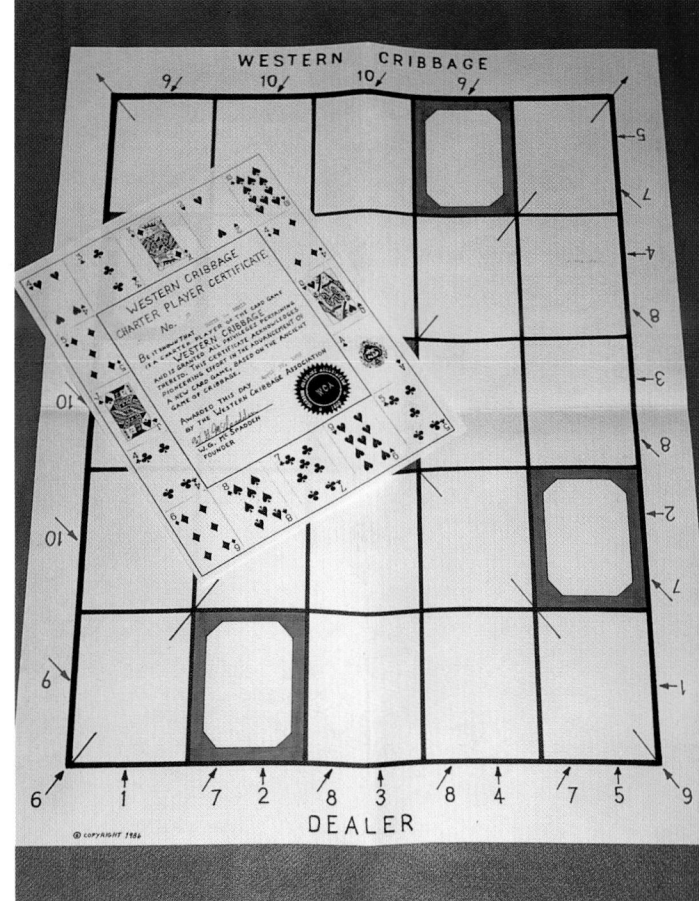

Chapter III. U.S. Cribbage Board Manufacturers and Distributors

There have been many manufacturers of cribbage boards in the United States over the past 150 years. In some cases, the companies were small and existed for the purpose of manufacturing just a few products, and tracing their history has been nearly impossible. In other cases, the companies held high visibility in their respective communities, but after they went out of business, their history disappeared along with them. Piecing together a manufacturer's history can sometimes be frustrating, but when the pieces fall into place and a history emerges, no matter how scant, then the search has been worth the effort. We know a lot more about the cribbage boards that were manufactured than we do about the manufacturers themselves, and the following chapter will list the boards that were produced by them.

Distributors have also played an important role in the cribbage board industry, especially in recent years when we have seen the manufacture of our most popular boards, such as the "29" board, moving to the Far East. American distributors, however, frequently have their logo and name applied to the boards, thus facilitating the identification process. Distributors such as the John N. Hansen Co. will continue to play an important role in the preservation of board styles as the manufacture of the more common styles continues to shift to the Far East.

Abbreviations used in this section are as follow: GW; Games Won; 2P; Two Player; 3P; Three Player T.A.; Twice Around; CMP; Current Market Price

Board model numbers are listed when known and **No.(Unk)** is used when the manufacturer normally used a model number, but it is unknown.

Data on some boards is incomplete because it has been provided only in writing from an owner of the board. Such boards are included, however, for they contribute to a more complete listing and allow the collector to be aware that these boards exist. Some boards have been previously photographed at other sites, and the photos are not as clear as desired. I have included them so that the general characteristics of the boards can be viewed.

A & L Manufacturing Co.: Brooklyn, New York

A & L manufactured higher end game products, such as cribbage boards. Their product line was carried by upper-class stores such as FAO Schwartz.

The company was bought by Crisloid, Inc. in 1970. *Royal Games* was the company's trademark.

Adco Creation:

Racetrack Cribbage: 3P once-around Brooks style track style; tracks are red-blue-green; 7 GW holes each color, boxed at one end; 3 starter holes each color; 15.5" x 3.5". $5

George C. Allis Company: Derby, Connecticut

1) 2P, T.A.; Polished brass cut out board with "claw feet"; 9 GW holes in circles at both ends center; 11.5" x 4". $50

2) *The Princeton:* 3P, T.A.; silver with extended feet; marked *"The Princeton"* on underside; 11" x 3.5". $200

ALPSCO (Adult Leisure Products Corp.): Locust Valley, New York: c. 1966

No. 40: *"Cribbage in the Round."* © 1966; 7.5" Diameter. $35

American Foundation for the Blind, Inc.

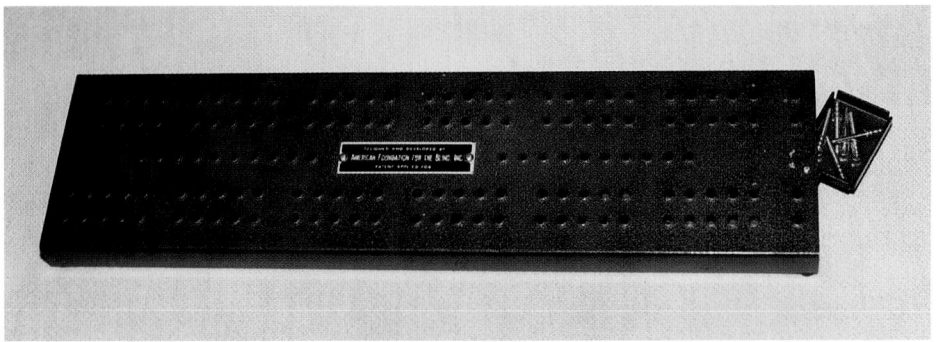

Metal, hollow; raised holes for touch; 14" x 3.75". $25

American Manufacturing Concern: Falconer, New York: c. 1920

Manufactured advertising boards. One classic style is known, which was used for boards which advertised products such as *Lash's Bitters*, *Priest's Indigestion Powder*, *Urban Shoe*, *Buffalo Brewing Co.*, and *Clover Gum*.

Priest's Indigestion Powder. 12.75" x 4.5". $75 - $100

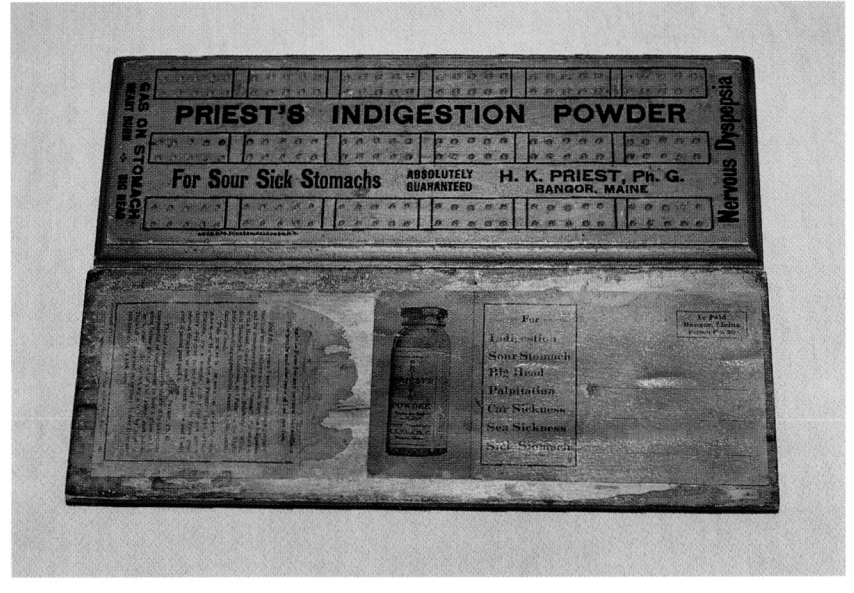

34

Buffalo Brewing Co. 12.75" x 4.5". $75 - $100

Are-Jay Game Co. Inc.: Cleveland, Ohio; c.1940 - 1973

Purchased by Crisloid, Inc. in 1973. Crisloid eliminated duplicate styles of cribbage boards and continued to manufacture many of the others. Crisloid also adopted the concave sides originally used by Are-Jay for use on many of their boards. Most boards were marked *Are-Jay.*

No. 01: *Big D:* 2P,T.A.; 2 starter holes each player; Checkerboard design down center, split by 5 GW holes each player; 9.75" x 2.5". $25

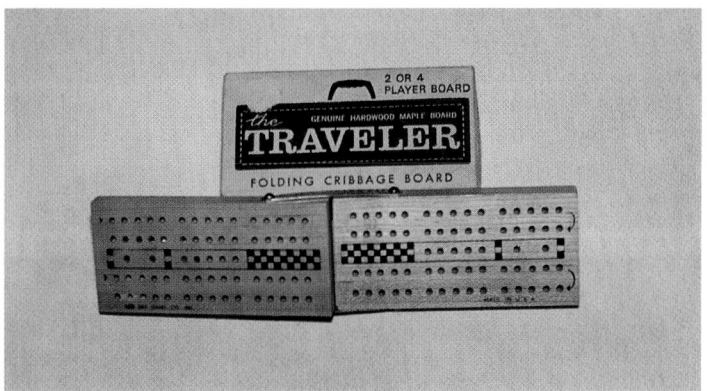

No. 021: *The Traveler:* folds by use of swivel bars on either side, which store both sides of the board face side up; 9" x 2.12". $25

No. 88: 2P; continuous track, 8 boxed GW holes each end; "Continuous Race Track Cribbage Board No. 88" stamped between tracks; identical to Crisloid #1012. 13.5" x 3.5". $25

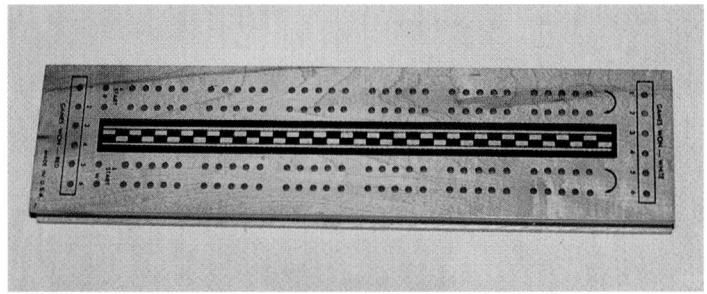

No. 101: Identical to Arthur Popper Games, Inc. No. 101; 11.75" x 3". $15

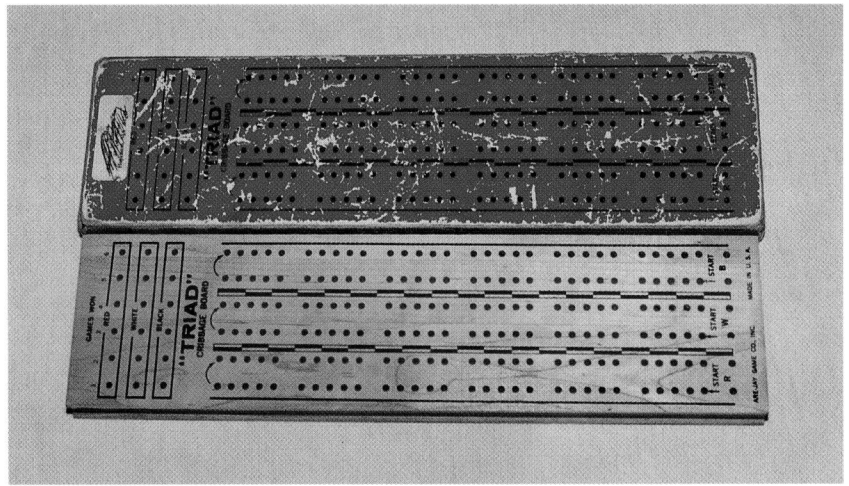

No. 303: *Triad:* rules printed inside box; 12.5" x 3.25". $20

No. 614: *Champion:* 2P, continuous around outer edge; center of board has peg holes for Games, Skunks, Legs, Total Points; 14" x 6.75". $20

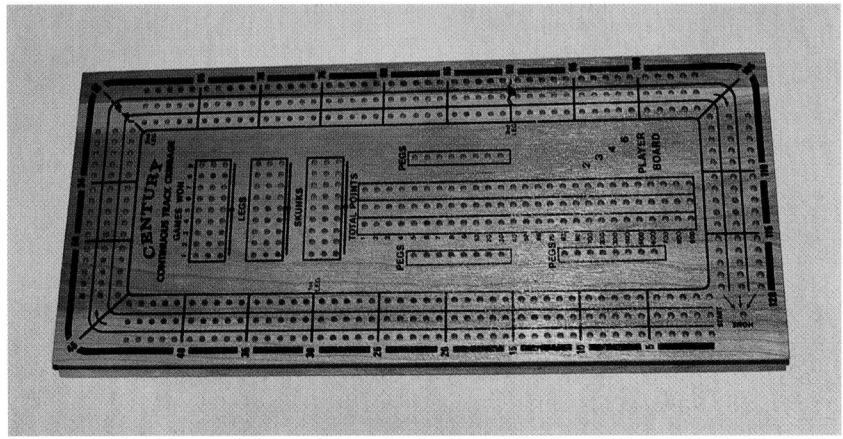

No. 715: *Century:* identical to Crisloid No. 1018; 14.5" x 6". $25

No. (Unk): 2P, continuous track; *Triumph continuous Track Cribbage;* center of board has peg holes for GW, Legs, Skunk. Identical to Baron No. 31/350 but has skunks instead of stars. 13.12" x 5.75". $20

Arrco Playing Card Company: Chicago, Illinois

A major manufacturer of children's card games, they distributed cribbage boards.

No. 150W: Japan; 11.75" x 2.85". $10

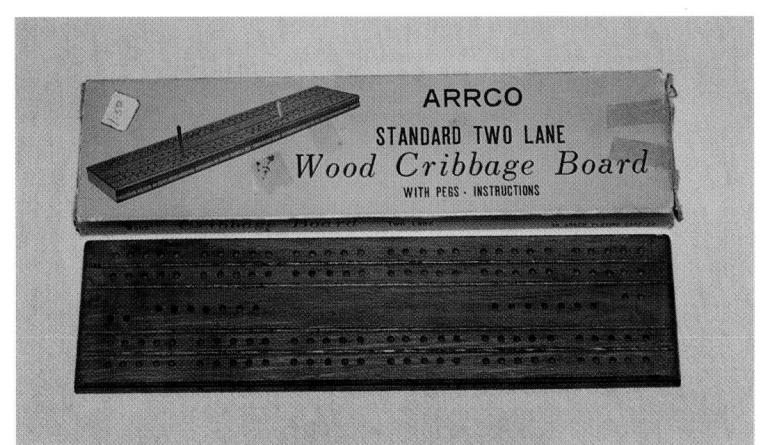

Arrow Cribbage Co.: St. Paul, Minnesota: c. 1941

2P, T.A.; black plastic board with white arrows surrounding each 5 holes; also blue, with black arrows. 5 GW holes each end in white rectangles; 2 starter holes each player in white rectangles at one end; wooden base pulls apart: Patent design # 127,917 was issued on 06/24/41 to Calvin D. Williams of Cloquet, Minnesota, with one-half assigned to Abner H. Nerhaugen of Duluth, Minnesota. 9.75" x 2 .75 x 1.5". $30

Artek Reproductions: Peterborough, New Hampshire: c. 1975 - present.

Artek's *"Save the Whale"* creations, including man-made "ivory" scrimshawed cribbage boards, are the focus of their product lines. Many are reproductions of ivory cribbage boards which can be found in nautical museums, and they are recreated to exact detail. The double 5 holes on all boards are outlined with black scrimshawed lines. Metal pegs with all boards. The company merged with Dahle USA in 1996.

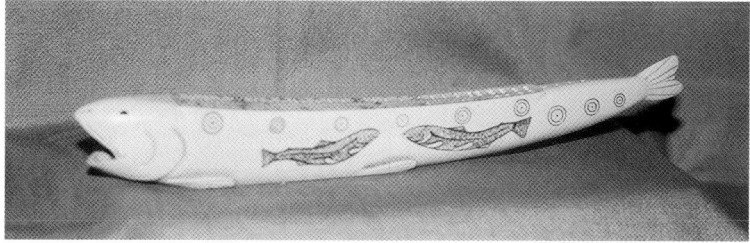

No. M532: 8" x 1". CMP

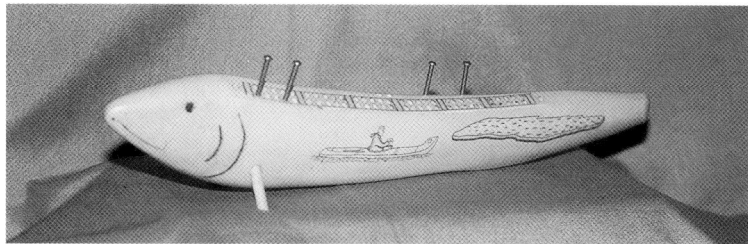

No. M534: 14" x 1.5" x 2.5" h. CMP

No. M538: 2P, T.A.; three dimensional walrus with tusks; Eskimo scenes scrimshawed on sides; 2 starter holes each player; 11" x 1.5" x 1.5"H. CMP

No. M541: 2P, T.A.; flat whale mounted on hardwood base; various scenes scrimshawed on face; 1 starter hole each player; 12" x 4". CMP

No. M542: 2P, T.A.; three dimensional tusk; various figures scrimshawed on face; 10" x 1.25". CMP

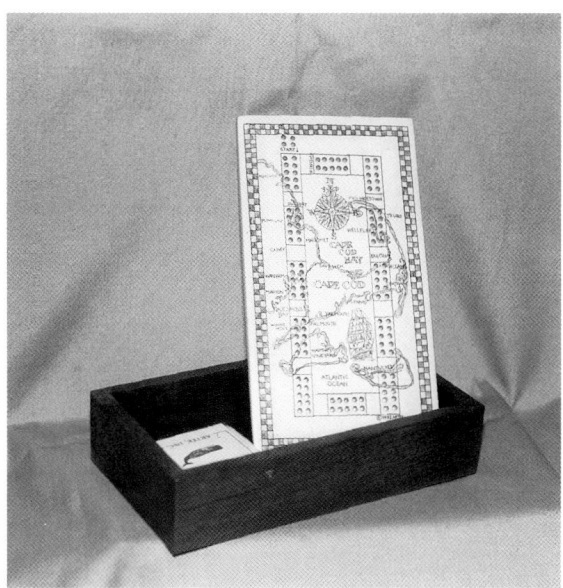

No. 897: 8.5" x 5" x 2.25"H. CMP

Arthur Popper Games, Inc.: NY 12, New York

Distributor of cribbage boards.

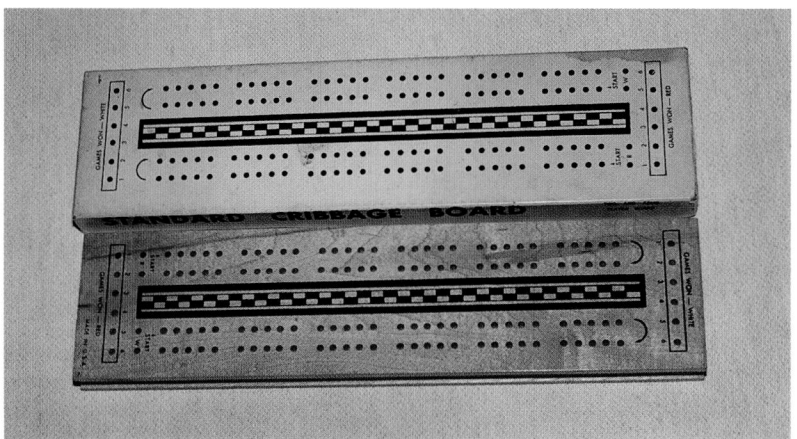

No. 101: Identical to Are-Jay No. 101; 11.75" x 3". $15

AP Games:

Distributor of cribbage boards. AP Games and Arthur Popper Games, Inc. both distributed cribbage boards from well-known manufacturers. Although their names are similar, there is no evidence yet that the two companies were related.

No. 885: 2P, T.A.; black grommets in all pegging holes; white grommets in 12 + 1 GW holes each end center and in the 4 starter holes. 11" x 2.5". $20

No. UNK; Identical to Horn No. C18; 11.5" x 2.5". $20

H. Baron Co. Inc.: 233-4th Ave. New York 3, New York: 1930s - 1972

H. Baron Co. Inc. was located in New York City for many years, and the factory was located in Long Island City. They were involved in the manufacture of cribbage boards, other game products, and miscellaneous items such as steel balls.

Over the years, Baron acquired several other manufacturers of cribbage boards, and with several of the acquisitions, the name of the company was altered to reflect the purchase. Some of the manufacturers purchased by Baron were Rottgames of NYC, John Samuels Co. of NYC (listed only as J.S. Co.), and Metro Mfg. Co.

When Baron quit the manufacturing business in 1972, Crisloid, Inc. purchased Baron's factory equipment and the rights to manufacture the cribbage boards. Crisloid continued to manufacture most of the cribbage board styles that had been previously made by Baron. Baron, by the way, converted his Long Island City factory into a motel and entered the business.

The Baron boxes are identified with the model numbers and the name of the company, but the boards themselves are not marked. Unless the board is purchased in the box, some research will be required to complete the profile. The boxes were printed in many designs, with no one design appearing to dominate in use. Some of the boxes pictured the enclosed board, while other boxes were printed with a leather grained pattern.

Most of the boards are of wood, but at least two models are plastic or Bakelite. Some of the board styles have a rectangular checkerboard pattern running down the center, some divided, some reaching from end to end. The positive identification of a Baron board with this pattern is the addition of two separate, staggered lines at the outer edge of the pattern, which was used only by Baron. Many of the newer models had concave sides.

Baron's cribbage board models, as well as those of the companies that they purchased, are included in this list, since many of Baron's styles were identical to ones manufactured by the old firms. Model numbers are identified for both firms, where known. One Baron board, No. 31/350, was sold in a box which pictured a board marked Are-Jay Co. Are-Jay and Baron were both purchased by Crisloid in the 1970s.

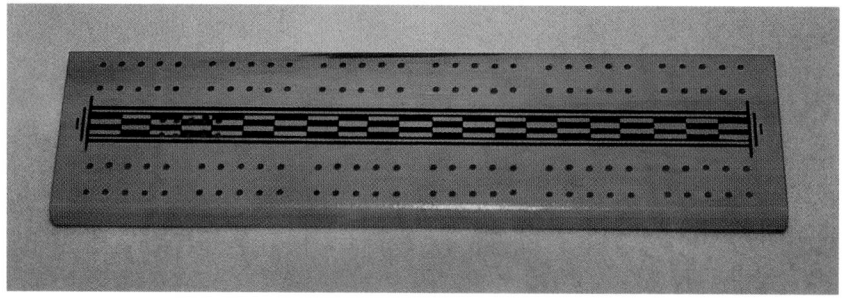

No. 1062B: (Rottgames); 11.5" x 2.6". $25

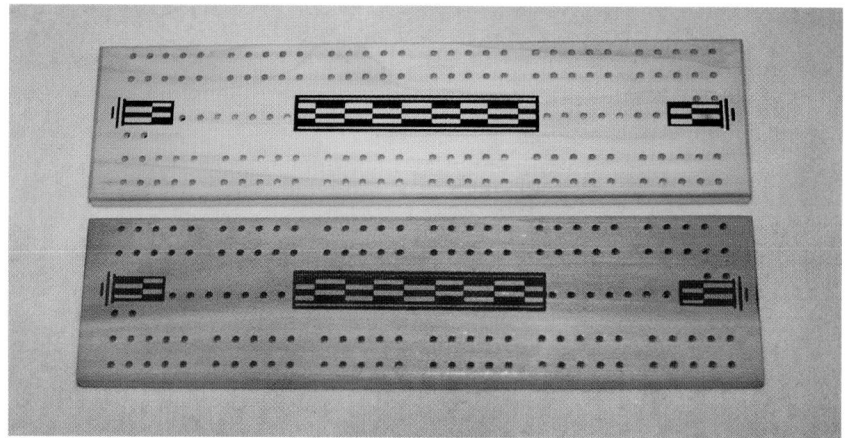

No. 5-1062-100: (H. Baron Co., Inc.) (Baron, Rott, and Samuels, Inc.); brown or black broken Baron checkerboard design down center; 11.5" x 2.6". $25

No. 6-1062/150: 3P, T.A.; 5 x 2 stenciled lines dividing streets and double 5 holes; 2 starter holes each player. $25

No. 14: (H. Baron, Co.); black Baron checkerboard design; was originally manufactured by Rottgames (No. 1052B). 8.25" x 2.25". $20

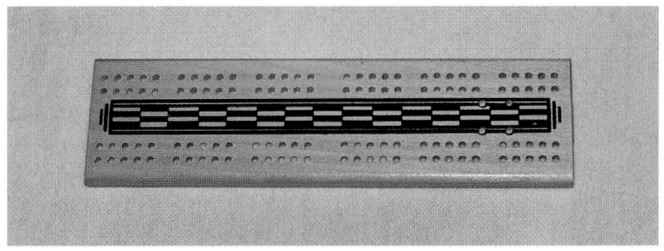

No. 14-4/80 (Baron, Rott and Samuels, Inc.): Same as No. 14, but checkerboard is brown. $20

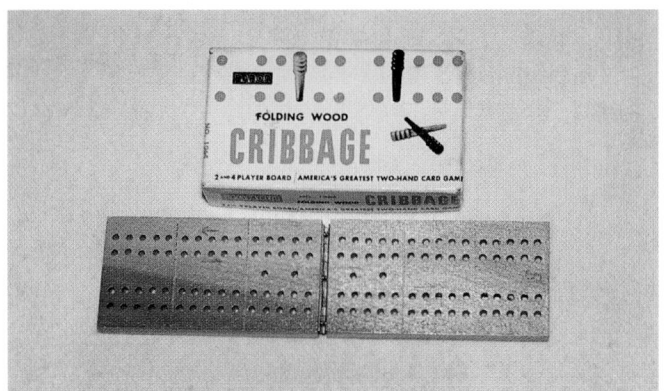

No. 1064 (H. Baron Co. Inc.): 7.5" x 2" open. $20

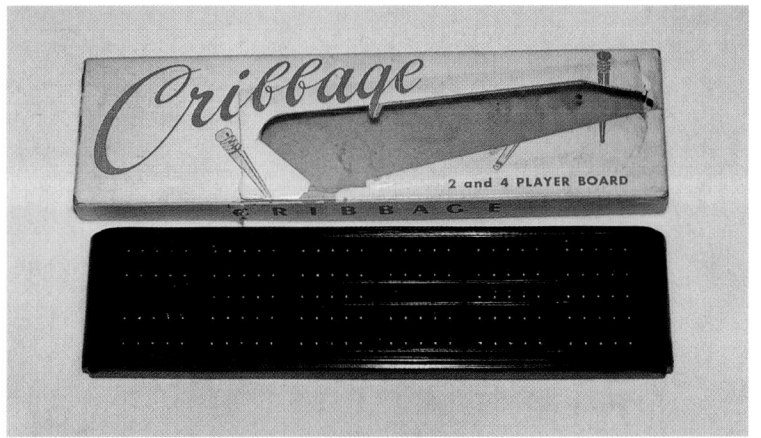

No. 17/100 (H. Baron Co.): Black molded Bakelite board; letters *"WPM"* molded in plastic under peg cover; originally Metro Games No. 17; 10" x 2.5". $20

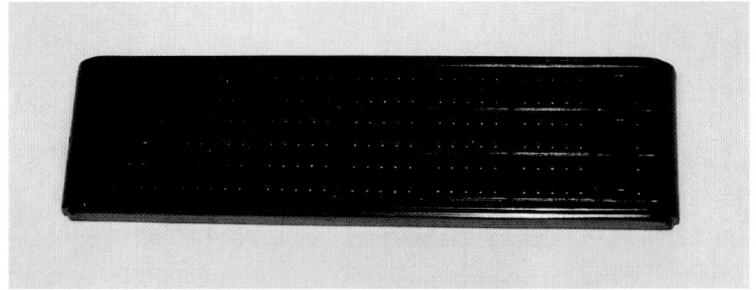

No. 18/100 (H. Baron Co.): Black or brown molded Bakelite board; letters *"WPM"* molded in plastic under peg cover; originally Metro Games No. 18; 10.75" x 3". $20

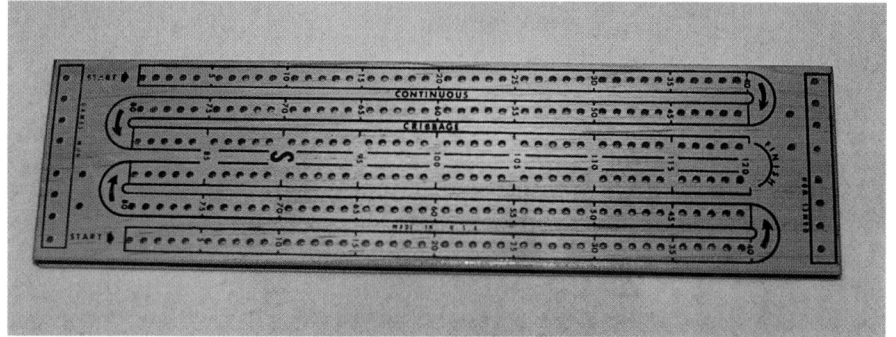

No. 28/250 (Baron, Rott, and Samuels, Inc.): Japan. Crisloid made identical board, No. unknown; 13.5" x 3.5". $20

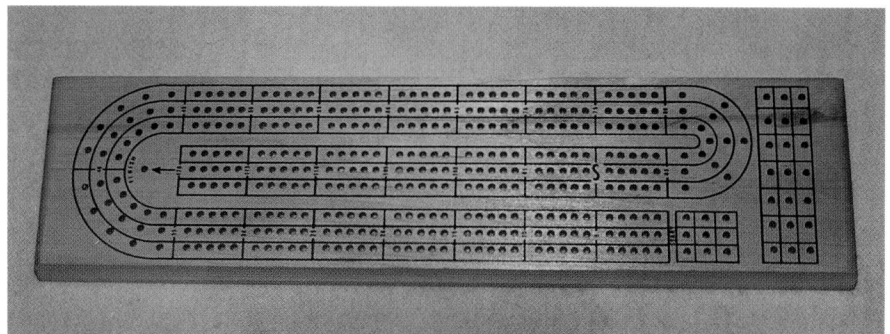

No. 30/350 (Baron, Rott and Samuels, Inc.): 14.5" x 3.75". $20

No. 31/350 (Baron, Rott and Samuels, Inc.): *"Tournament Continuous Play Cribbage"*: 14" x 6". $25

No. (Unk.): (Rottgames): Game box with various game pieces; small 2P, T.A. cribbage board included; Box 15" x 10" x 4.5". $25

No. (Unk.): (John Samuels Adult Games; 34 West St.; New York, New York): 2P, T.A.; leather folding with snap/flap closure; board is made from 5 layers of leather; mfg. in 1952; brown box with marbled surface; 9.35" x 2.5" open. $20

Baron /Scott Enterprises, Inc.: Columbia, Maryland: - present

Baron/Scott is a distributor of cribbage boards which are of foreign manufacture.

No. 3003: 3P once-around Brooks style track with each player's track color-coded (R-G-B); 7 boxed GW holes at one end for each player. Upper sides of board are grooved. CMP

No. 3005: 3P once-around rectangular board with each player's pegging holes color-coded (R-G-B) for all scoring; marked *"Continuous Track Cribbage"*; concave sides; scoring areas in center for GW, Legs, Skunks, Total Points. 14" x 6". CMP

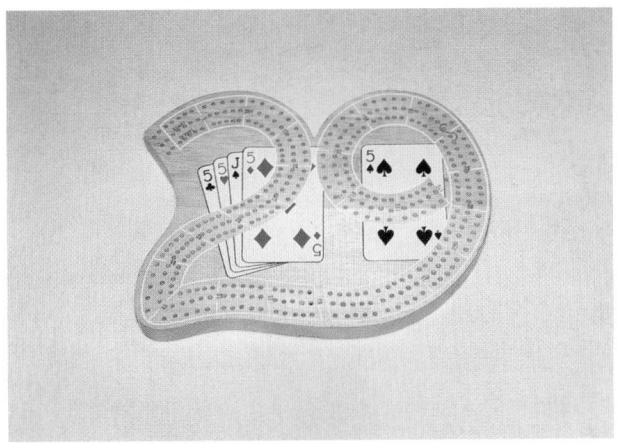

No. CL29: Taiwan; 9.5" x 7". CMP

Baron, Rott & Samuels:

    See H. Baron Co.

The Board Room: Hebron, Maine: 1993 - present.

    The company was originally founded by William Thompson in 1993, and after his death it was re-organized by Jim Mavor. The company manufactures boards of cedar and other woods, and they have brass eyelets in all pegging holes. The double 5 holes are outlined with stenciled rectangles of various colors. Pegs are solid brass. All boards have one starter hole for each player.

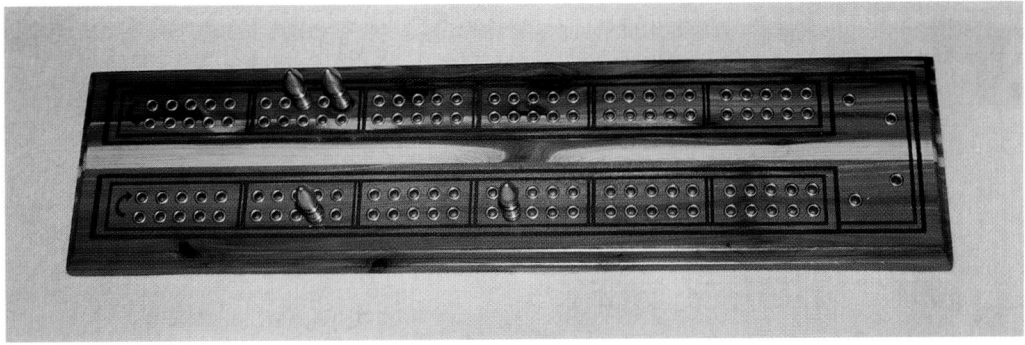

Board Room Classic: 2.5" pegs; 21.5" x 5.5". CMP

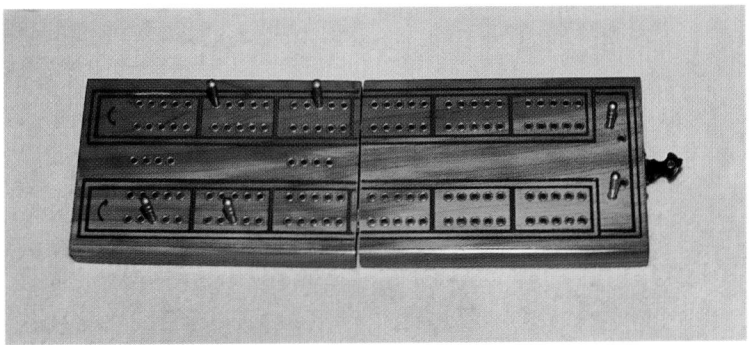

Folding Travel: 11.75" x 3.75". CMP

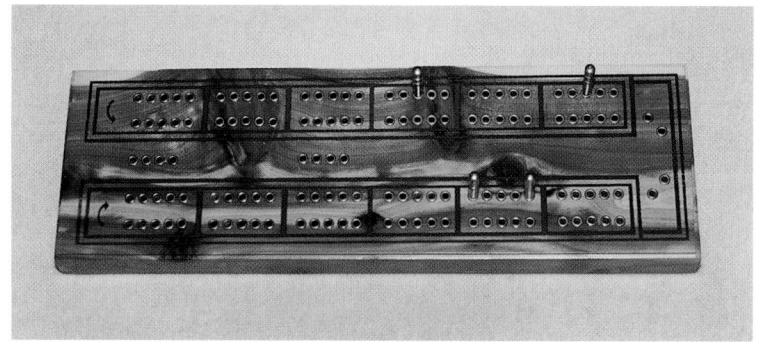

Small straight board: 11.85" x 3.75". CMP

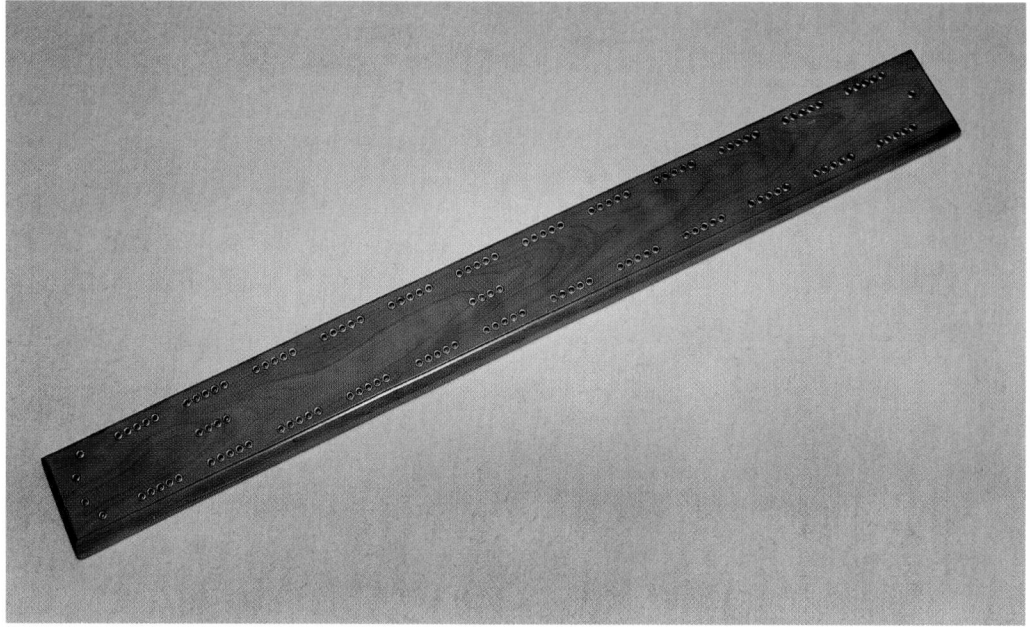

Street variation: single row of 12 sets of 5 holes on each outer edge; 2 starter holes each player; 23.5" x 2.5". CMP

Bonus Cribbage Co.: Minneapolis, Minnesota: c. 1959

Manufactured a game variation called *Bonus Cribbage*, which was © in 1959 by Blaine G. Danielson.

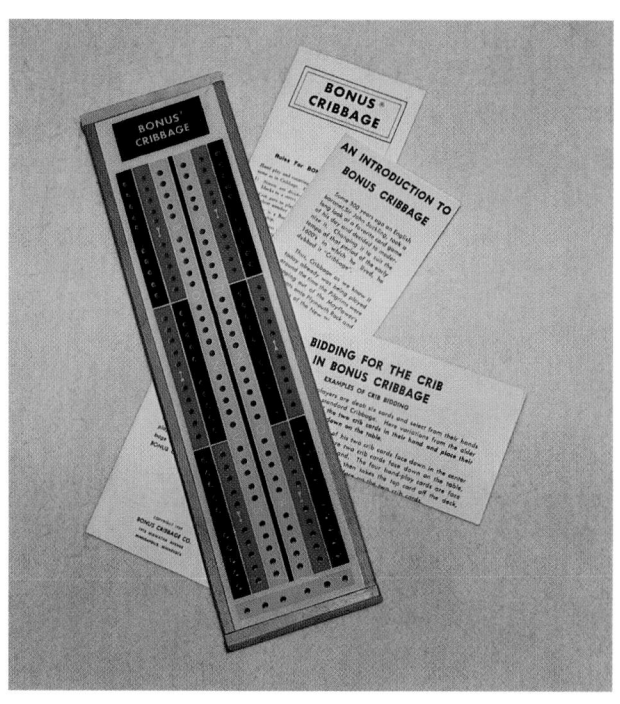

"Bonus Cribbage": 2 sizes; 11.75" x 3.25" or 15.75" x 4.75". $20

Charles A. Brewer & Sons: Chicago, Illinois: c. 1925

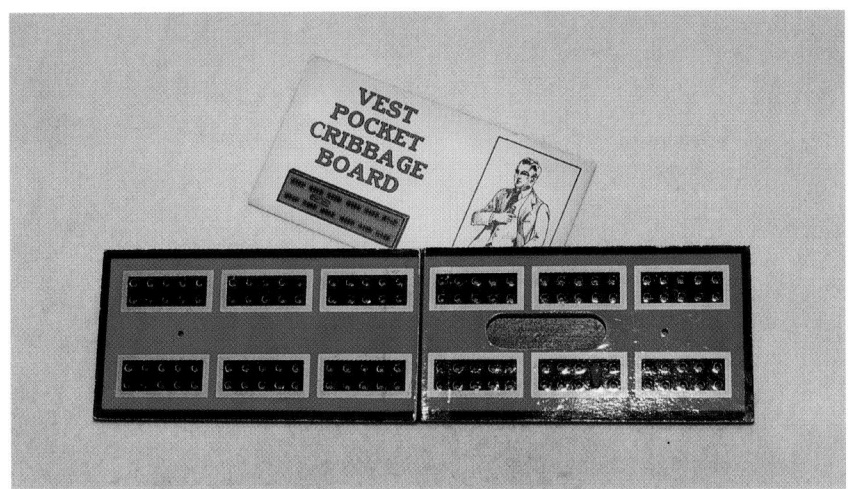

Pressed paper folding advertising board: name of company found in bottom of peg storage area; red background, with black rectangles; 9.5" x 2.5". $20

Brookstone: Peterborough, New Hampshire Distributors

No. 11995: 4P walnut board, continuous play around outer edge; was manufactured for them by Drueke; 15.35" x 7.12". $15

No. Unk: Key chain cribbage board, manufactured for them by TNM, has *Brookstone* on face. 3.75" x 1.25". $15

Cape Shore Inc.: Yarmouth, Maine: - present.

Produced cribbage board scorepads in different designs, some packaged with pencils and deck of playing cards with matching design.

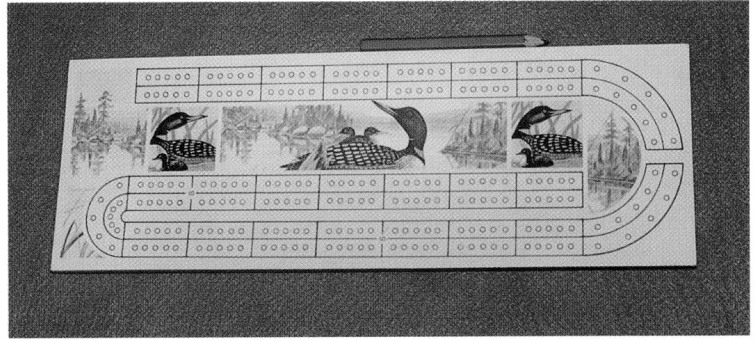

Scorepad of 50 sheets: 8.5" x 3.75"; 25 sheets: 11.75" x 4". $4

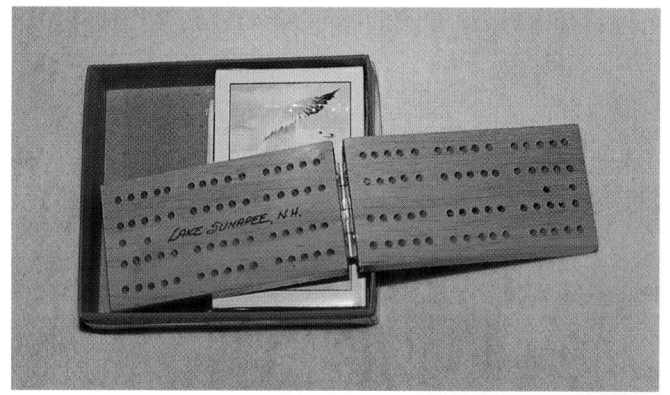

Souvenir Traveling Cribbage Set with cards: 7.5" x 2" open. CMP

Cardinal Industries., Inc.: Brooklyn 11, New York, then Long Island City, New York. 1945: - present.

Cardinal Industries was founded by Les Berger in 1945, and the family continues to own the business to this day. The company is a major contributor in the board game industry. The older boards have the old Cardinal logo (which is an encircled Cardinal on a branch) and step-down sides. The newer boards have *Cardinal* stenciled on them.

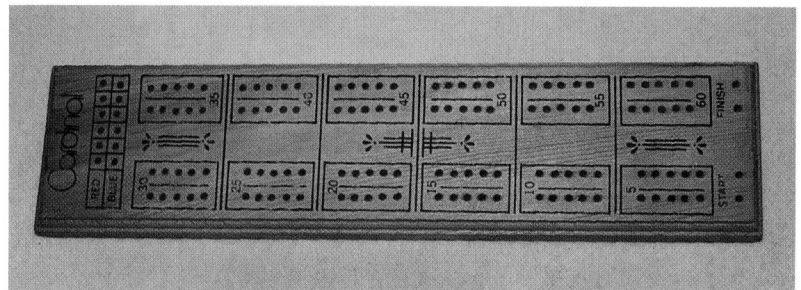

No. 61 (old): USA; 11.75" x 2.5". $15

No.61 (new): Has *Cardinal* stenciled at top, step-down sides; GW holes stenciled in red and blue; Taiwan; 11.75" x 2.75". CMP

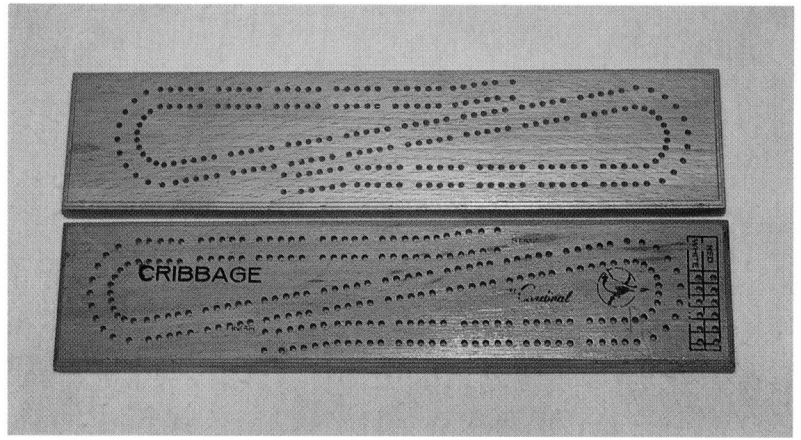

No. 62 (old): USA; was also made without stenciling; 13.5" x 2.85". $15

46

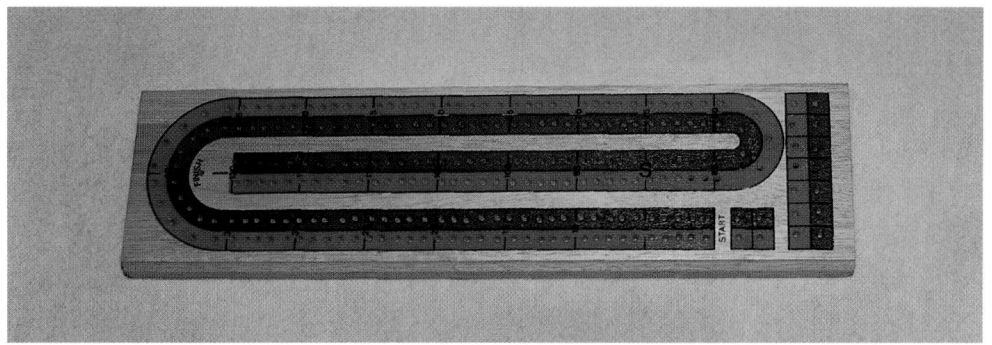

No. 62 (new): Indonesia; 13.5" x 3.5". CMP

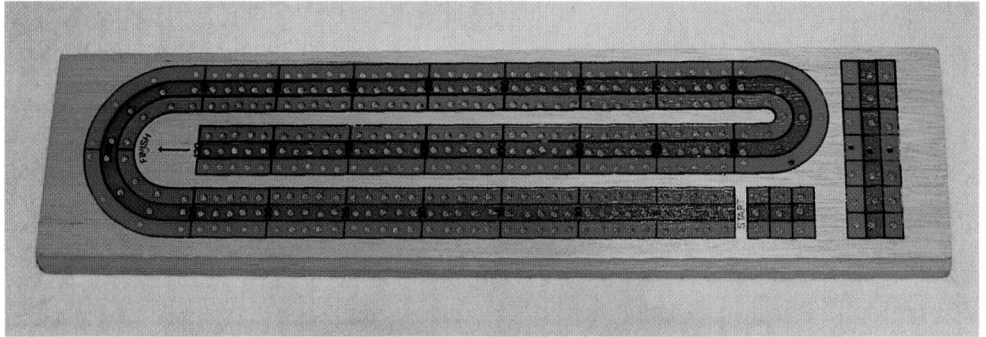

No. 63: Indonesia: 14.75" x 3.75". CMP

No. 6311: Identical to No. 63, but box includes deck of cards. CMP

The Carrom Co.: Ludington, Michigan: 1889 - present

The company was originally called the Ludington Novelty Works and was founded in 1889 by Henry Haskell for the purpose of manufacturing a brand new board game called Carrom that he had patented. It was renamed Carrom Co. in 1910 when the business was sold. Carrom has never directly manufactured cribbage boards. The firm purchased the Drueke Co. in 1992 and Drueke continues to manufacture most of their old product line, including cribbage boards. *See Drueke.*

G. H. Cook, Co.: Arlington, Washington: 1980s - present.

The company was founded by Gordon H. Cook, who is known internationally as a sculptor. The company manufactures man-made ivory products, which are individually scrimshawed. The cribbage board was manufactured until 1993.

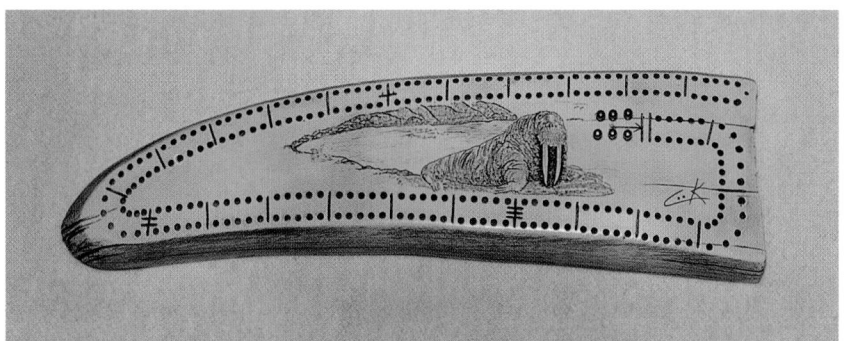

No. GC1: Various designs, such as sailing vessels, walrus, the state of Alaska, scrimshawed on face. 12" x 3.5". $55

Cornwall Products: South Paris, Maine

The company was founded by Hamilton Oxley Cornwall and was purchased from him by his son Stanley Hamilton Cornwall in 1967. Stanley owned the business until he sold it in 1974 and during these manufacturing years, the company was feted as the largest manufacturer of wooden giftware in the USA, growing from 65 employees to 350 employees before being sold. The company manufactured several models of cribbage boards, made mostly of pine. Besides cribbage boards, they also manufactured other game boards, such as checkers, chess, and tic tac toe. The company is still in existence, but it ceased the manufacture of cribbage boards many years ago. Most boards have the Cornwall logo stamped on the underside.

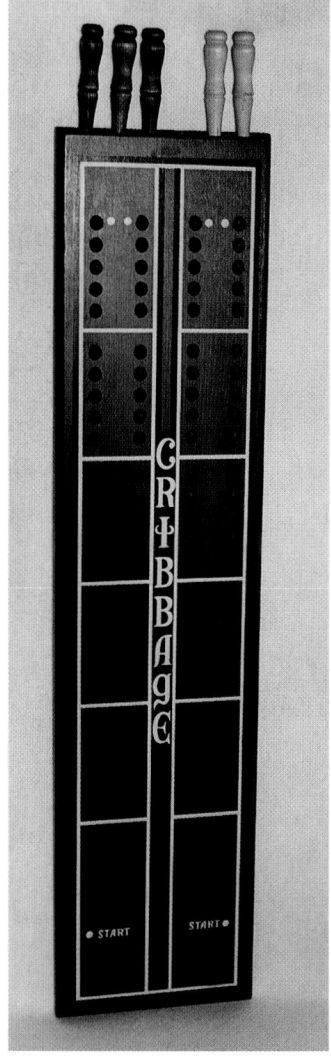 

No. 417: 28.25" x 6.5". $25   **No. 417A:** 16" x 4.5". $20

No. 418: Cribbage table; similar to wall model No.417. $40

No. 418A: Cribbage bench made from a tree slab; 17" H, 47" L, 9" W. $60

No. 554: *See models 554A & B. No legs.* $25

No. 554A: Executive Table; same as # 554B, but straight black legs. $30

No. 554B: Executive Pine Coffee Table Board; edge of table is "wavy." Could be purchased with S. & H. green stamps in the 1970s; 29" x 9.5" x 16.5". $30

No. 910: Stub legged board. 23.5" x 8". $25

Country Woods Co.: Hayward, Wisconsin: - present

Country Woods manufactures a variety of wood inlay boards, which can be found in the marketplace.

Crestline Manufacturing Co.: Santa Ana, California

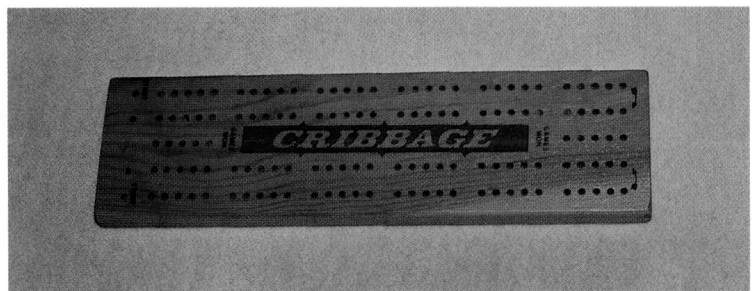

No. 111: Stenciled solid blue center panel; 10.5" x 2.75". $15

No. 114: 2P, Brooks style track; 6 GW holes each player; solid stenciled red line between tracks; Identical to Kent No. 5053. 13.25" x 4". $15

Crib-Derby Co.: 1449 Laurel Ave., St. Paul, Minnesota: c. 1948

The Crib-Derby Company manufactured a wooden oval race track style cribbage board in the 1940s. On 6/08/48, Design Patent # 149,863 was issued to Rhys Orville Evans of St. Paul, Minnesota for the design of the board. Interestingly, the board pictured on the patent was a hollowed out version, identical to the board that was later manufactured in plastic by E. S. Lowe, Co.

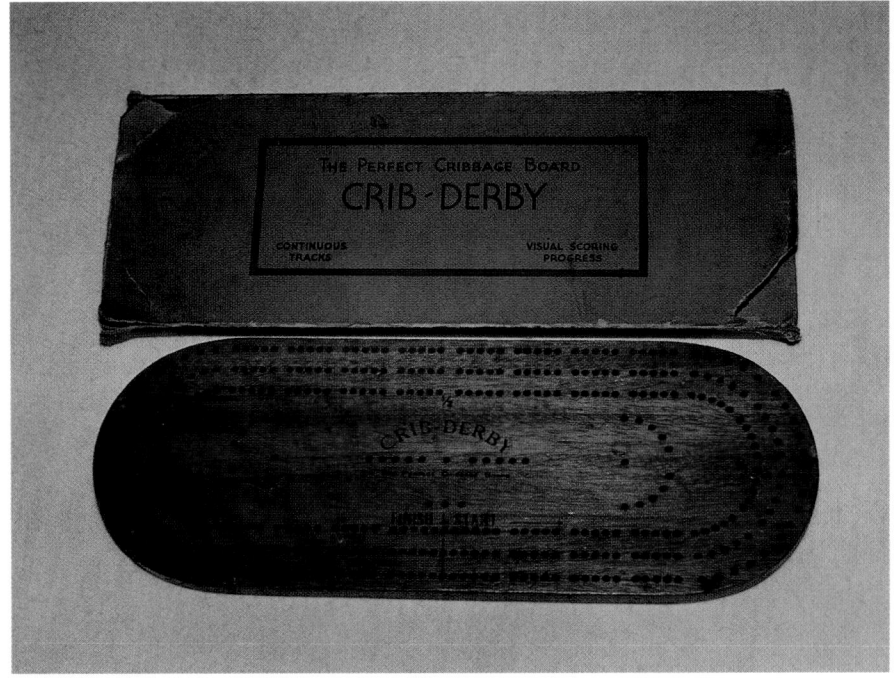

Stenciled *"Crib-Derby The Perfect Cribbage Board"*. 14" x 5". $50

Crisloid, Inc.: Providence, Rhode Island: 1947 - present

Crisloid, Inc., formerly known as Crisloid Plastics, Inc., bought out several board manufacturers in the 1970s, including A & L Mfg. Co. in 1970, H. Baron & Co. in 1972, and Are-Jay Game Co. of Cleveland in 1973. Some of the board styles from these former companies are still manufactured by Crisloid. The Brooks-style track boards (No. 1030 and 1031) are still manufactured by Crisloid, the last to be "Made in the U.S.A." Unless otherwise noted, Crisloid boards feature concave sides, which was originally found on both Are-Jay and Baron cribbage boards. Most of their boards are manufactured in their factory, which is located in Providence.

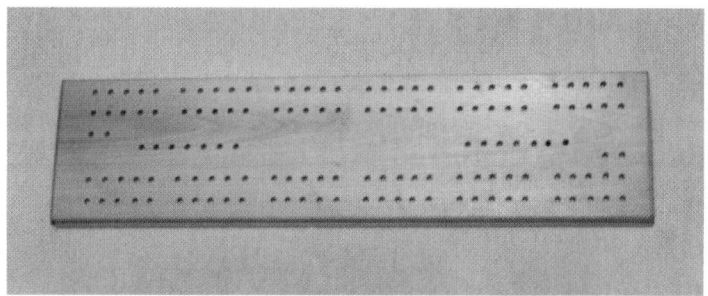

No. 987: Japan; 11.5" x 2.35". $15

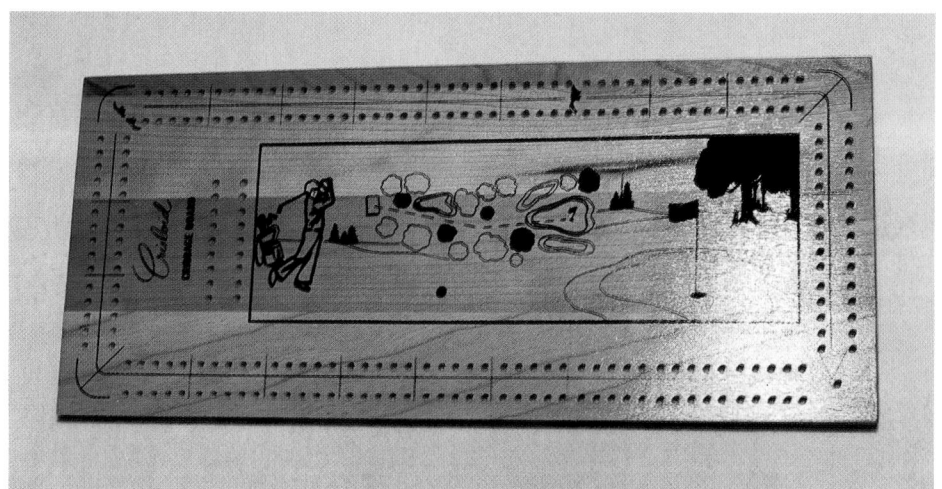

No. 1017: Silk screened decal of golfer; 14" x 6". CMP

The following boards are same style as #1017, with different decals.

No. 1002: Reclining cat. CMP

No. 1003: Still life of fruit and pitcher. CMP

No. 1004: Mallard. (actually a Loon) CMP

No. 1005: Haley's Comet. CMP

No. 1007: Wildlife. CMP

No. 1009: Seashore with lighthouse. CMP

No. 1010: Barnyard. CMP

No. 1011: Black Angus. CMP

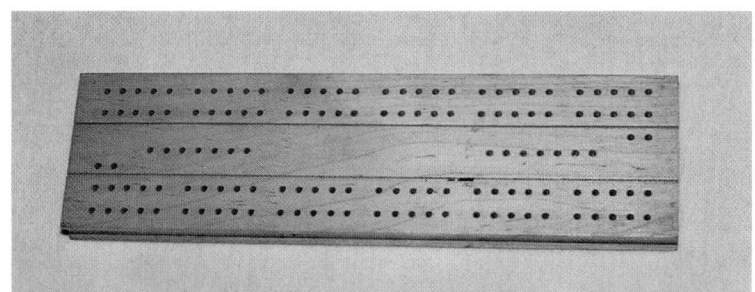

No. 1006: Grooved each side of center; 11.5" x 3". CMP

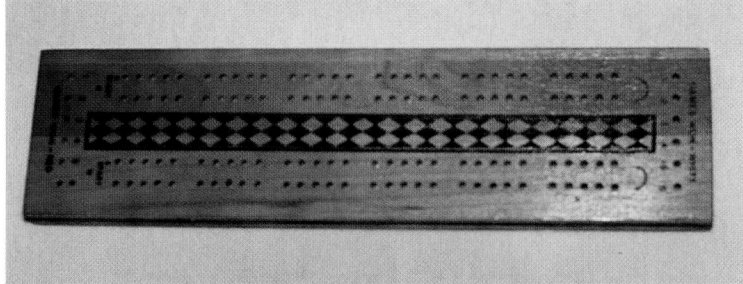

No. 1008: Stenciled diamond pattern; 11.5" x 3". CMP

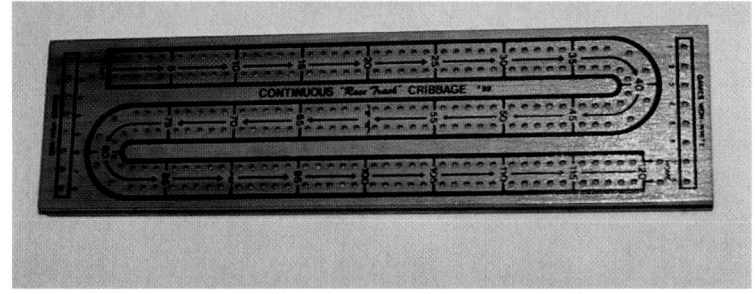

No. 1012: 13.25" x 3.25". CMP

No. 1014: 2P, continuous around outer edge; marked *Champion Continuous Track Cribbage:* center of board contains various sets of holes marked *Games Won, Skunks, Total Points: Pegs:* 14" x 6". CMP

No. 1015: 2P, T.A.; folding walnut; 2 starter holes each end center; 7.5" x 2.12" open. CMP

No. 1016: Identical to No. 1014 except players' scoring tracks and center holes are color coded red or blue. CMP

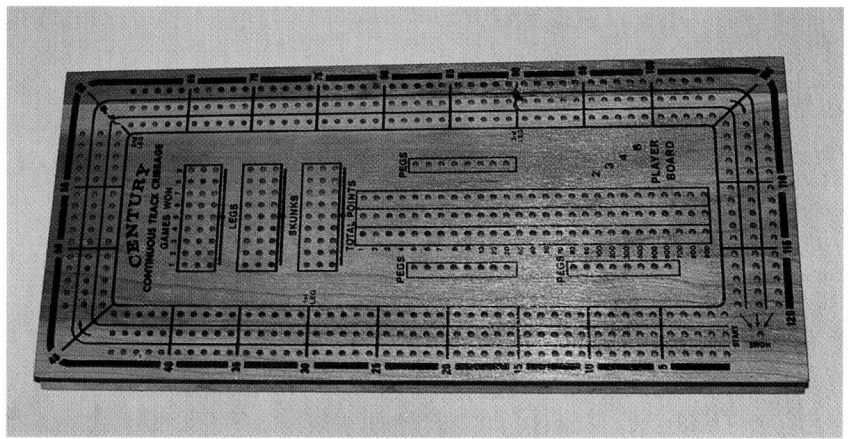

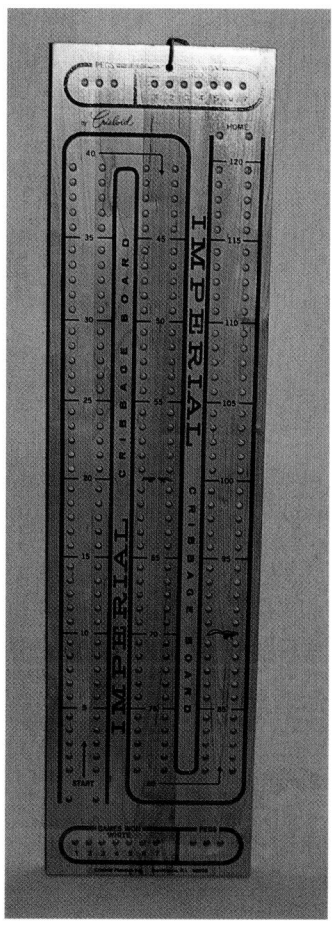

No. 1018: *Century*; identical to Are-Jay No. 715; 14.5" x 6". CMP

No. 1020: 2P, stenciled; 29.5" x 7.6". CMP

No. 1019: Identical to No. 1018 except players' scoring tracks and center holes are color coded red, yellow or blue. Similar to Baron #31/350. CMP

No. 1022: 3P, continuous track; stenciled white; 14.5" x 6.5". CMP

No. 1025: 2P, T.A.; folding; stores in leatherette case with deck of cards; board identical to No. 1015. CMP

No. 1026: 2P, T.A.; folding, velour bag with deck of cards; board identical to No. 1015. CMP

No. 1028: 2P, T.A.; walnut box with center top swivel; brass plate in center; card and peg storage in box; 2 sets of 7 GW holes and 2 starter holes down center; 11.5" x 3.35". CMP

No. 1030: 3P, continuous Brooks style track; 3 sets of 9 GW holes, boxed at one end; 3 sets of 3 starter holes, boxed; peg out hole marked *Finish*; 14" x 3.6 ". CMP

No. 1031: Identical to No. 1030 except players' scoring tracks and GW holes are color coded red, yellow, and blue. CMP

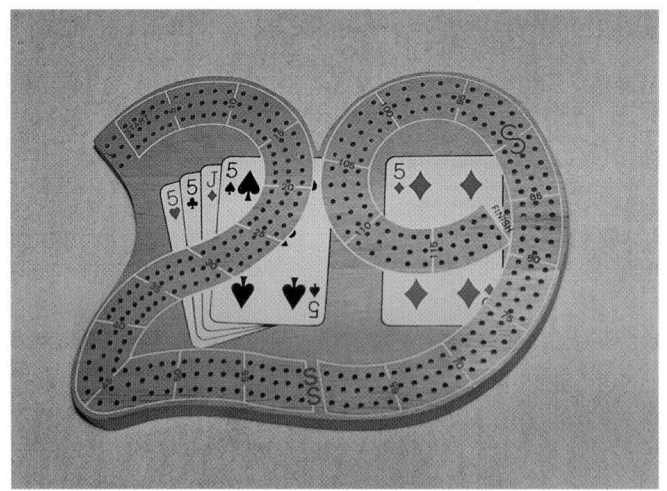

No. 1040: *Official Mister 29 Cribbage Board:* imported; 9.5" x 7". CMP

No. 1044: *Royal Four Player Cribbage:* same style as No. 1045, but streets not color-coded; 14" x 6". CMP

No. 1050: 2P, continuous miniature "29" board; marked *Official Mister 29 Cribbage Board:* 5 diamonds cut card; imported; 6" x 4.25". CMP

No. 1071: 2P, rue buck. CMP

No. 1072: Wood ducks. CMP

No. 1073: Pintail duck. CMP

No. 1080: Center polymer insert of scrimshawed schooner; 14" x 6". CMP

No. 1081: Center polymer insert of Clipper Ship; 14" x 6". CMP

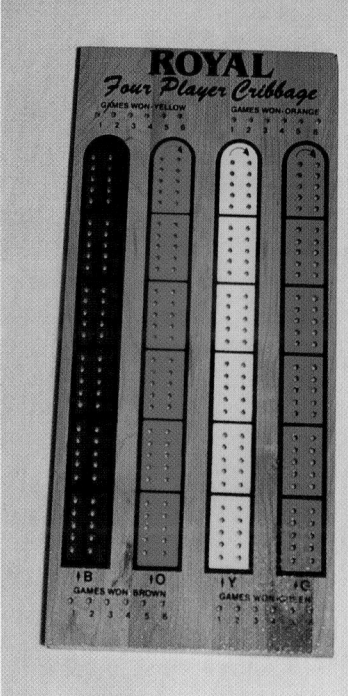

No. 1045: Stenciled brown, red, yellow, and green. CMP

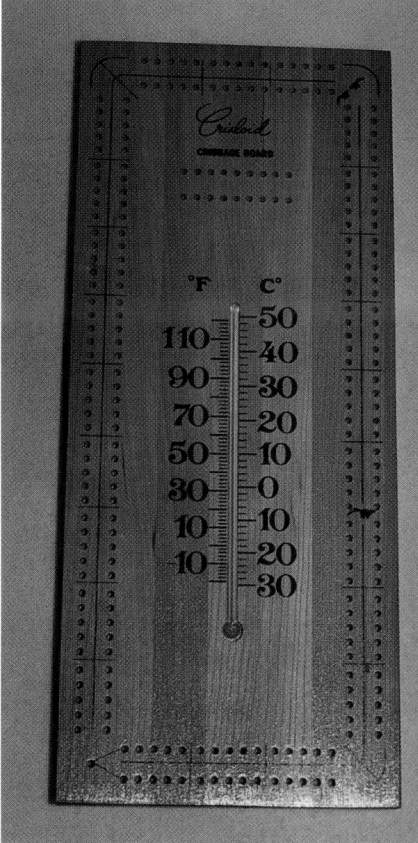

No. 1355: Working thermometer located in center of board; board style identical to No. 1001. CMP

No. 1082: Seaman; 14" x 6". CMP

No. (Unk): 2P, continuous by jumping through 40 holes each line; 8 GW holes each end with solid black line; marked *Made in USA* and *Continuous Track Cribbage* between rows; identical to Baron No. 28/250. 13.5" x 3.5". $20

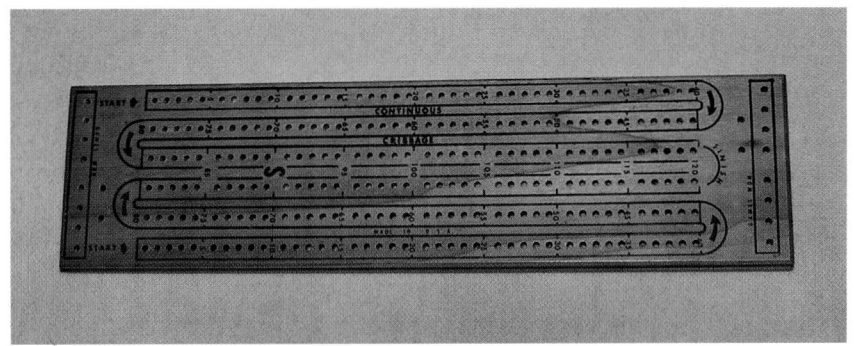

No. (Unk): Marked *Continuous Cribbage.* 12" x 3". $20

No. (Unk): Brown plastic box, hinged cover; stores cards, dice, chips and pegs: 8.75" x 2.5 ". $20

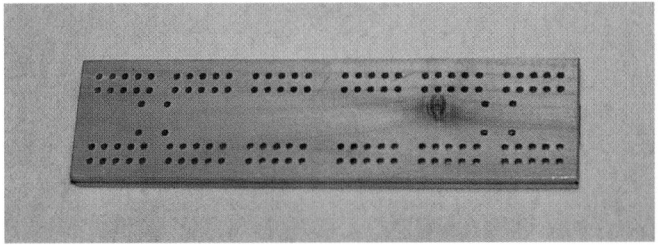

No. (Unk): 8.5" x 2.12". $15

Curtis Products Co.: No. Woodstock, New Hampshire
and Leominster, Massachusetts: 1951 - 1970s

On May 1, 1951, a Game Scoring Device was patented by Wilfred A. Curtis of North Woodstock, New Hampshire. The patent number for this game scoring device, better known as the Curtis Cribbage Counter, is No. 2,550,675. Although the board was used primarily for scoring in cribbage, it could also have been used to keep score for other games such as Bezique, Whist, Pinochle, and Dominoes. As late as 1973, it was still being advertised in Yankee Magazine.

The board was manufactured in molded plastic with a slot along either side of a numbered game scoring register. The board consists of two of these sets, one set for each player. A movable plastic dial, which cannot be removed from the board, slides along the slot, registering the count for the game being played. One might wonder why each player had two slots and dials. Quite simply put, the player started out by moving the outside dial with the first count. When scoring the second time, the first dial remained intact and the inside dial was moved from the point of the outside dial's score onward. For the third move, the player returned to the outside dial, continued where the inside dial had left off, and so on. This system allowed for a review of the last count, but in reality, was probably a rather cumbersome system. That assumption may account for why so many of the boards that have been located are in such good condition!

The instruction sheet which accompanied these pegless cribbage boards listed the following factors among the positive assets:

    no pegs - no holes
    nothing to wear out
    simplifies keeping score
    eliminates error
    sliding dials for easy scoring.

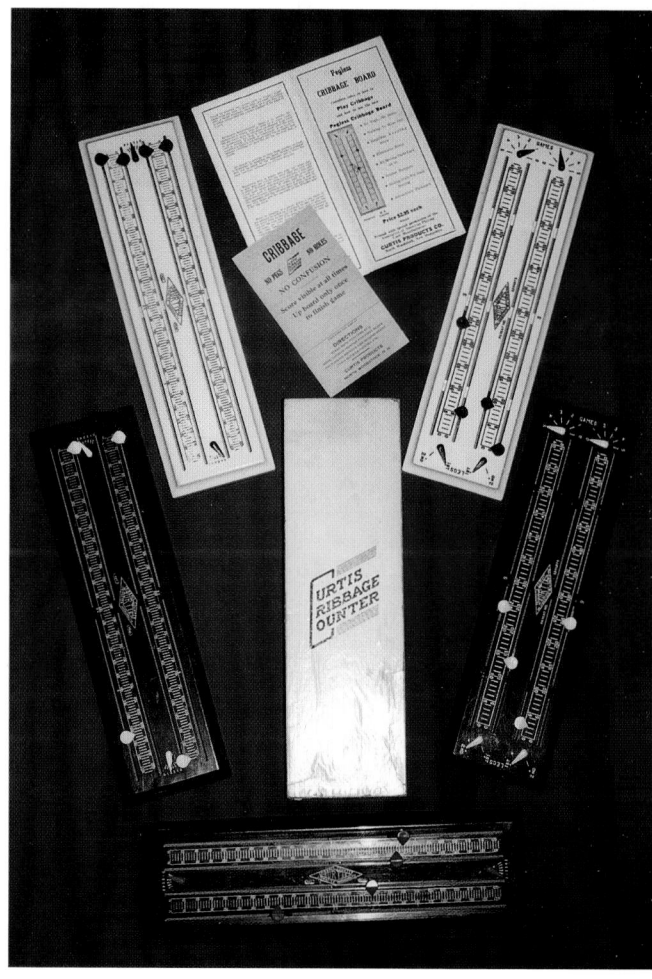

The various color combinations and street styles. $40-50

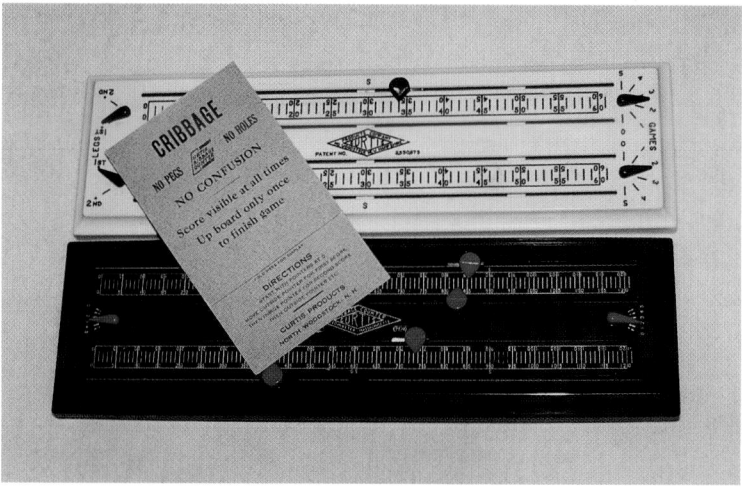

White board, pegging for 60 holes. Black board, pegging for 120 holes. Both styles are 14" x 4". $40

Curtis Way Co.: Meriden, Connecticut

Manufactured advertising boards

The New Hotel Brinkman: 3P, T.A.; wooden; black rectangular border surrounding the double 5 pegging holes; routed upper edge; 13" x 4.35". $50

Custom Cribbage, Inc.: Forest Lake, Minnesota: 1995 - present.

The company was founded by Joe Jasicki and Dan Alm in 1995 after Jasicki bought a bowling pin cribbage board for them to play on. They enjoyed the board so much that they decided that golfers might like to have a board designed just for them! They designed and sold a board which resembled a nearby golf course, and production took off from there to include a variety of subjects, such as sports (including the NFL Series), wildlife, American landmarks, popular products, and others. All boards are finished with a clear coating and have a hanger for wall display. These boards come in a variety of sizes and shapes.

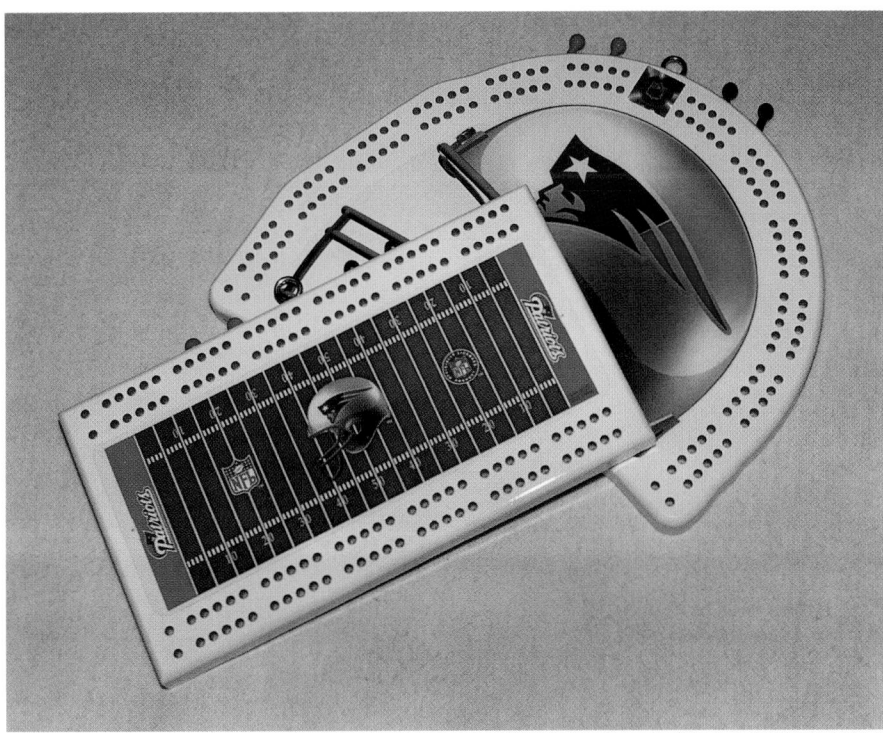

NFL Series: field; 11" x 6"; helmet; 12" x 11". Both CMP

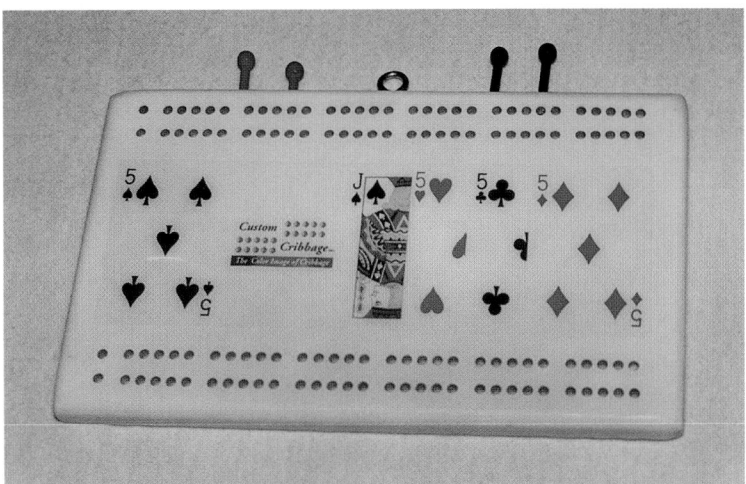

"29" hand; 11" x 6". CMP.

Daybranch, Inc.: Plainville, New York

        No. OCF 750: 2P, T.A.; folding; © 1985; made in Taiwan. $20

Wm. F. Drueke and Sons: Grand Rapids, Michigan: 1914 - present

        The Drueke Company was established in 1914 by William F. Drueke, and it passed through three generations before being sold to the Carrom Company in 1992. Drueke manufactured a diversified product line of games and game pieces, and the first games ever manufactured by them were chess sets. During World War II, Drueke manufactured over one million cribbage boards for the men in service. After *Carrom* purchased the company, the corporate offices were moved from Grand Rapids to Ludington, Michigan, but the well-known Drueke line of products are still sold under the name of Drueke. The model numbers for the cribbage boards that are still manufactured have been changed, however, and the name Drueke and the model number are no longer imprinted on the boards.

        The Drueke trademark was a knight chess piece and could be found imprinted on their cribbage boxes. The oldest board boxes are black, while the newest ones are dark green. The older boards were usually made of solid walnut and were imprinted with the company name and model number of the board. In later years, a black and gold sticker with the knight chess piece trademark, the company name and the model number was placed on the boards for identification. Some board models, old and new, have the name Drueke as well as the model number incorporated into the design on the face of the board. Most of the boards manufactured today have no identifying marks on them.

        Although there are some variations, the boards described below represent the most common characteristics of each model number identified. Boards that are still available are valued as current market pricing (CMP).

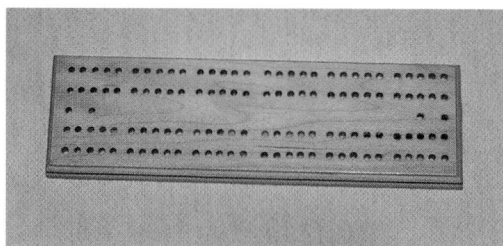

No. 1: 7.5" x 2.12". $15

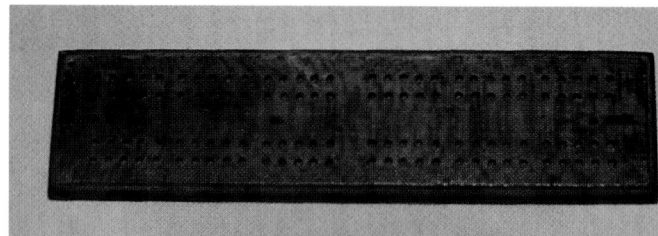

No. 4: 10" x 2.5". $25

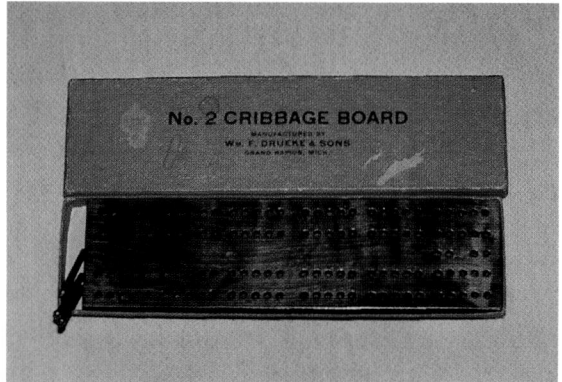

No. 2: 7 7/8" x 2 7/16". $15

No. 5: 2 x 6 grooved or plain top; 11" x 2.75" plus slight variations. $25

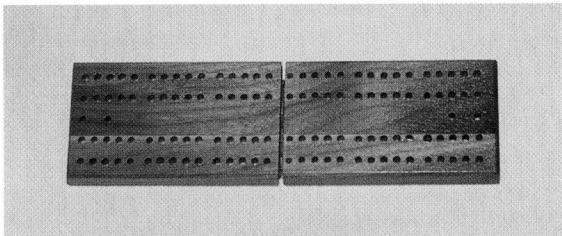

No. 6: Folding board; 7.5" x 2". $15

No. 6B: Boxed, with room for deck of cards; 7.5" x 2". $15

No. 7: Folding board with spring hinges; 2P, T.A.; 2 starter holes each end center; black leather case, snap closure, stenciled "*CRIBBAGE* " and *Drueke No. 7* in gold. $35

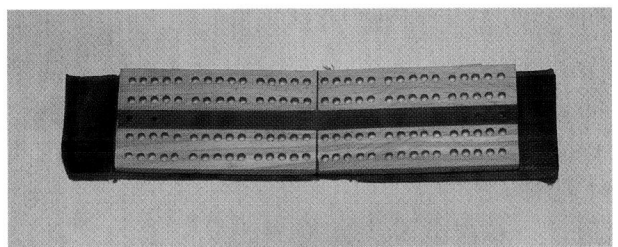

No. 8: Folding board (old); leather back with flap closure; 7.12" x 1.6" open. $30

No. 8: Folding board (new); 2P, T.A.; stored in leather pouch; plain center; 7.12" x 1.6" open. CMP

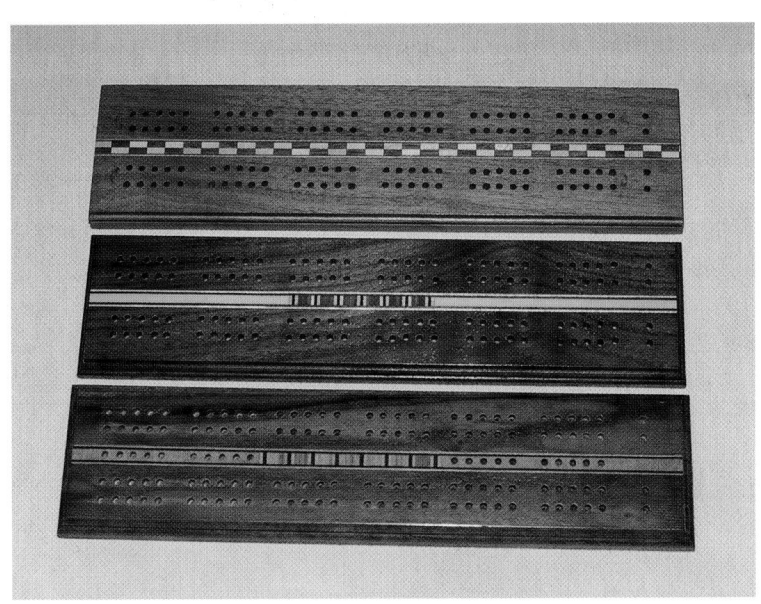

No. 9: Various center inlays; 11" x 2.75". $20

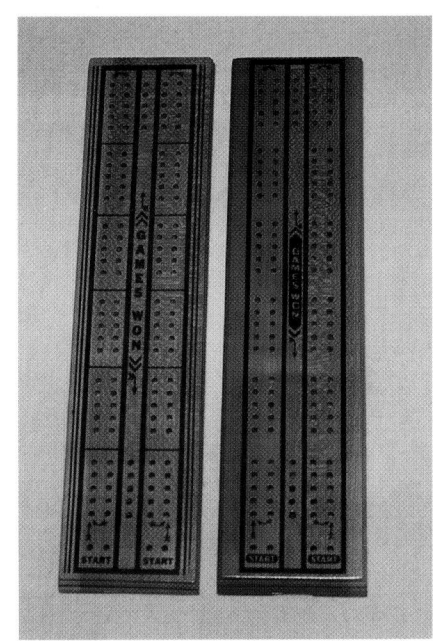

No. 10: 11" x 2.75". $20

No. 10SP: Same as No. 10, but used for advertising. $25

No. 11: *Travel Cribbage*: 2P, T.A.; 2 starter holes each, outer end and center; walnut; 7.5" x 2.12". CMP

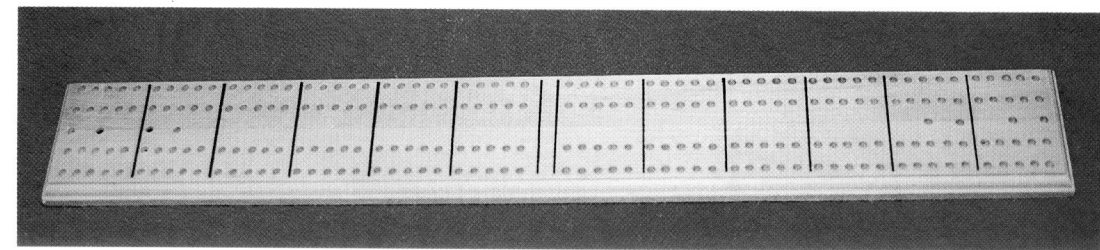

No. 11X: Original tournament board manufactured by Drueke; 15" x 2". $25

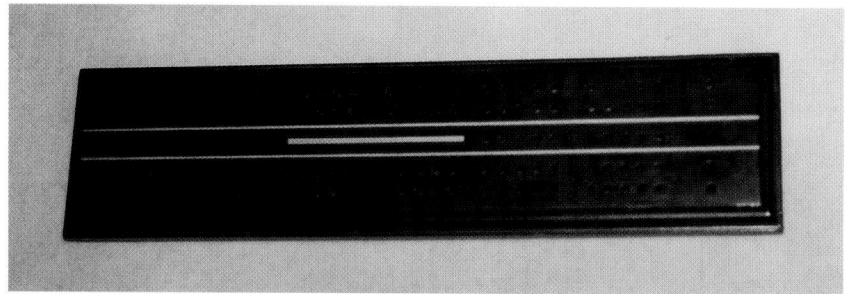

No. 12: Blackened hardwood; 11.12" x 2.75". $30

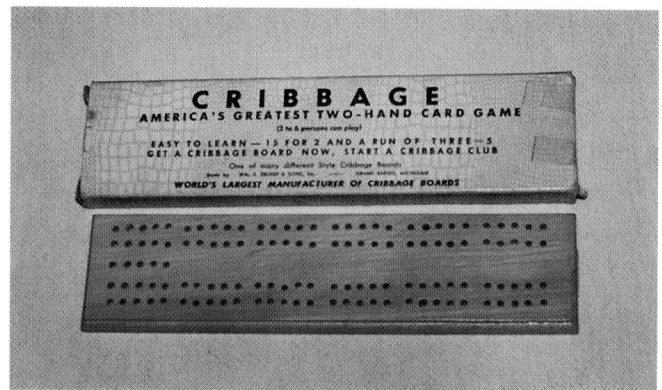

No. 14: Plain box or in Drueke advertising box; 9.5" x 2.25".
$20 - $35

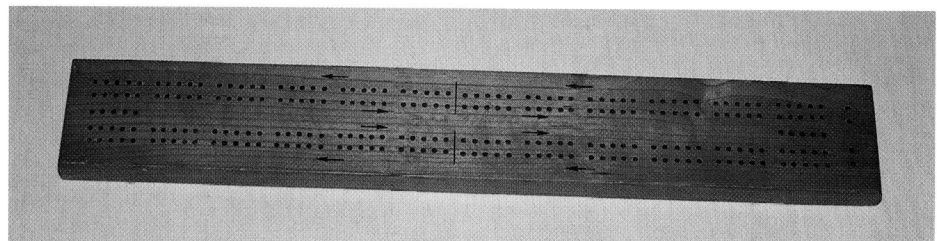

No. 15-2: *The Official Tournament Long Board*; 18.75" x 2.75". CMP

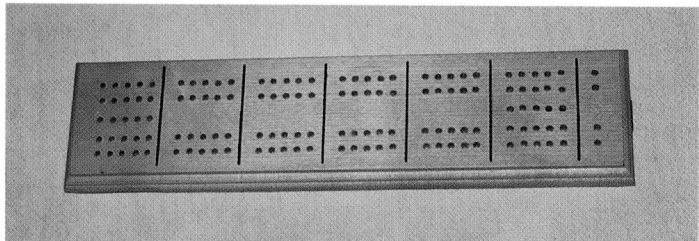

No. 18: Stenciled cross dividers; 11" x 2.75". $20

No. 23: 2P, T.A.; yellow and black stenciled center design and lines separating double 5 holes; 5 GW holes one end; 2 starter holes other end; 11.25" x 3". $35

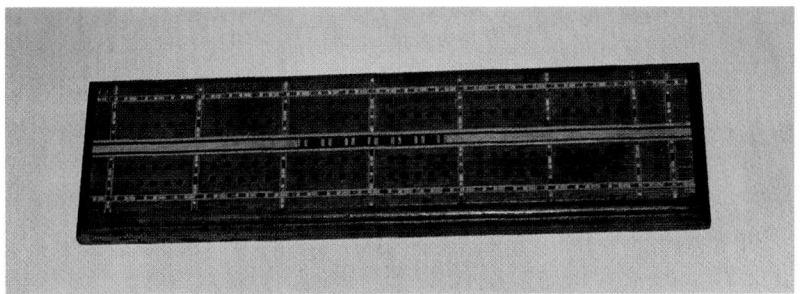

No. 26: Stenciled or inlaid; 11.75" x 3.25". $35

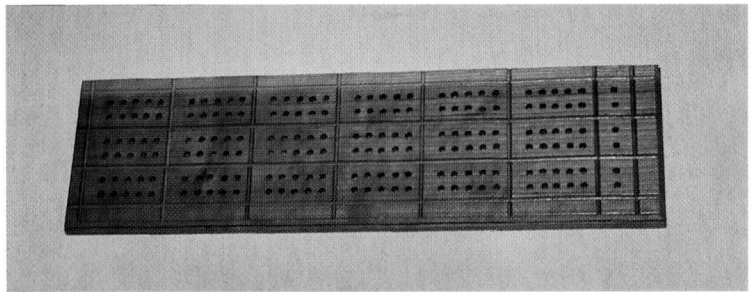

No. 27: Grooved; 12" x 3.25". $15

No. 28: Stenciled with black, blue, yellow, or green; 12" x 3.35". $25

No. 31: 3P, T.A.; narrow black stenciled lines separating double 5 holes; 5 GW holes; has also been found with 8" x 4" grooves; step-down sides; 11.75" x 3.25". $25

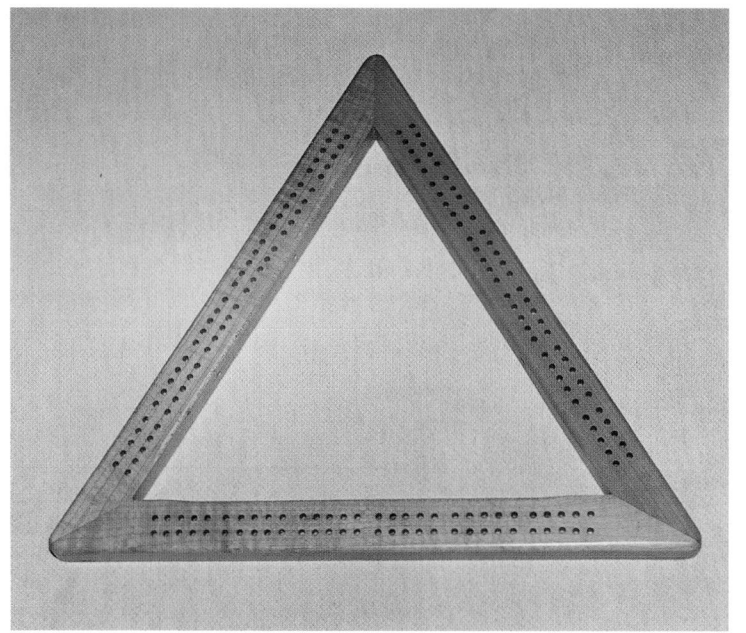

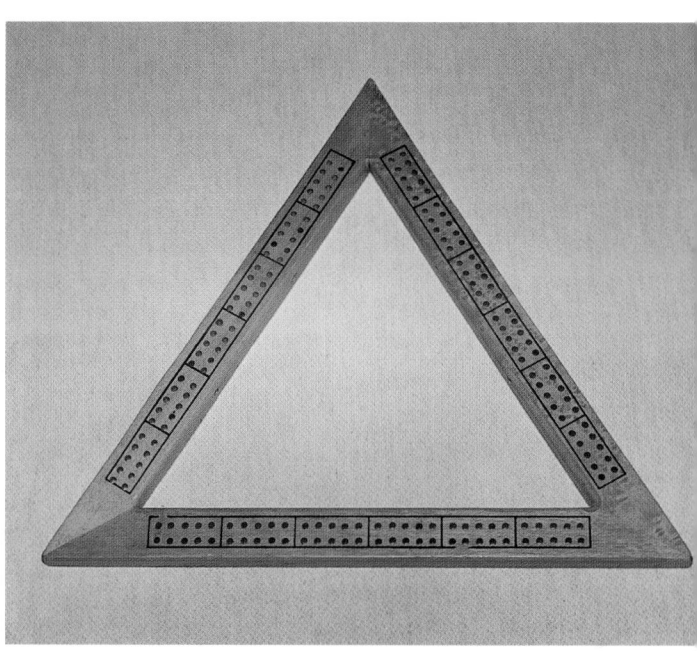

No. 38: Grooved; open triangle; 12 .25" x 1.25". $50

No. 39: Stenciled; open triangle; 12.6" x 1.25". $50

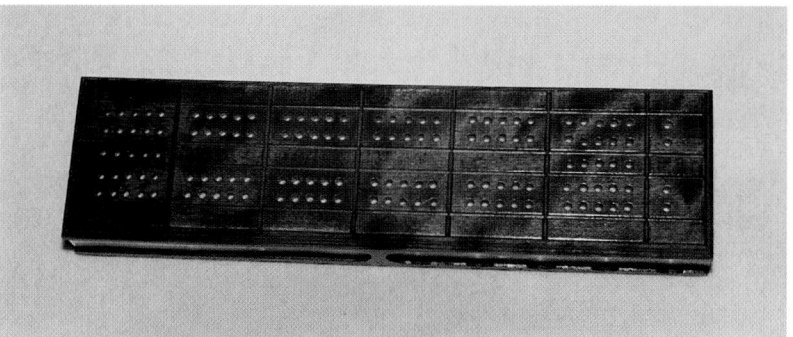

No. 042: Game box; 11.12" x 3.12 " x 1.5". $40

No. 42: (not 042); 11.12" x 3.12" x 1.12". $40

No. 43: 3P, T.A.; folding, with clasp closure; fold is held together by two springs, and board folds to outside; inside hollowed to store cards and includes a brass covered slot for peg storage; 9.35" x 3.35" open. $35

No. 43: 2P, T.A.; box with slider on side to hold cards and pegs; Drueke used same number for two different styles; 11.75" x 3" x 1.35". $35

No. 44: 3P, T.A.; folding, hinged in middle; cards and pegs store inside; brass hinges and snap closure; red felt along the edges; 9.75" x 3.35" open. $35

No. 45: 3P, T.A.; folding box; *Cribbage Board and Gin Rummy Combination*; 10" x 3.5" x 1" open. $50

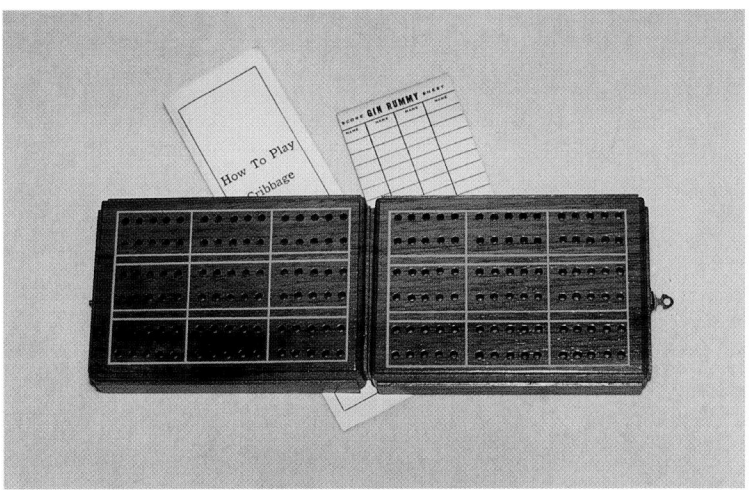

No. 46: 3P, T.A.; box included Gin Rummy Score Pad, Gin Rummy and Cribbage instruction sheets. 10" x 3.5" x 1" open. $50

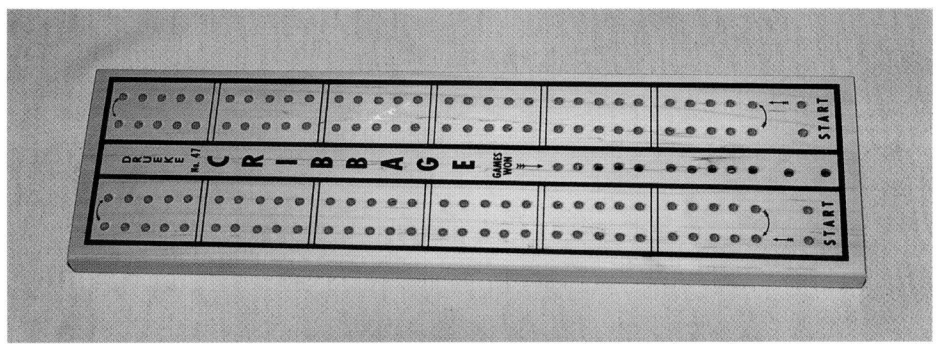

No. 47: 2" pegs; 15.5" x 4.6". CMP

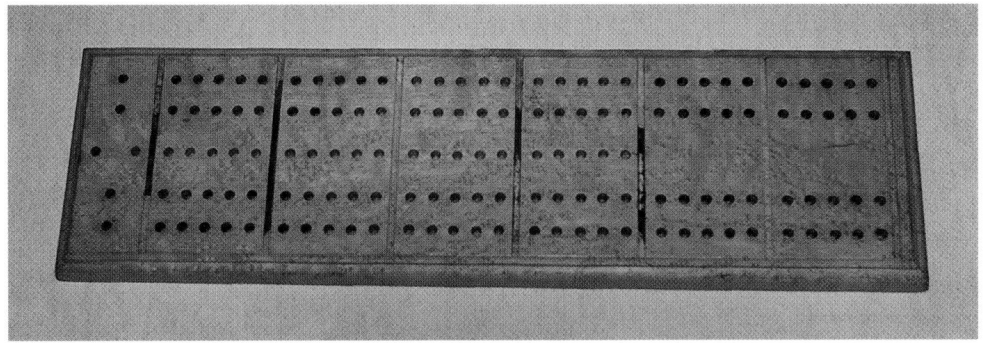

No. 48: Inlaid; 15.75" x 4.5". $35

No. 49: 2P, T.A.; flat leather, doesn't fold; 9 x 6 grooved indents with 6 "boxes" down center containing 2 starter holes in outer ones and clover design in the others. 4.8" x 2". $25

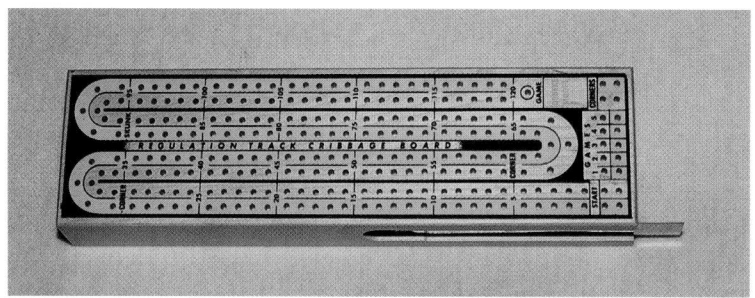

No. 050: Game box; 11.85" x 2.75" x 1.5". $40

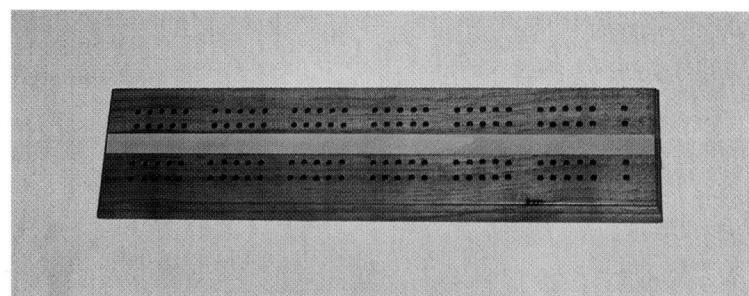

No. 99X: Center inlay; 11.25" x 2.75". $20

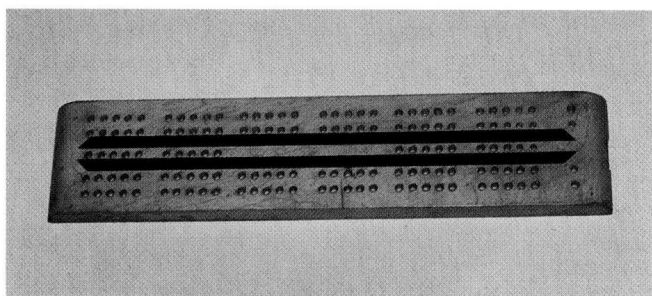

No. 105: Stenciled; 11" x 2.5". $25

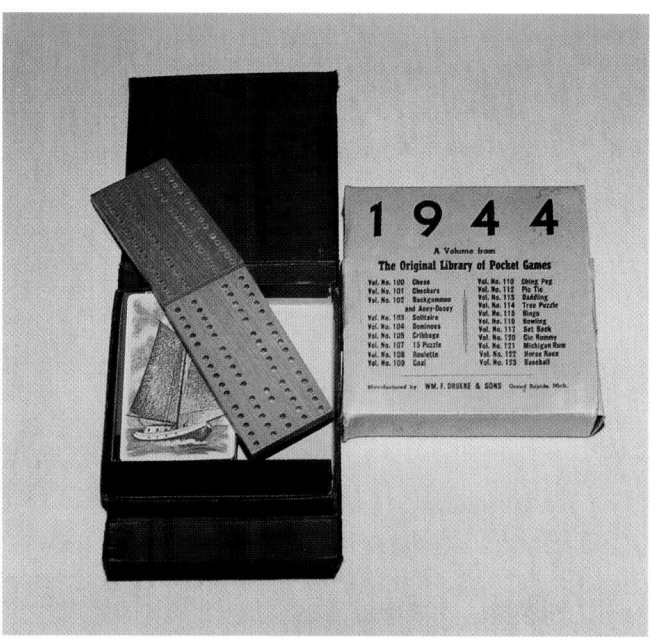

VOL. 105: Folding, cloth back; deck of playing cards included; This board was one of a set of 22 game volumes called "The Original Library of Pocket Games" and were sold as "The Ideal Gift For the Men in the Service". Boxes were 4.5" square and were packed in a special mailing carton. Board; 7.25" x 1.85" open. $35

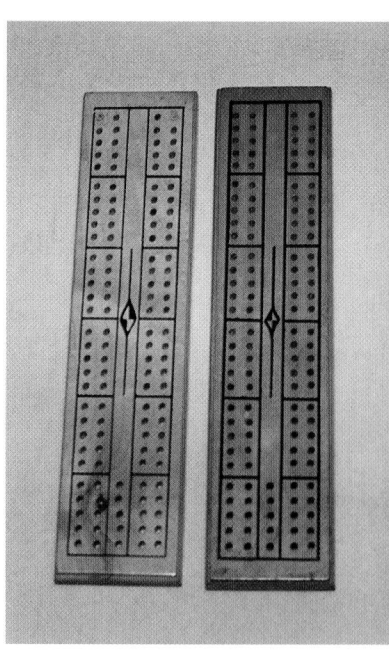

No. 114: Stenciled; 9.35" x 2.25". $35

No. 205: Game box; 12" x 3.25 " x 1.65". CMP

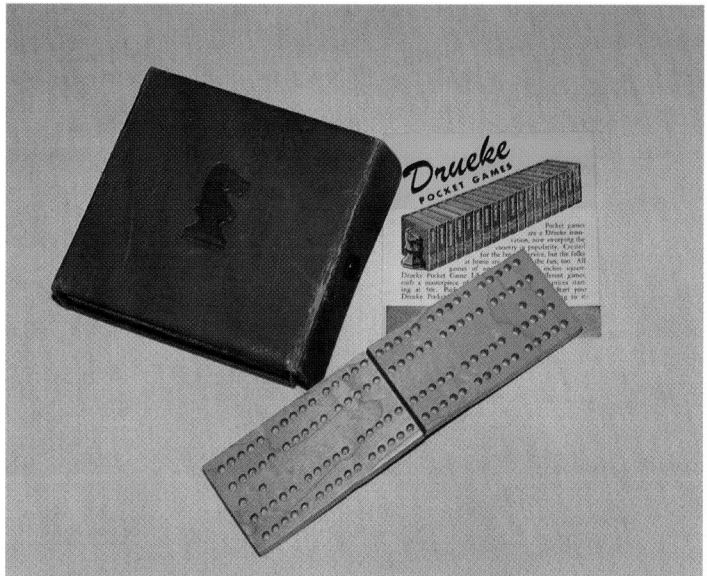

Vol. 405: Same as Vol. 105, but box is leather. $30

No. 515: Identical to No. 47, but was made of walnut. $25

No. 770: Mahogany or fruit wood table with drawer: 3" pegs; 5 GW holes each end center; 2 starter holes each player; brass drawer pull; 18" x 37" x 14". $175

No. 888: 4P, T.A.; cherry box; marked *The Foursome Cribbage Board* down center; thin black stenciled lines dividing double 5 holes; directional arrows at each end of streets; 2 starter holes each player; card and peg storage on side. $40

No. 957: 2P, continuous M-shaped track; 5 GW holes each player at end, center; 2 starter holes each player one end side; 2 corners holes each player other end side; stenciled black lines dividing double 5 holes and outer edge of playing field; used 2" club pegs; 15.75" x 4.75". $20

No. 957W: Identical track to No. 957, but board is stenciled white; *Cribbage* stenciled at one end. CMP

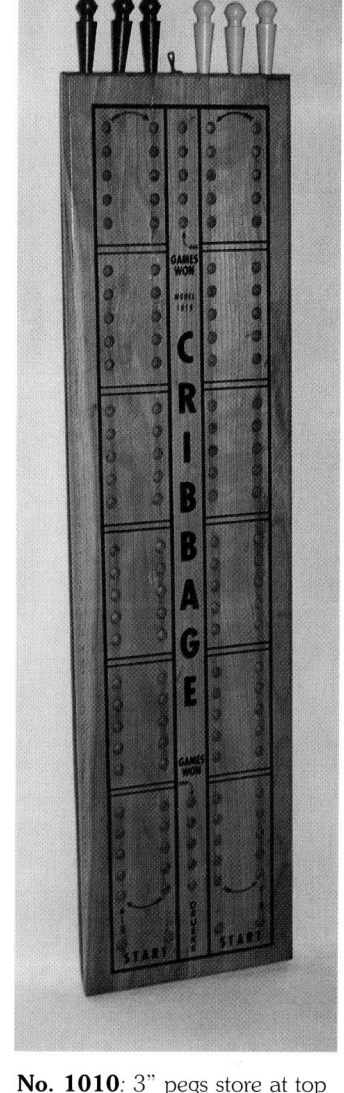

No. 1010: 3" pegs store at top of board when hung on wall; 31" x 8". CMP

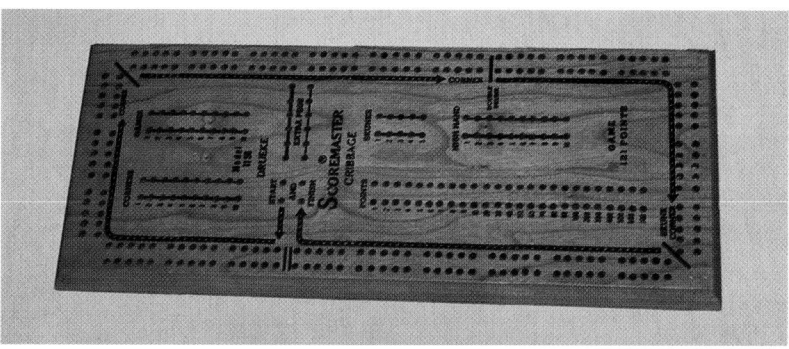

No. 1150: stenciled; 13.25" x 5.5". CMP

No. 1949: 2P, T.A.; oval *Race Track Cribbage:* combination game board with 3rd inner track containing fewer holes, designed to play "Race Track" cribbage in addition to regular game; Patent # 2,415,073, ©1946 by A.H. Buffmire; 10.5" x 3.75". $30

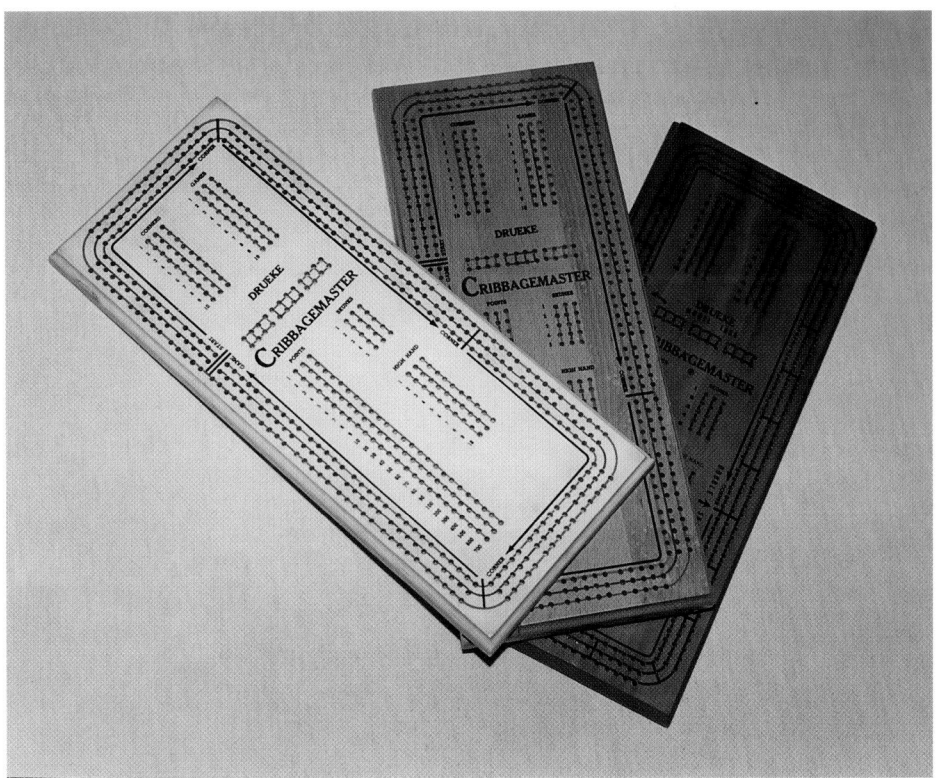

No. 1950: 14.5" x 6.5". CMP

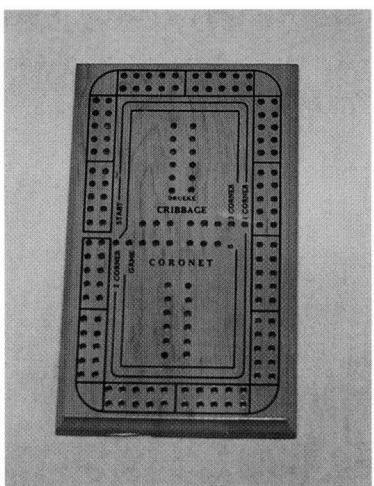

No. 1951: *Drueke Cribbage Model 1951 Coronet:* 7" x 4.25". $25

No. 1957: 2P, once-around M-shaped track; marked *CLUBMASTER* at top of rounded end of board, which has a hole for hanging on wall; 5 GW holes center 1 end, with 4 *Start* holes 1 side, and 4 *Corners* holes other side; tracks are stenciled yellow and natural; 1.6" pegs; 16.75" x 4.5". $25

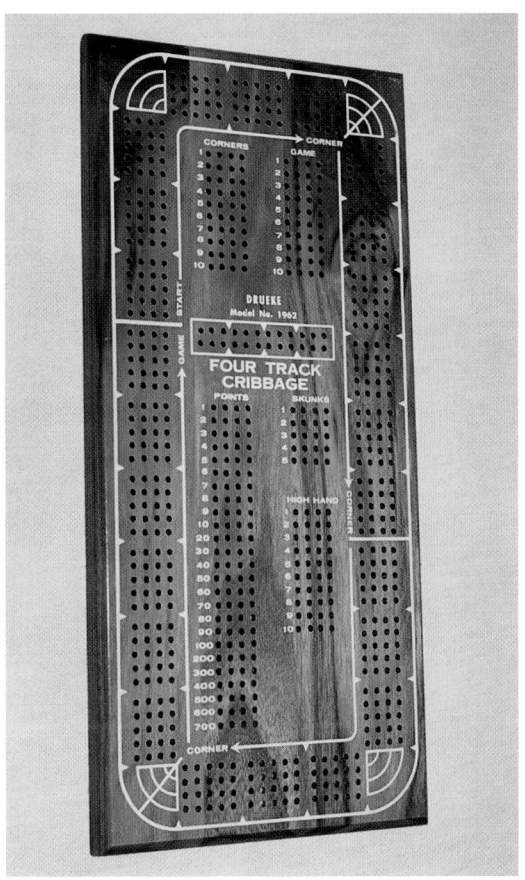

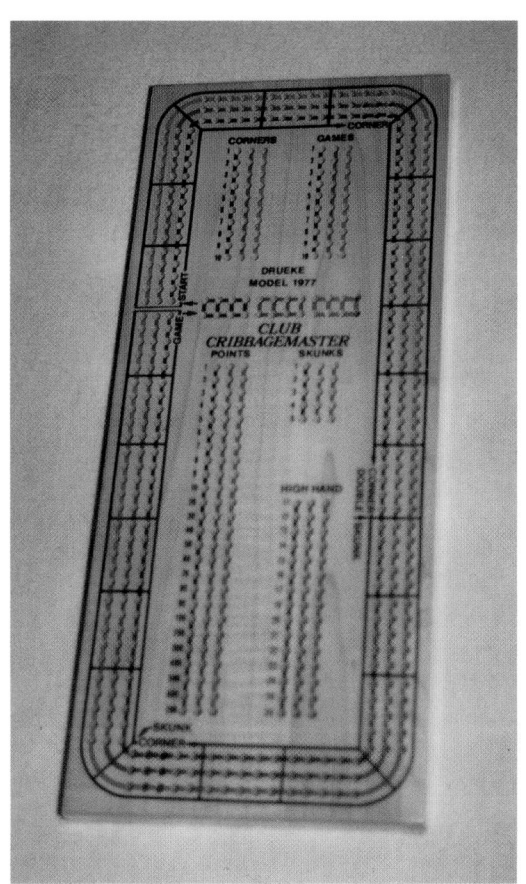

No. 1962: *Four Track Cribbage:* 15.5" x 7.12". CMP

No. 1977: 17.5" x 8". CMP

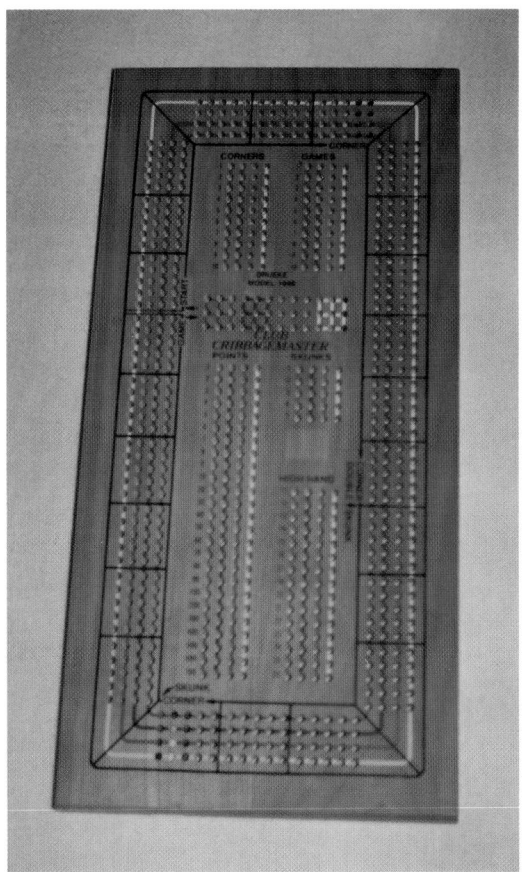

No. 1988: 19" x 9.25". $30

No. 2029: "29" shaped board; 3P, continuous track; 9.5" x 7". $25

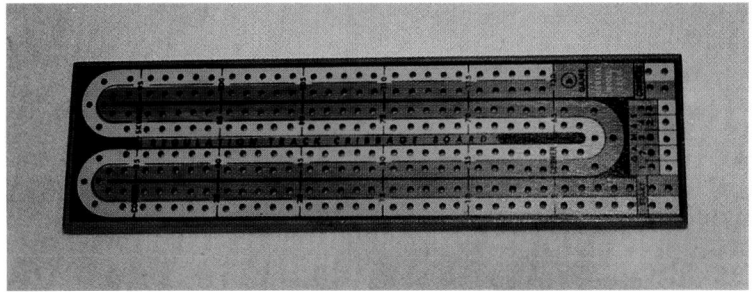

No. 2050: 12" x 3.25". CMP

No. 4444: Wide walnut board stenciled *FOUR SCORE CRIB-BAGE ONCE AROUND* in center at end of game hole; all stenciling done in gold; 4P Brooks style track; 2 starter holes each player. $30

No. 5005: Game Kit in leatherette and wood storage box; Game pieces for Backgammon, Acey-Ducy, Chips, Michigan Rummy, Roulette wheel, Chess, Checkers, deck of cards, and 2P, T.A. cribbage board. 9.25" x 1.75". $50

Duncan's Woods (formerly Gameboards Unique)**:** Portland, Oregon: - present

Most of their boards are made of exotic woods.

Box with card storage; inlay; 5" x 3.5" x 1.5". CMP

Eddy, S.C.: Kalamazoo, Michigan: c. 1940

Mr. Eddy patented and manufactured the *"Saves Argument"* board (Patent #2204177, issued 7/11/40) which may be the earliest 120 hole once-around cribbage board patented in the United States.

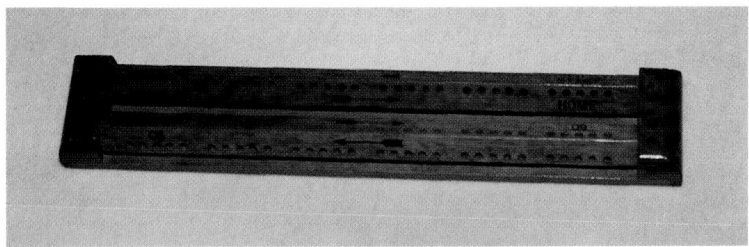

11.25" x 2". Boxed $60

Evan Johnson Co.: Grand Rapids, Michigan: c. 1950

1): 2P, T.A.; folding leather boxed board, top lifts off; blue and white pegs:similar to WWII library box games; 4.75" x 4.75". $25

Famus Corp.: Brooklyn, New York

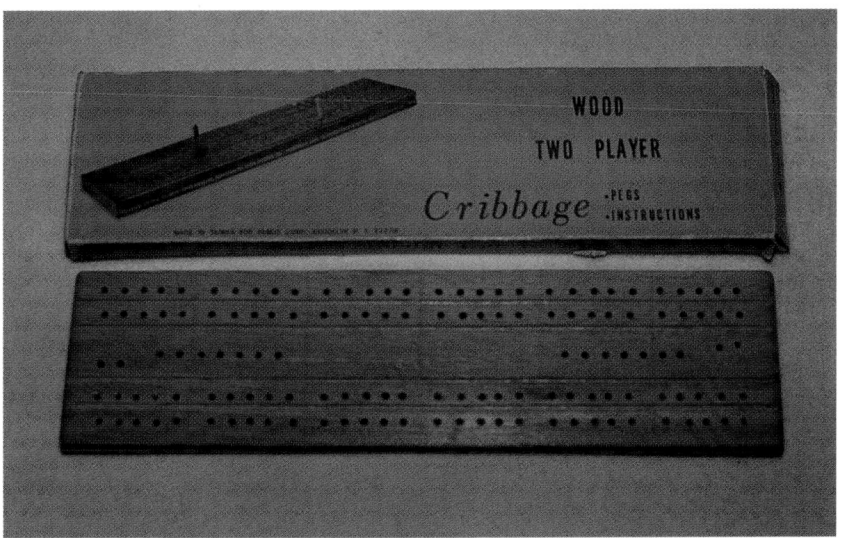

Grooved; identical to Arrco No. 151W; 11.5" x 3". $10

Field Manufacturing Co. Inc.: New York City, New York

Field's logo was a crowned crest containing **"F"** and **"M"**. The company name was printed below the crest.

No. 101: 2P, T.A.; company crest in center of board; 6 GW holes each end center; 2 starter holes each player; concave sides; 11.75" x 2.75". $20

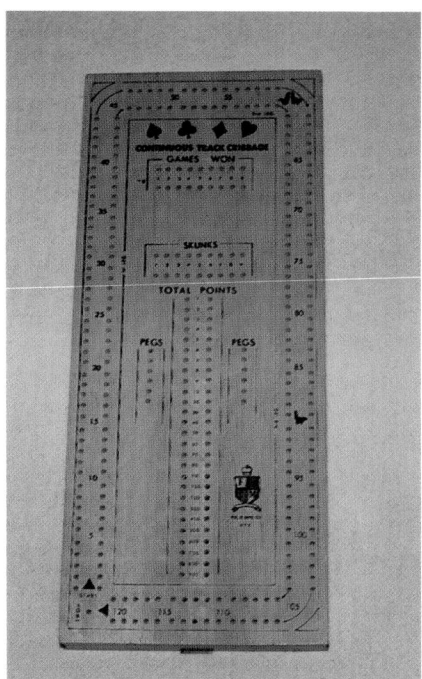

No. 614: Taiwan; 14" x 6". $20

Fred Roberts Co.: San Francisco, California

> Distributor of cribbage boards. Name appeared as assignee on several cribbage board patents.
>
> **1)** 2P, T.A.; both players start on one side and finish on other side of board, pegging holes are numbered in blocks of 5; Thailand; 12" x 3". $15

GerardCraft: Cape Elizabeth, Maine: 1975 - present

> GerardCraft is a small manufacturer of high quality hand-crafted boxes, including cribbage boards, most of which are made of pine.

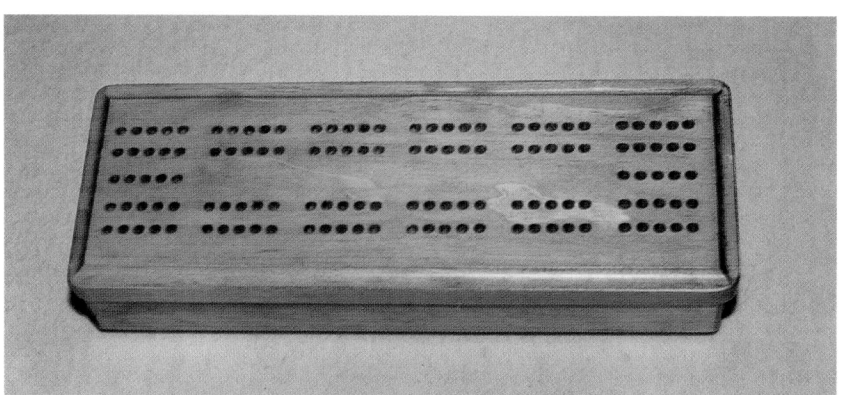

No. J2: 12" x 4.25" x 2.25". CMP

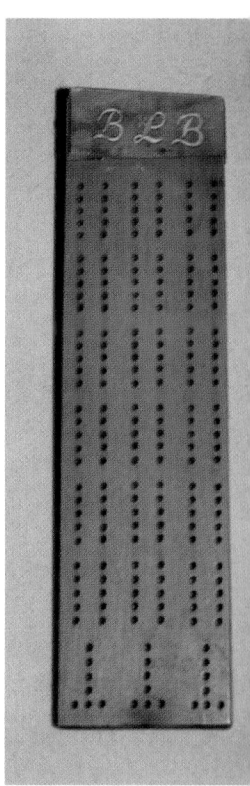

No. (Unk): End pivots to reveal peg storage. 12.5" x 3.25". $40

Gibson Art Co.:

> Bought W. C. Horn, Bros. & Co. in the early 1960s and continued the manufacture of Horn's games, including the cribbage boards for a short time. *See Horn for listing of boards.*

Glanson Games: NY 12, New York

Glanson Games introduced the first mass-produced continuous track boards (the Brooks style) sold in the USA. Acme Ruler & Adv. Co., Ltd. of Toronto originally manufactured the continuous track style. Glanson first distributed, then manufactured them, in identical styles, but changing the shape of the ends and sides. Brooks, Aristocrat and Triumph boards were all manufactured under the Glanson label, possibly after the companies were bought by Glanson. The history of these names isn't yet clearly understood. The early boards were marked "Made in Canada", and the later ones "Made in USA".

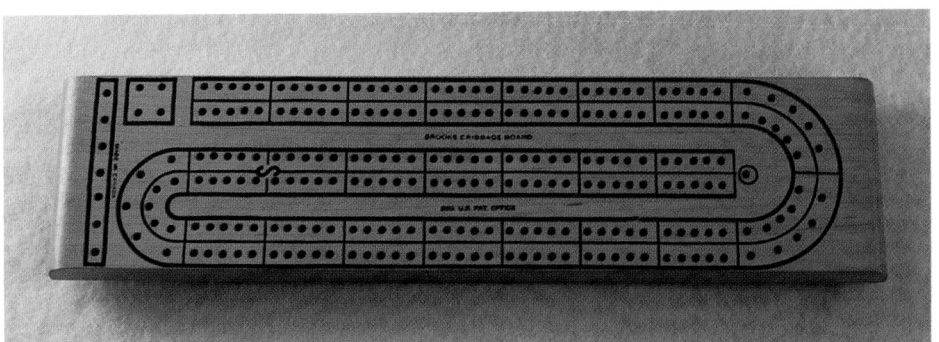

No. 18: 13.5" x 3". $15

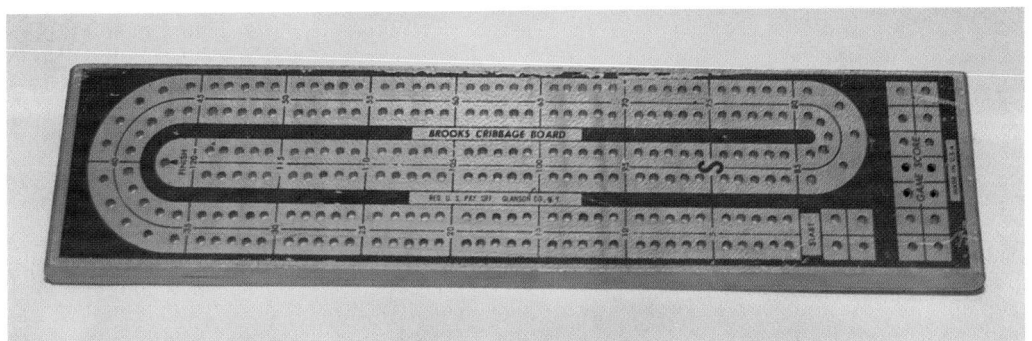

No. 28: Maroon, natural, or black; Des. Pat. Reg. No. 11544; 13.5" x 3". $15

No. 36: Triumph: Identical to Acme's Aristocrat, Jr. 13.35" x 3.5". $15

Acme X300: 14.5" x 3.5". $25

Grand Rapids Dowel Works: Grand Rapids, Michigan

Manufactured cribbage boards until the 1940s.

No. 202: 2P, T.A. blond wood; 10 GW holes each end center; no starter holes; grooved sides; with pivoting wooden peg cover; "stub" legs. $30

No. (Unk): 2P, T.A.; 8 x 4 cross wood inlays; 10 GW holes each end center; "stub" legs; peg slot has pivoting wooden cover. $30

Great American Trading Co.: York, Pennsylvania: - present

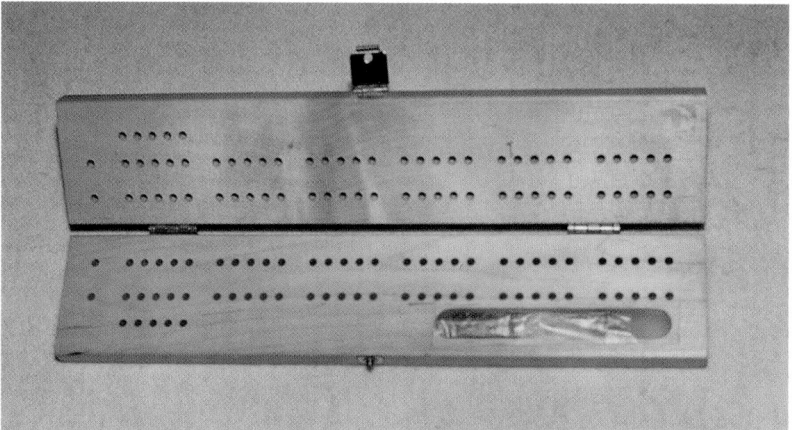

No. 22080: Folding maple travel; 10" x 4.12" open. CMP

No. 22081: 2P, T.A.; folding maple travel; 5 GW holes, 2 starter holes each player 4 x 1 grooving separating the double 5 holes; peg and card storage when folded; 17.12" x 6.5", open. CMP

No. 22083: 4P, T.A.; folding travel; 2 starter holes each player; peg storage when folded; 12" x 2.75 " open. CMP

Great Western Enterprises: Aberdeen, Washington: c. 1983-present

Founded by Spencer Abersold, who still owns the company.

A variety of designs used — advertising (no longer manufactured; value $70), wildlife, sports. Plastic peg pod set in underside; 16.5" x 7.5". CMP

Green Mountain Mfg., Inc.: Trout Creek, Montana

Green Mountain Mfg. sold large hand crafted cribbage boards which were often mounted on stub legs. The company name was on a small label which was secured to the base.

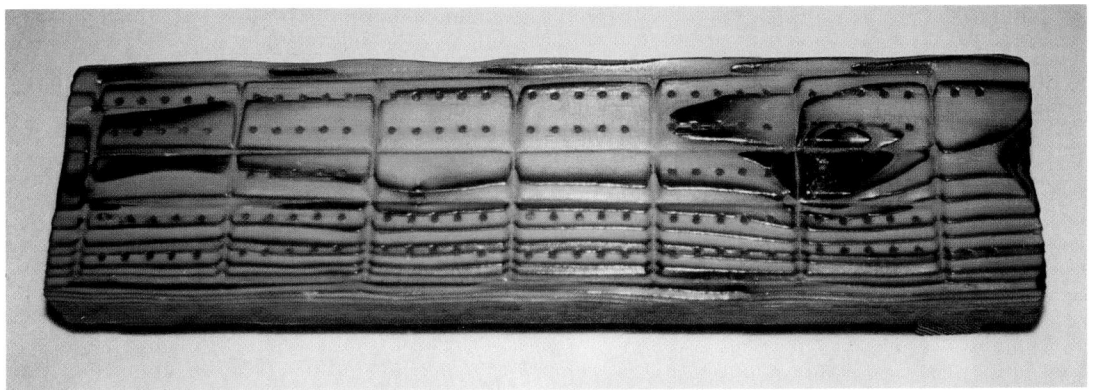

Stub legs; 18.75" x 5.25". $20

Hamilton Mfg. Co: Minneapolis, Minnesota

Hamilton manufactured the Candy store punch-out cribbage board. Holes were drilled through to the bottom, held papers with numbers, which were pushed through by the customer. The board was the grand prize after all the holes were punched and winner determined. Attached cardboard placard advertised ***Cribbage Board Jackpot Deal,*** and each punch cost $.25. The identical board, different color on outer edge, was manufactured by Harlich Mfg. Co..

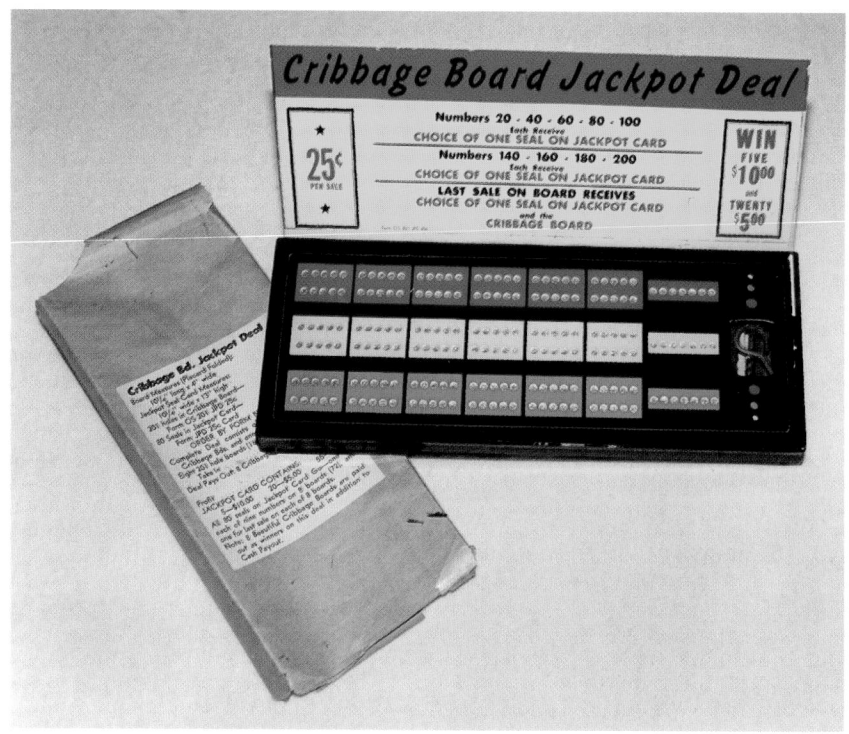

Red, yellow, blue streets; 10.25" x 4.25". Un-punched: $50; with wrappers: $80

John N. Hansen Co.: Millbrae, California: 1947 - present

Hansen has been a major distributor of cribbage boards manufactured in Taiwan since 1975 when they introduced 5 or 6 models to their product line. Mr. Hansen, who founded the business, died in 1995. All boards are manufactured of hardwood, most have metal pegs, and some bear the Hansen logo (H formed by squat J at top and upside down U at bottom). All Hansen boards are styles most commonly used by players, none are exotic or uniquely crafted.

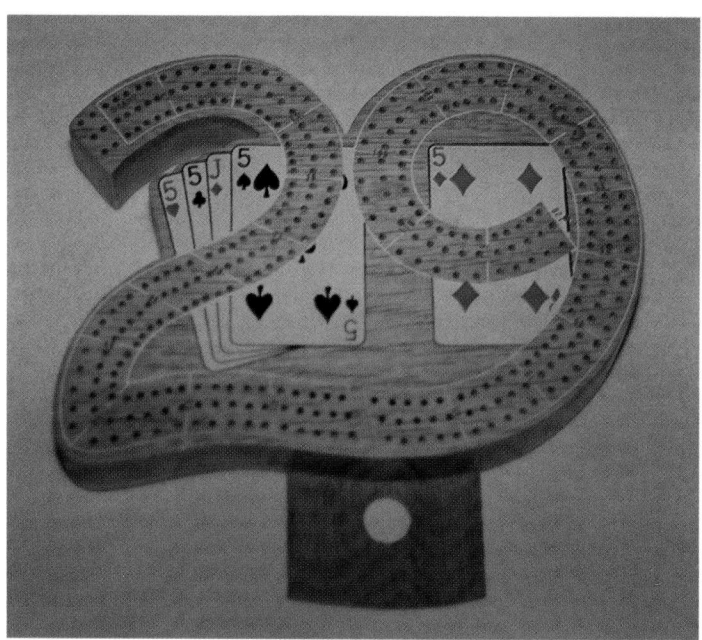

No. TR 29: Playing card storage; 9.5" x 7". $20

No. TR 29M: Mini "29" board: 6" x 4.5". CMP

74

No. TR290: "29": same as TR29, but no card storage; 9.5" x 7". CMP

No. **TR50**; *Standard Cribbage:* 2P. TA.; 6 GW holes at each end. $10

No. TR66: 2P, continuous Brooks-style track; 7 GW holes each player, 2 starter holes each player; each 5 holes surrounded by thin rectangular block; natural wood color; 13.25" x 3.5". CMP

No. TR77: 3P, continuous Brooks-style track; designed same as TR66; natural color; 14.25" x 4.5". CMP

No. TR88: 2P, continuous track set up same as TR66, only one street is blue, the other white; 13.25" x 4.25". CMP

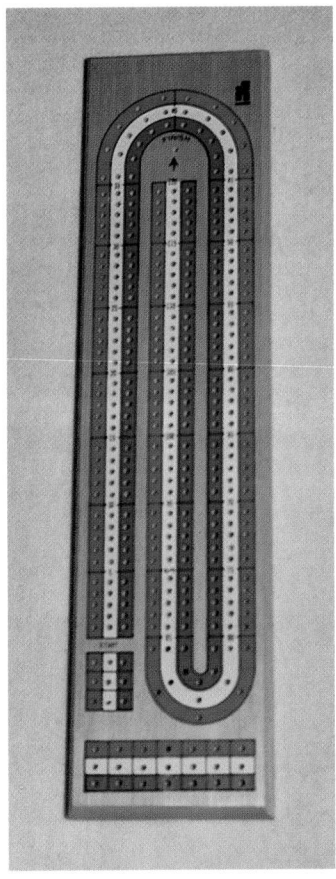

No. TR99: Tracks are red, white, and blue; 14.25" x 6.5". CMP

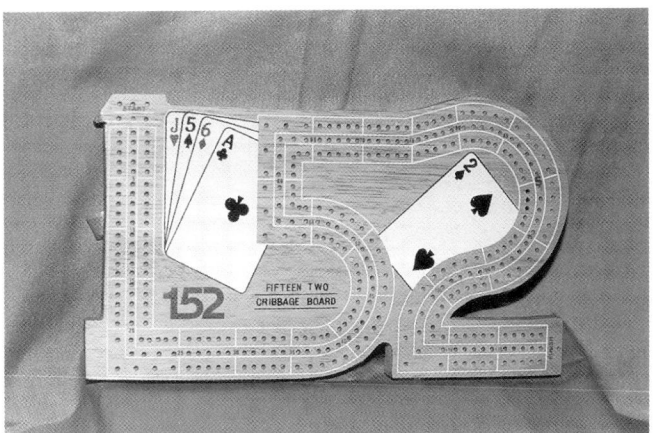

TR152: 11.5" x 6.5". $25

No. TR400: 15.5" x 7.5". CMP

No. 00297: 7 in 1 Game case includes GS7459 cribbage board. CMP

No. 00298: Same as 00297, but game case is different color. CMP

No. 00301: 6 in 1 Game case includes GS7459 cribbage board. CMP

No. 00500: Travel Trio zippered case includes GS7459 cribbage board, dominoes and cards. CMP

No. 8907: 2P, T.A.; box with cribbage board top, holds cards and dominoes; brass plate in center; 11.5" x 4.5" x 2.5". CMP

No. 8908: 2P continuous inverted S-shaped track; large metal pegs; stenciled gold lines outlining track; *Ambassador Cribbage Board*; 13.75" x 3.5". CMP

No. 9046: 2P, T.A.; plastic box holding 12 in 1 games; 2 GW holes each end center; board has center Spade, Diamond, Heart, and Club design; bottom opens for storage of cards, pegs, other pieces; 7.12" x 1.6". CMP

No. GS7459: 2P, T.A.; folding travel; 7.25" x 2" open. CMP

No. B1038: Folding travel in pouch. CMP

No. H1750: Game case; stores TR88 board, dice, dominoes, and cards. CMP

No. TM7460: 2P, T.A.; folding travel board; stored in leatherette case with deck of playing cards; 7.25" x 2", open. CMP

Hardwood Creations of California: Davis, California: 1980s - present

Hardwood Creations was founded by David Levy, and all products created by him are done with inlays of exotic woods such as Padauk and Peruvian walnut

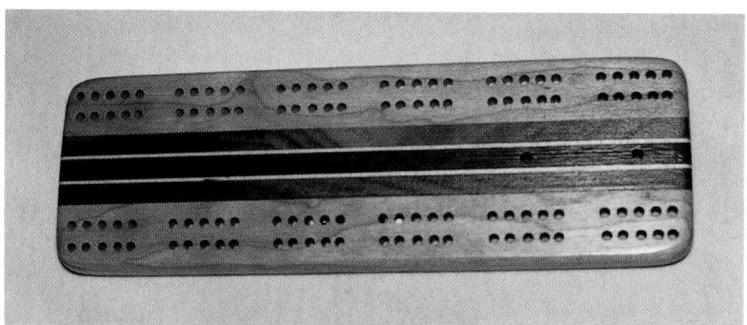

No. G2: 12" x 3.75". CMP

Harlich Mfg. Co.: Chicago, Illinois

Manufactured a candy store punch-out cribbage board identical to one made by Hamilton Mfg. Co., only the outer edge is burgundy.

Heald Mfg. Co.: Worcester, Massachusetts

> **1)** 2P, T.A.; steel; grooved around upper edge, down center, and around each double 5 holes; steel plug at end holds steel pegs; 11.25" x 2.5". $25

Heines House TDC Co.: Minneapolis, Minnesota

> **No. CB101:** "*Pla-Trac*": 2P, T.A.; each individual street, as well as 2 sets of 5 GW holes in center, confined in a narrow inlaid strip - for a total of 6 narrow inlays on the board; copyright 1975; 12.5" x 3.35". $30

Heartwood Creations: Rockwood, Illinois; est. 1978

Manufactures most boards with inlays, which are done with exotic woods.

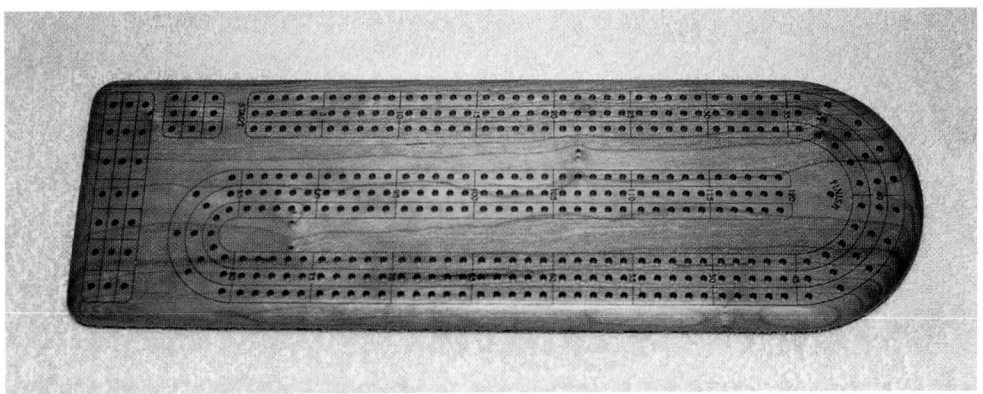

14.5" x 4.5". CMP

W.C. Horn, Bros. & Co.: Newark, New Jersey; 1846 - 1962

The W. C. Horn, Bros. & Co. was established in 1846 and was originally known as Koch Sons and Co. It was founded by William C. Horn's uncle and was located at the corner of William and Ann Streets in New York City. The firm specialized in stationery products such as postcard albums, autograph books, and they also provided general purpose order files for the U. S. Government.

Shortly after the Civil War and at the age of 23, William C. Horn joined the firm as a salesman. Eventually, Horn was named president, and the name of the firm was changed to W. C. Horn, Bros. & Co. When he died in 1902, his son, William. C. Horn, Jr., 21 years of age and a student at Yale, was named president.

In 1924, the factory was moved to a larger building located on 571-577 Third Street in Newark, New Jersey. The corporate offices, however, remained on 5th Ave. in New York City until the company ended business. Although there was some production of games while the factory was located in New York City, the product line increased after it was moved to Newark. Some of the games which Horn manufactured included cribbage boards, backgammon sets, chess and checker boards, dominoes, and Carla Derby (a horse racing game). The company also added lodge equipment such as gavels, sound blocks, ballot boxes, ballot cubes, and balls to their product line. In spite of their diversified line of games, they are known today primarily for their cribbage boards. Limited manufacture of the cribbage boards probably began sometime around 1915, which is supported by dates found on the early instruction sheets.

Whether or not Horn bought out R.F. McCrillis Mfr., of Norwalk, Ohio, is not clearly understood, but McCrillis did design cribbage boards for Horn. Horn's fine line of cribbage boards was made basically of hard maples, including curly and birds-eye maple. The craftsmanship was of excellent quality, with many of the early boards boasting grooved sides, inlays or grooves separating the streets in a variety of ways, and many boards having indented arrows showing the direction of the streets. Almost all Horn boards were identified on the underside with an indented logo, most boards marked with a "C" (for cribbage) number. Later, when McCrillis was "bought," the McCrillis name was added to the imprint. The Horn "C" has a standard number for each different model. The second letter and number found on many boards, and which varies from board to board, possibly represented the lot number.

William C. Horn, Jr. remained president of the firm for over 50 years until 1957, and he died in 1959. After his death, W. C. Horn, Bros. & Co. was sold to the Gibson Art Co. of Cincinnati, Ohio, manufacturers of greeting cards and other stationary products. Only a few cribbage boards can be found with the Gibson marking "KC" added to the Horn logo, indicating that this product line was phased out with the change in ownership.

Horn manufactured some of their models without the Horn imprint on the bottom, and these boards were sold to venders for distribution. Two known distributors of Horn-manufactured boards were *Kingsbridge* and *AP Games*. If you check their listings, you will find the Horn model numbers included.

Horn manufactured other game boards with the "C" numbers. Because it is felt that there was a chronological "C" product number up to at least No. C84, it is noted that the following numbers were used for other games; **C44:** Eight Men on a Raft; **C49:** Tick Tat Toe; **C61:** Pinochle Counter; **C65:** Pinochle & Bezique Counter.

To facilitate the review of the following boards, the following features should be noted; 1) In some cases, boards with identical model numbers are so different in style that they are listed separately. 2) KC numbers were used after the Gibson Art Company bought Horn. 3) Horn-style starter holes are very distinctive and are found on many of their boards. See illustration in Chapter 1.

No. 1: No data. $30

No. C2: Inlaid; 12" x 3". $30

No. C3: 2P, T.A.; 6 x 4 grooved dividers; first Horn board mfg. with streamlined ends; 10 GW holes each end center; some have Horn starter holes; 11" x 2.35". $20

No. C5: Inlaid or grooved; Various lengths; 10.25" to 11.25" x 3". This was Horn's most popular board style and was manufactured for many years with progressive changes in design. $20

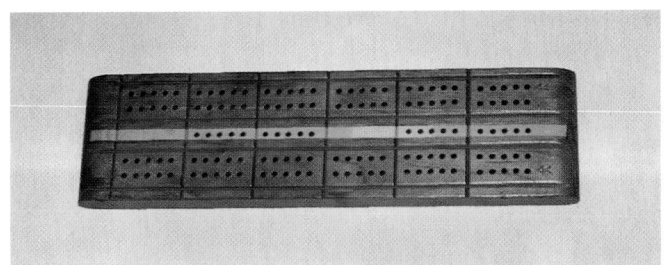

No. C6: 11" x 3". $15

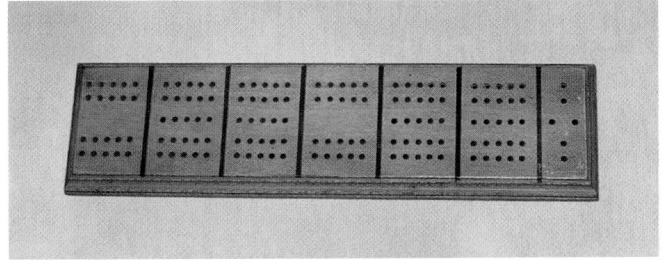

No. C8 (old style): 11.5" x 3". $20

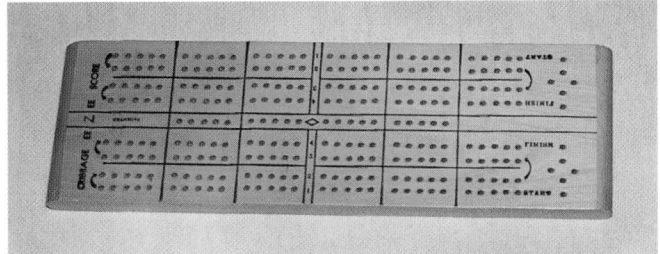

No. C8 (new style): 12" x 3.5". $20

No. C9: 11" x 3". $22

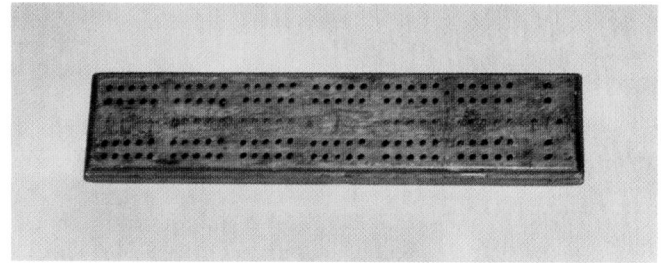

No. **C10:** 11" x 2.5". $30

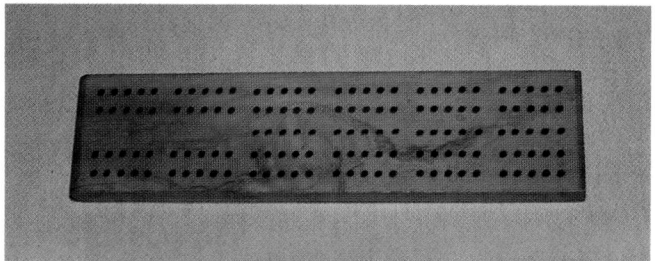

No. C11 (old): Wooden slider - WWII Board; 9.5" x 2.5". $20

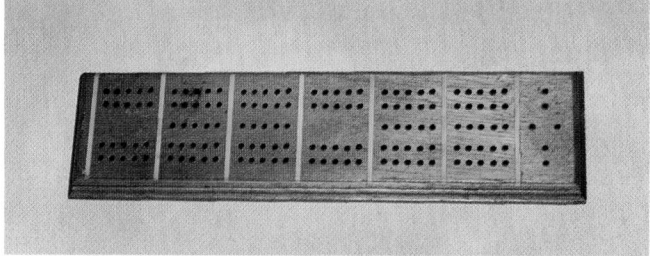

No. C11 (new): Inlaid; 11.5" x 3". $30

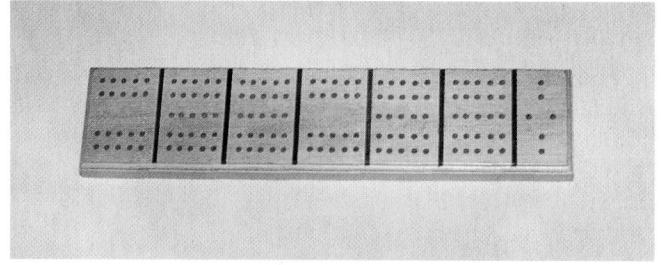

No. C12 (old): Grooved, inlaid, or plain; 11.25" x 2.5". $20

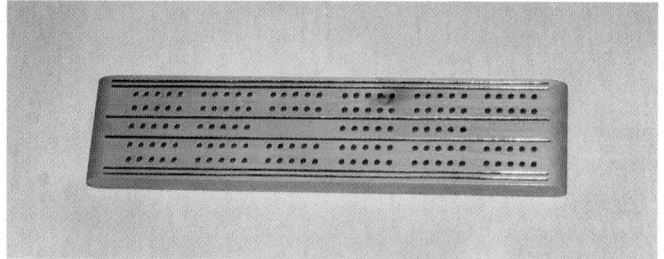

No. C12 (new): Grooved, with silver stenciling; 11" x 2.35". $20

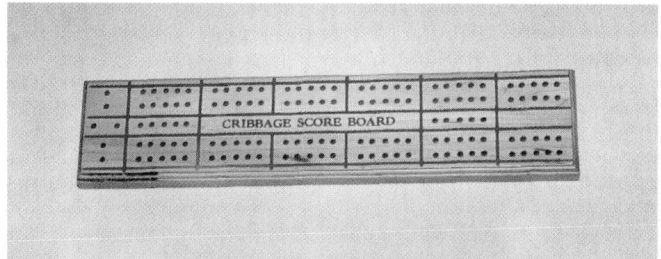

No. C14: Plain top or red stenciling. 11" x 2.5". $15

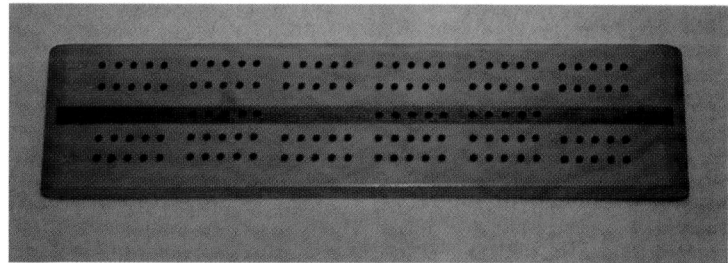

C15: 11" x 2.5". $20

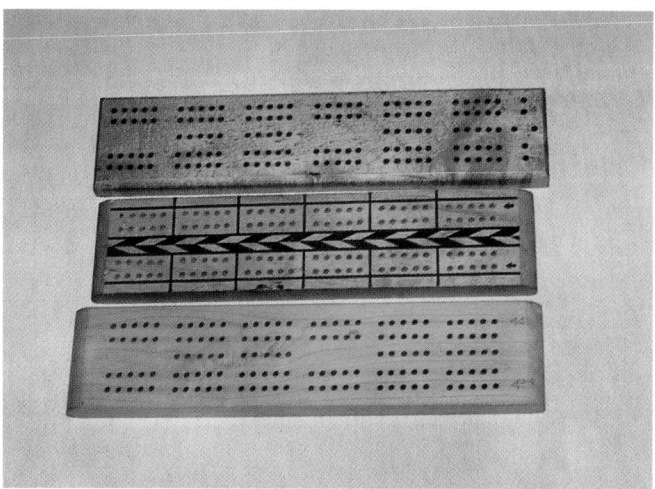

No. C16: Stenciled or plain; 10.5" x 2". $20

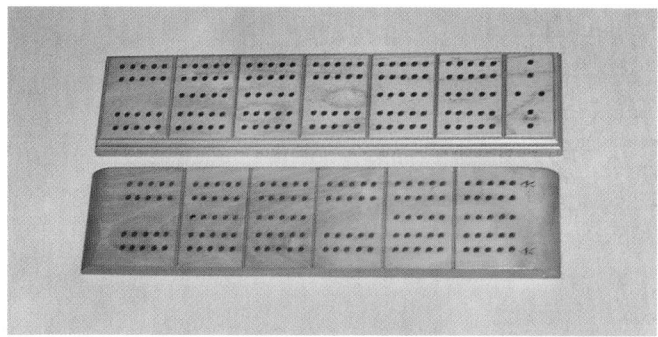

No. C17: Grooved or plain; 11" x 2.5". $20

No. C18: Grooved or stenciled; 11" x 2.5". $20

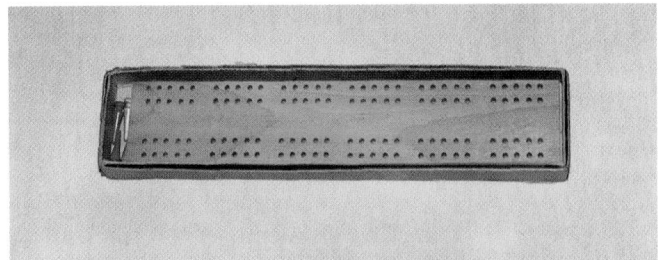

No. C26: 9.75" x 2". $15

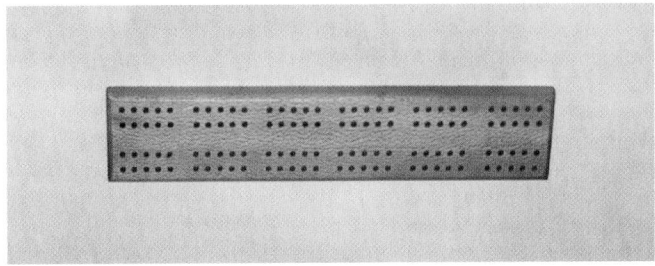

No. C27: 9.5" x 2". $15

No. C33: 3P, T.A.; 3 different wood inlays for tracks with 3 crosswise inlays at one end; 8 GW holes and 3 starter holes each track; 2 wooden slot covers; 12.25" x 2". $40

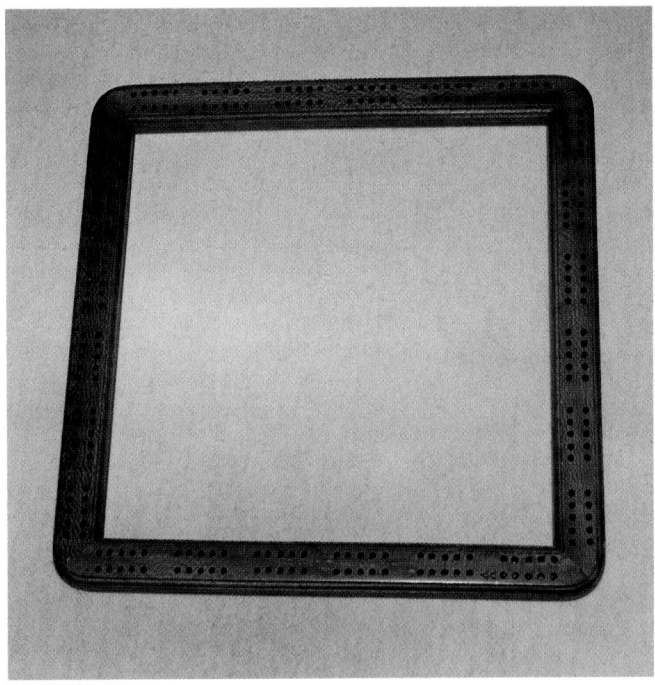

No. C34: 11.5" x 11.5" x 1" w. $50

No. C35: No data. $25

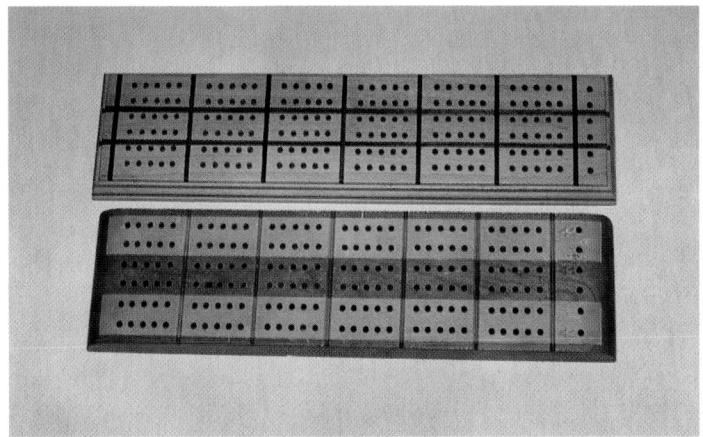

No. C36: Stenciled or inlaid; 11.25" x 3". $20

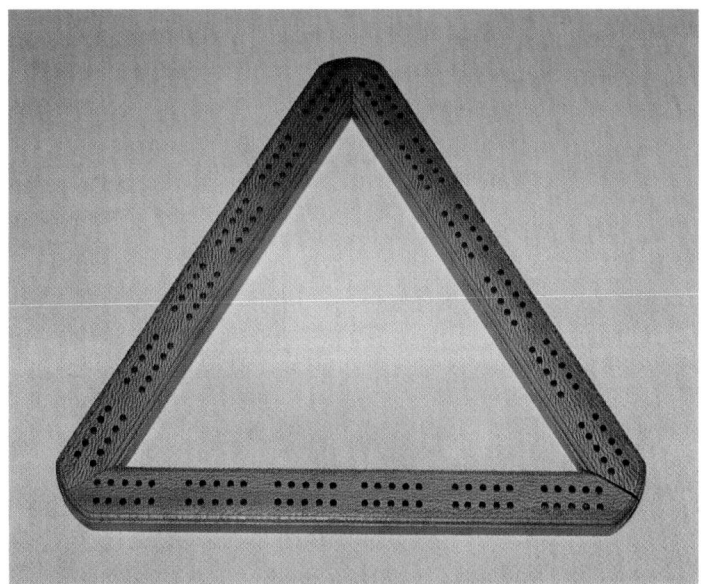

No. C38: 11" x 1.25". $40

No. C39: Grooved or inlaid; some wooden slot covers; 11" x 3". $15

No. C70: 2P, T.A.; folding inlay; 10 GW holes each outer end center; Holds deck of cards; 9.75" x 3.25" x 11.75" open. $35

No. C72: Folding box; 2P, T.A.; 2 starter holes each player; broken inlay down center; 9.12" x 3.12" open. $30

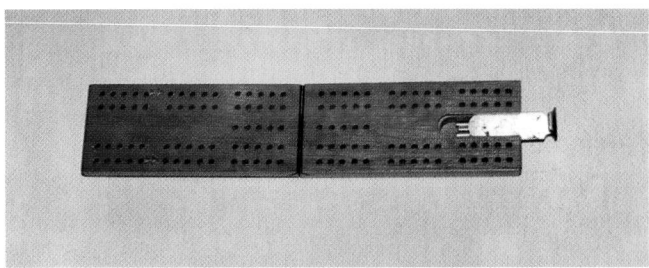

No. C82: 9.75" x 2" open. $35

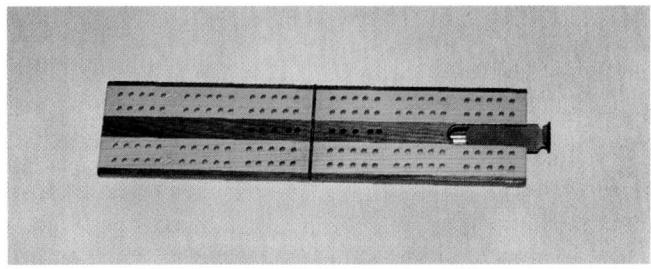

No. C83: Inlaid; 10" x 2.25" open. $35

No. C84: Inlaid; 9.75" x 2". $20

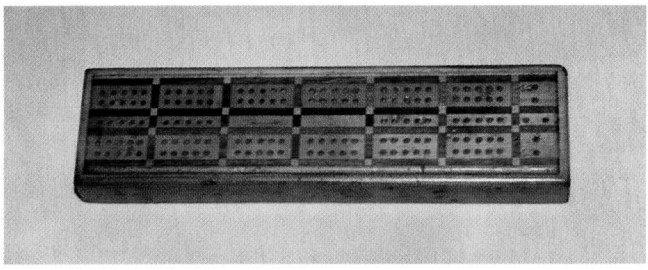

No. C230: Some wooden slot covers; 11.12" x 2.75" x 1.5". $30

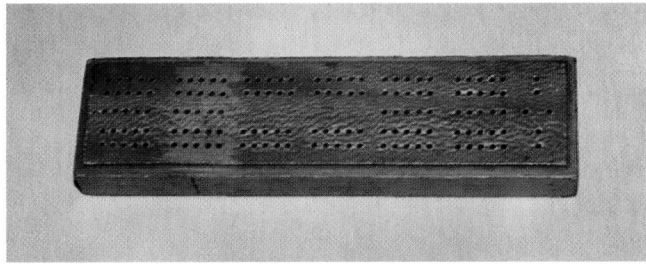

No. C231: Grooved or plain; 11.25" x 3" x 1.25". $35

No. C233: 2P, T.A.; card storage box; cards and pegs store in side slot; wood inlay down center; top edges grooved; center GW holes; 11.25" x 2.75" x 1.25". $30

No. C234: Box; 11.12" x 2.75" x 1.5". $30

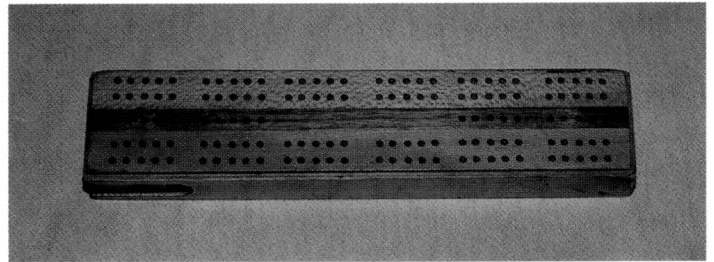

No. C235: 10.25" x 2.25" x 1". $30

No. C237: 2P, T.A.; card storage box; 10 GW holes each end center; no starter holes; 10" x 2.75". $20

No. C239: No data. $30

No. C240: Lift-off top box; 2P, T.A.; 6 x 2 grooves; feather inlay down center; 10 GW holes each end center; Horn starter holes; entire board has "lip" around middle of sides; 11.25" x 2.75". $40

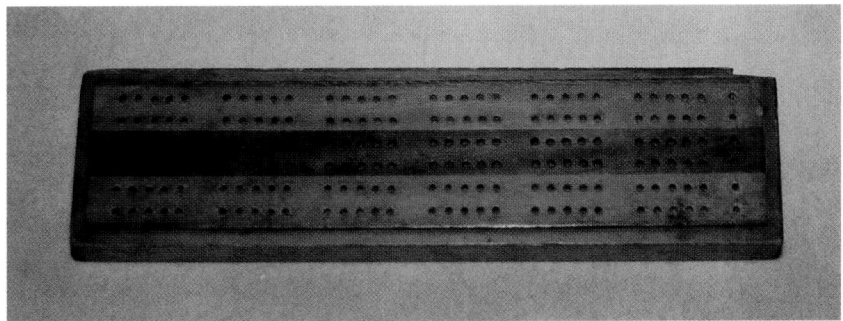

No. C245: Inlay; 11.5" x 2.85" x 1.25". $30

No. C271: 2P, T.A.; 11" x 3"; center inlay; 10 GW holes each end center; 11" x 3". $15

No. G1: 2P, T.A.; folding wood, leather back marked *Cribbage Board*; peg storage inside; no GW or starter holes. $20

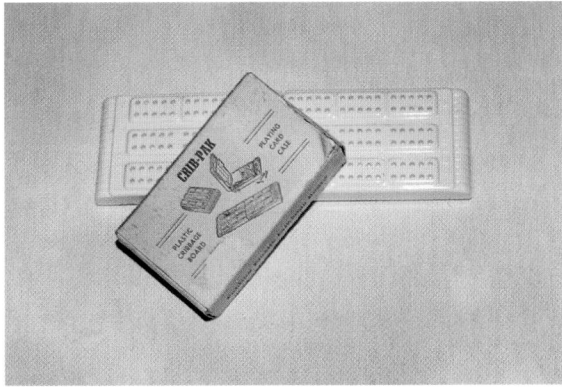

No. M76: *Crib-Pak:* ivory or maroon plastic; 9" x 2.75" open. $20

No. KC8(1): 2P continuous track; *Easy Score Cribbage* ; green and blue tracks curve to next row; stenciled *start* and *finish* ; 15 GW holes down center; identical to Kingsbridge No. 6759; 12" x 3.5". $15

No. KC8(2): 2P continuous track, arrows curve to next street; stenciled burgundy 6 x 2 divider lines; *Cribbage E-E-Z-E-E Score*; streamlined ends; 10 GW holes in center; 12" x 3.5". $15

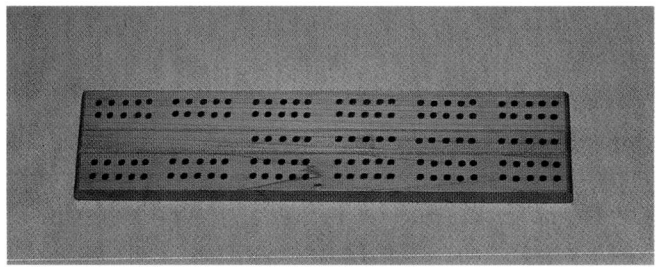

No. KC11: 9.5" x 2". $15

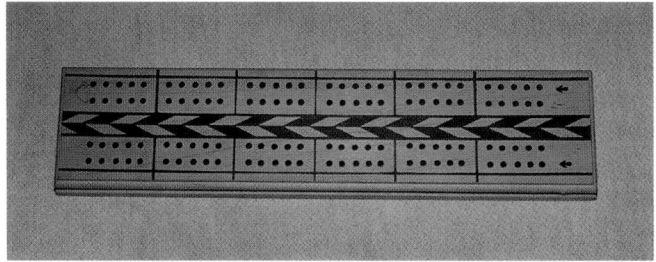

No. KC16: Stenciled; identical to Horn C16; 10.5" x 2.5". $15

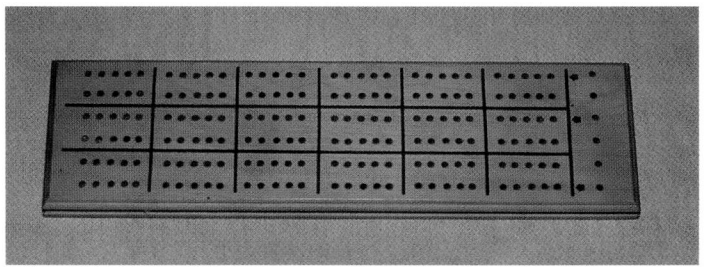

No. KC39: stenciled; 11.25" x 3". $15

No. KC184: 3P, T.A.; cherry base, inlaid with light wood; feather inlay and 7 x 4 strips separating double 5 holes; 2 starter holes each track; 11.5" x 3.75". $20

No. KC230: Identical to C230; metal slot cover. $30

No. 61 (No C): 2P, T.A.; Folding board with leather cover stamped *Cribbage Board*; peg storage inside; identical to Kingsbridge No. 6756; 10.6" x 2" open. $20

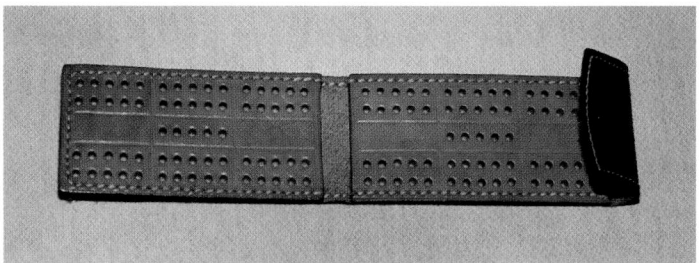

No. 88 (No C): Leather folding; sold during WW II; 11.5" x 2.12" open. $30

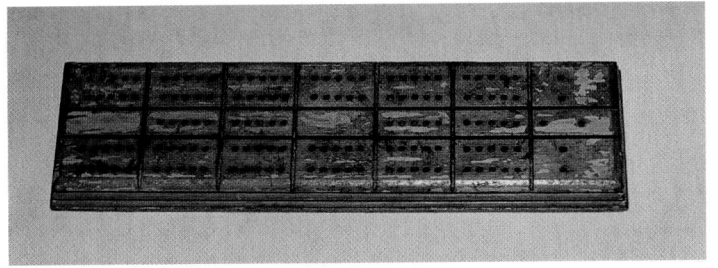

No. UNK: 11.5" x 3" x .75". $30

Hoyle Products: St. Paul, Minnesota

See Standard Packaging Co.

Jack Daniels: Lynchburg, Tennessee: - present

Cribbage boards are made from used Jack Daniels whiskey barrel staves, including metal bands, by local crafters, and sold locally.

2P, T.A.; oak; pegs made of hand cut iron nails; 21" long. CMP

John Gill Mfg.: New York City, New York: mid-to-late 1800s

John Gill was primarily a manufacturer of Piano-Forte hardware.

Hedgehog Board: *John Gill's Improved Cribbage Board and Whist Counter Combined Patented*: U.S. Patent # 40,999, 12/22/1863; 10.5" x 3.75" x 1.25 ". $300

John Samuels Co. (J.S.): New York City, New York

Bought by H. Baron Co., they manufactured boards under the *"Good Luck Brand"*.

Folding leather travel w/snap closure; mfg. 1952; 12" x 2.25" open. $25

Kencroft Assoc., Inc.: Buffalo 7, New York

Manufactured a plastic board patented by Ralph T. Rycroft (Patent No. D144417, issued 1947).

No. 30: 8.25" x 2.75" open. $40

Kent: St. Paul, Minnesota

See Standard Packaging Co.

Kingsbridge: by Atlantic Playing Card Co.: Long Island City, New York

The company was a distributor of cribbage boards made by other American manufacturers. Their cribbage board boxes were blue, unmarked.

No. 6756: 2P, T.A.; folding board with leatherette cover, flap for closing; peg storage one side; no starter holes; *Cribbage Board* on cover; identical to Horn No. 61; 10.6" x 2". $15

No. 6757: 2P, T.A.; 6 x 2 grooved dividers; 10 GW holes each end center; Horn starter holes; identical to Horn No. C18; 11" x 2.5". $15

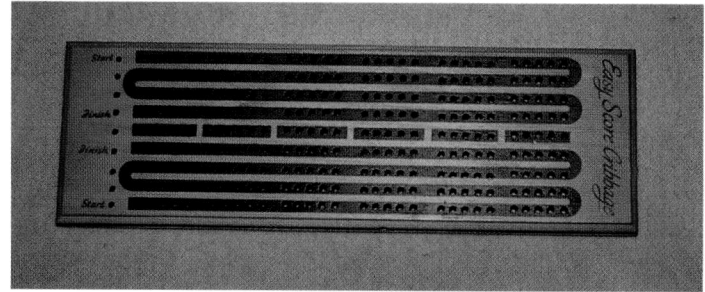

No. 6759: Identical to Gibson (Horn) No. KC8; 12" x 3.75". $15

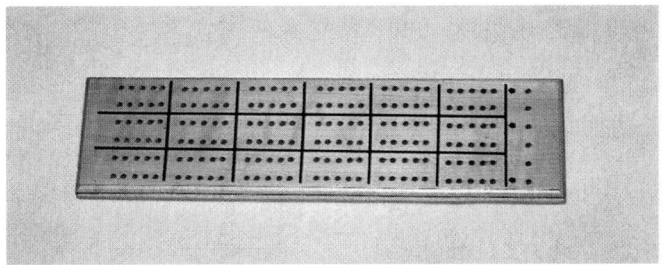

No. 6818: Identical to Gibson (Horn) No. KC39; 11.25" x 3". $15

Kingstone: 1980s - 1990s

Distributed *The Trainer Cribbage Board.*

No. CB106: Taiwan; 8.25" x 7". $15

Kingsway:

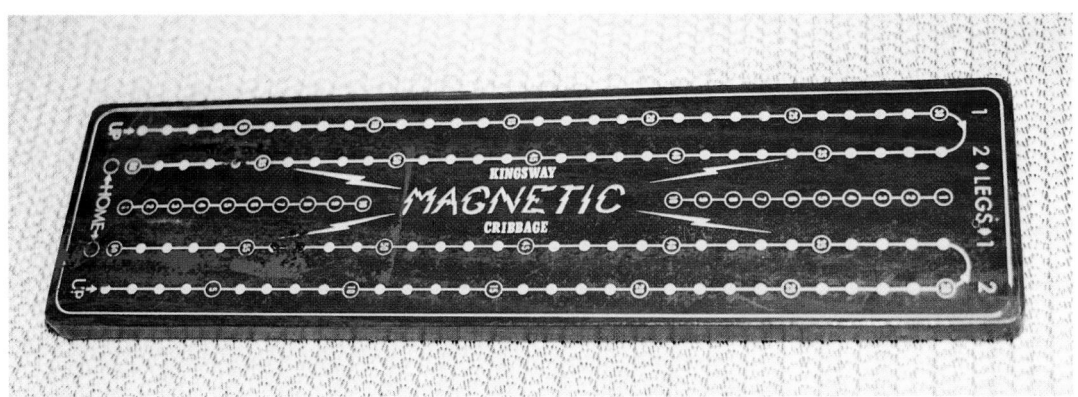

Kingsway Magnetic Cribbage: Magnetic game pieces; 12.25" x 3.25". $25

C.A. Kirk (House of Kirk):

Manufacturer of oversized pine cribbage boards, some 2" thick, which use a 3" peg. The company logo, a house with *c a kirk* below it, is branded on the bottom. Boards were manufactured in various designs, including abstract shapes and state outlines.

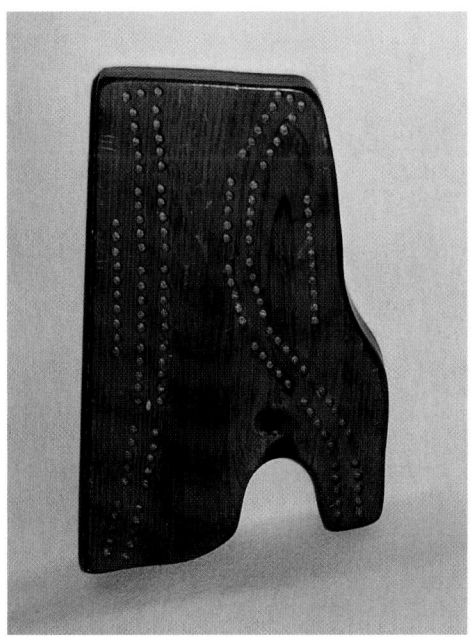

16.5" x 10" x 2". $30

B. Lamb & Co.: Plainville, Connecticut

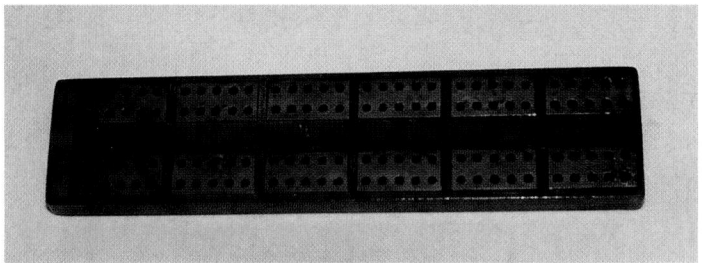

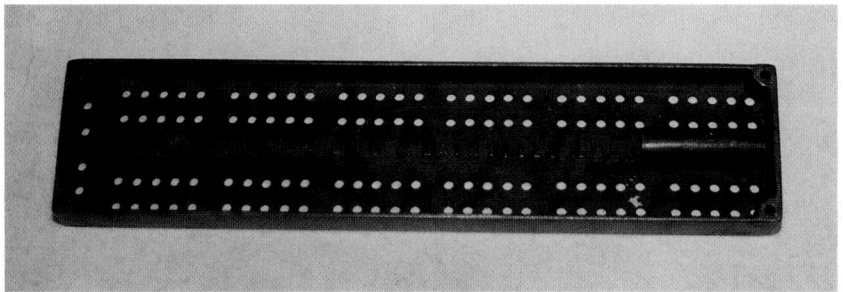

Hollow cast iron; underside imprinted *B. Lamb & Co.* cylindrical peg holder; 10.5" x 2.5". $45

Laraia & Co.: Worcester, Massachusetts

Laraia & Co. manufactured calendars and novelties. The cribbage boards were manufactured by the molded products division.

2P, T.A.; Bakelite board; 2 starter holes each player at one end; flat sides; box marked "Compliments of Belmore Beverage, Webster, Mass." $50

C.W. Le Count Co.: South Norwalk, Connecticut: 1863 - c. 1920

Established by Charles W. Le Count in 1863, the company began as manufacturers of machinists' tools and later added cribbage boards to the product line. A nickel-faced steel top with walnut base cribbage board was patented by Charles W. Le Count in September 1879 and again in July 1885. Although the boards were not given individual identification numbers, Le Count boards can be identified by one or more of the following marks:

1. Company name is on slider
2. Company name is imprinted on the side of the metal top
3. The name of the company and the patent date is a part of the face design.

In 1895, the business was taken over by a son, William G. Le Count, and the name was changed to W. G. Le Count Company. The factory moved to 246-278 East Avenue, East Norwalk some time after that. The cribbage boards continued to have the old company name imprinted on them.

One of the most fascinating and unsolved puzzles surrounding the Le Count cribbage board styles is that there also exists a board with a nearly identical face design to one of the Le Count boards, but "F. W. Quitman So. Norwalk CT." and a different center medallion is imprinted on it. We know that Frederick W. Quitman was born in Prussia in 1847, moved to the United States in 1870, and his occupation was listed as "machinist" on the 1900 South Norwalk census. One can only assume that Frederick Quitman originally designed the cribbage board and then sold the manufacturing rights to C. W. Le Count. The name F. W. Quitman was then removed after the board design was patented by C. W. Le Count.

The early C. W. Le Count cribbage boards included a set of rules that were written by E. C. Hazard of New York. Various board styles could be purchased through the Montgomery Ward and Sears Roebuck & Co. catalogs from the late 1800s to the early 1900s. The Le Count cribbage boards are still readily available, the abundance of which can probably be attributed to the fact that they could be bought wherever the catalogs were distributed.

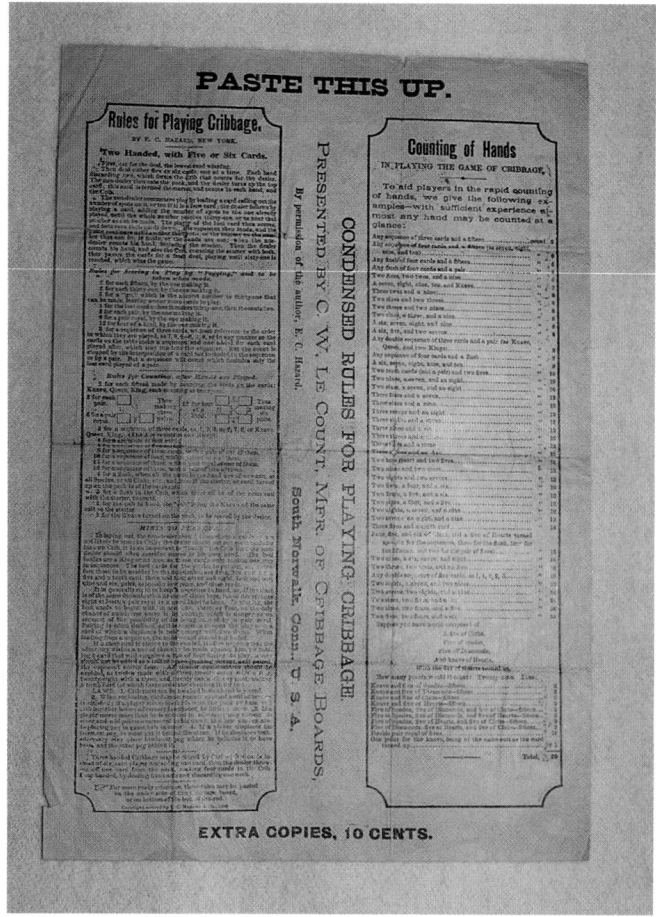

E.C. Hazard Instruction Sheet.

The boards have been broken down into three basic models, which appears to be the only way that they were identified. The size of the metal top is listed.

Model No. 1: 3P, T.A.; box board with 1 or 2 card slots on sides(s) for playing card and peg storage. The second slot was for storage of Pinochle cards.

Top

Bottom: showing game wheels; box marked *Combined Cribbage, Whist and Euchre Board;* 10.25" x 2.5". $100

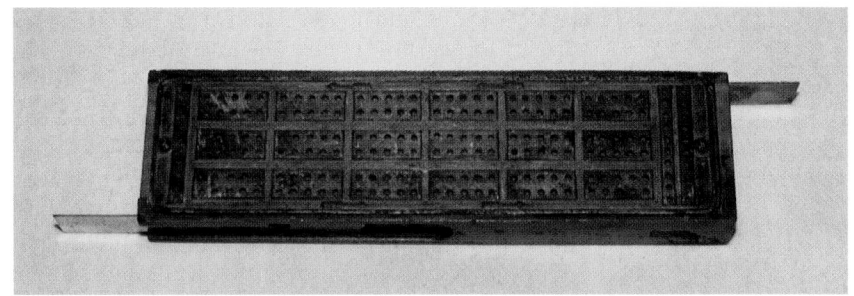

The "*Arrow*" board: two raised street directional arrows on each edge of the metal top; 10.25" x 2.6". $50

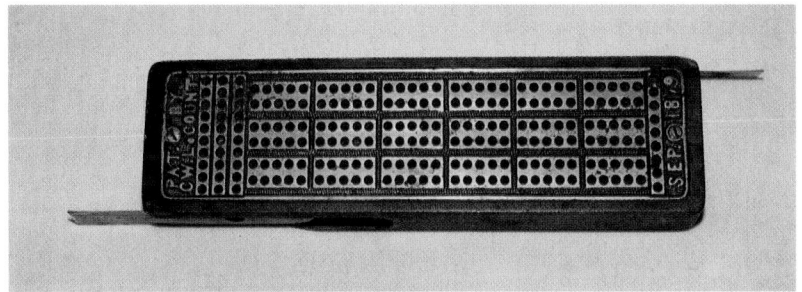

Advertised as *Le Count's New Patent Cribbage Board:* stamped *PAT. BY C.W. Le COUNT* at one end, *SEP.1879* at other end; 10" x 2.5". $40

Box: 3P, T.A.; 2 card slots; 3 sets 10 GW holes at one end, 9 starter holes at the other end, each surrounded by raised circle; each block of double five holes located in raised rectangle; in Montgomery Ward's 1894 Catalog for $1.00; 10.5" x 2.85". $40

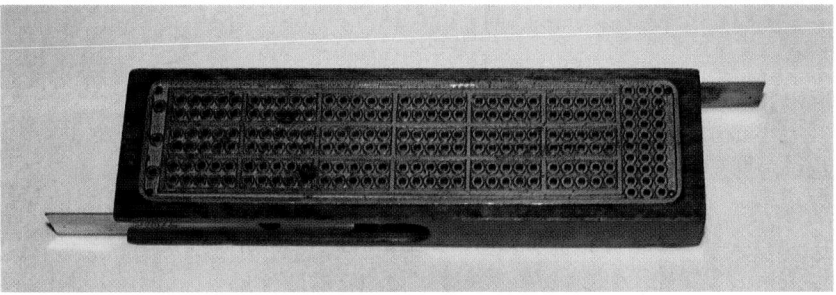

10" x 2.5". $40

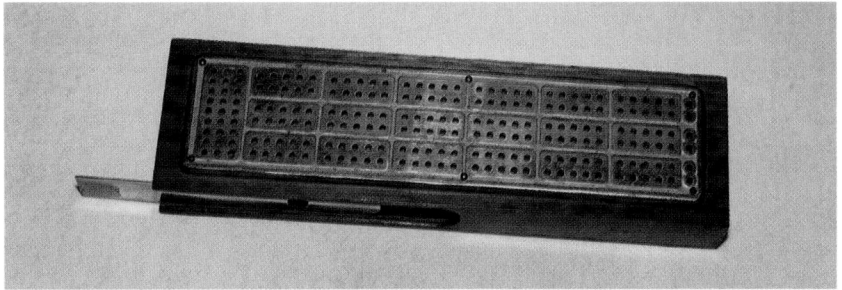

9.75" x 2.35". $40

Box: 3P, T.A.; 1 card slot; 3 sets of 10 GW holes at one end, 1 set 9 starter holes at other end, all in raised rectangles; each block of double five holes located in raised rectangle; in Sears Roebuck's Fall 1900 catalog for $.85; 10.5" x 2.85". $40

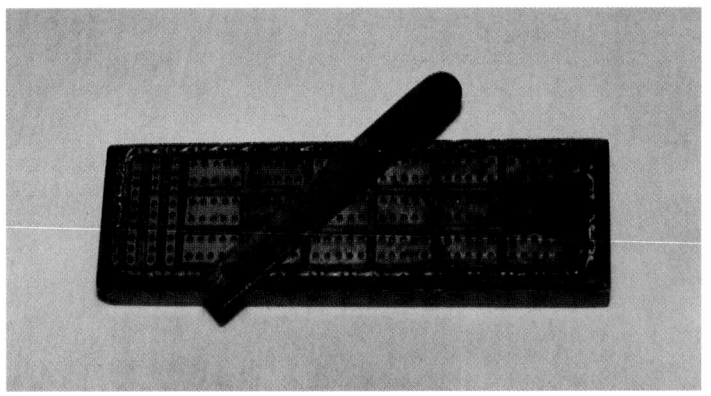

Edge of metal plate scrolled; wooden slot cover; 9.5" x 2.75". $45

Model No. 2: 2P, T.A. Box with 1 card slot on side for playing cards and peg storage.

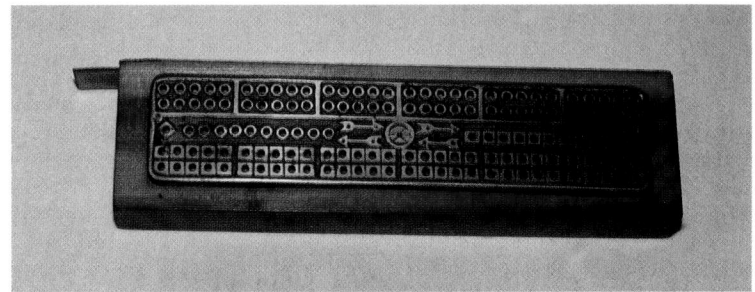

Advertised as *Le Count's Climax Cribbage Board:* 9.5" x 2.25". $50

Model No. 3: 2P, T.A. board; peg storage on underside.

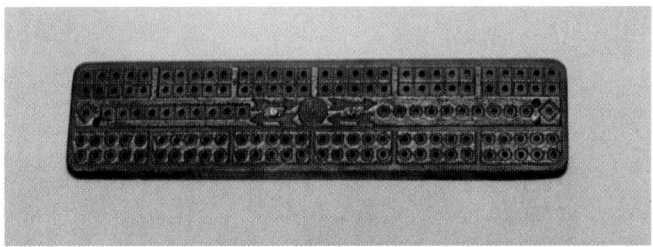

Soft wood base: sold in Montgomery Ward's Winter 1894-95 catalog for $.50; 9.85" x 2.25". $30

F W. Quitman board: 2P, T.A.; see No. 3 board for basic board description, *except for center. Each side of center medallion is printed F.W. Quitman SO. NORWALK CT.; .75" drawer on side for peg storage; 9.75" x 2 11.75". $150*

Life's Games Corp.: Great Neck, New York: c. 1990 - present

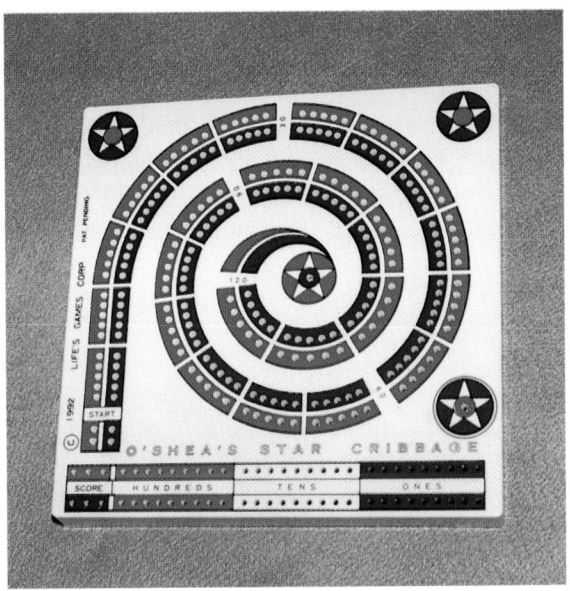

O'Shea's Star Cribbage: plays *Yankee Doodle Dandy* when winner pegs out; 8.5" x 8.5". CMP

Lion Rock Ltd.: c. 1979

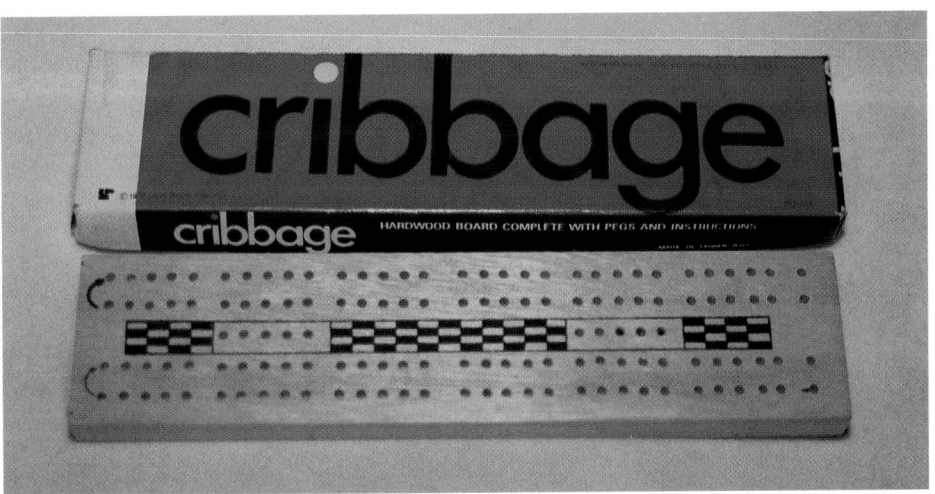

No. 002: Taiwan; © 1979; 9.25" x 2.12". $5

E.S. Lowe Co., Inc: New York City, New York: 1920s - 1974

    The E. S. Lowe Company, Inc. was founded by Edward S. Lowe, and the corporate offices were located at 27 W 20th St., New York City. The company manufactured a diversified line of cribbage boards, including boards made of plastic, leather, and wood. The older instruction sheets carried the phrase *"For Those Who Know, It's Games By Lowe"* but the only games other than cribbage boards that are readily recognized today are those that were carried in the company's series called Bookshelf Games.

    Bookshelf Games was a series of games manufactured primarily for use by the servicemen of WWII. They were enclosed in small cases which resembled a book, and packed easily. Other manufacturers of games, including Drueke and Metro Mfg. Co., also produced similar sets. Bookshelf Games came in two versions. One was an economical set, had covers of pressed cardboard and sold for $.50 to $1.50. The Deluxe Edition was bound in "top-grain genuine cowhide" or simulated leather and cost $3.00 to $5.00.

Lowe acquired the Crib Derby Company of St. Paul, Minnesota, the manufacturer of the first known race track-style cribbage board and manufactured a plastic version of the board.

In 1974, the offices of Lowe were moved to Springfield, Massachusetts, when the Milton Bradley Company purchased it. Most of the Lowe board styles continued to be sold by Milton Bradley, with some minor changes made to the styles. Prior to the take-over, the boards were manufactured in this country, but under Milton Bradley, they were manufactured in Taiwan and Japan.

The Lowe logo was a diamond with an "L" or "Lowe" contained within it. Both the boxes and the boards were identified with the logo. The model numbers are found only on the boxes. After the Milton Bradley take-over, the famous Lowe diamond logo continued to be used, with some minor changes. "E.S." was added to Lowe, and "A Milton Bradley Company" was added outside the diamond. Eventually, the Lowe board styles were discontinued.

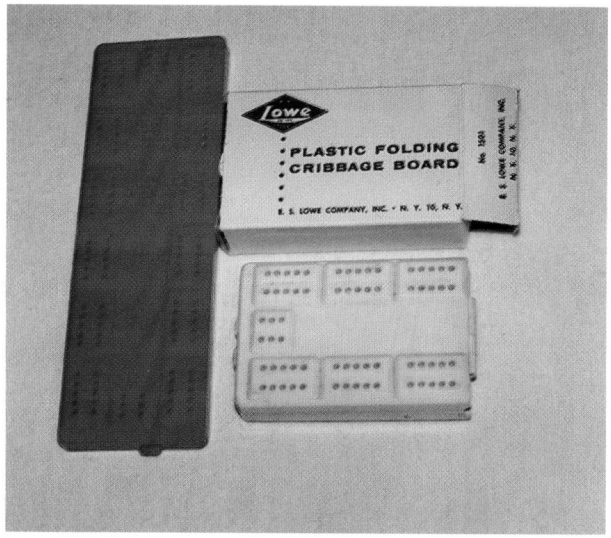

No. 1501: Red or white plastic; (renamed Folding Travel Cribbage Board under MB); 9" x 3" open. $25

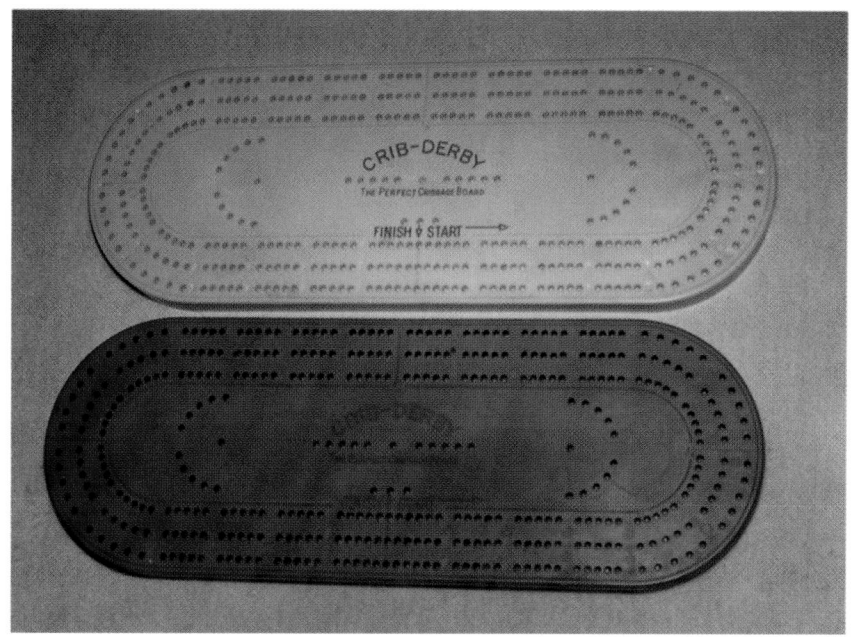

No. 1502: *Crib Derby:* tan or white plastic; underside hollow and marked *Pat. Des. 149863 Made in USA*; 14" x 5". $30

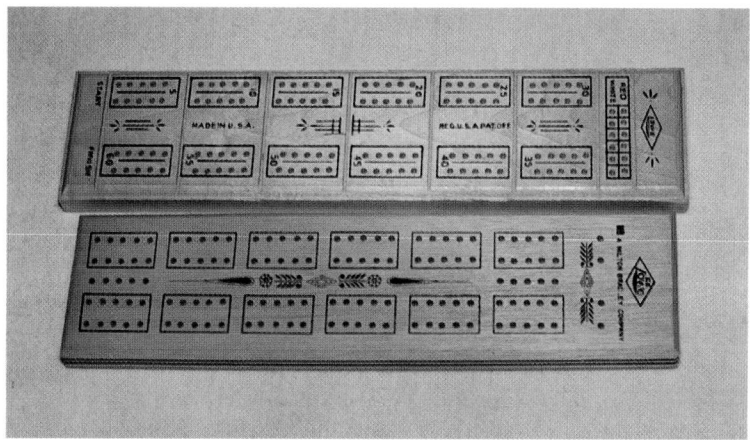

No. 1503: Stenciled; 12" x 2.75". $10

No. 1504: Deluxe version of No. 1503. $15

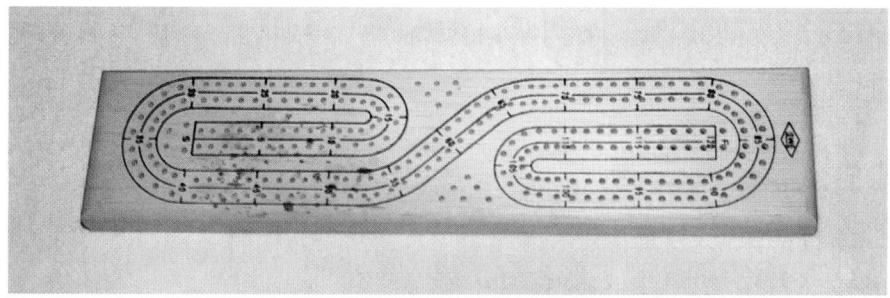

No. 1505: 13.5" x 3". $10

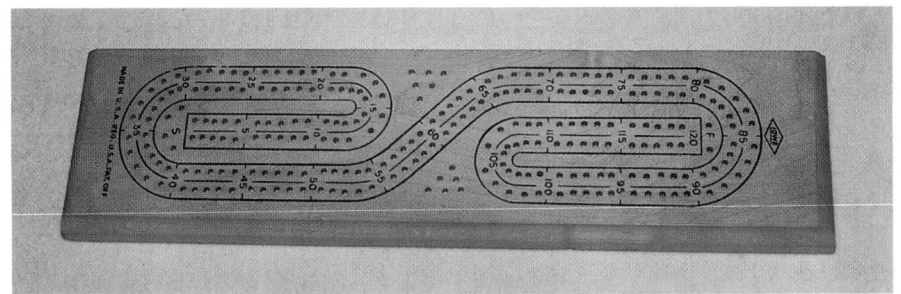

No. 1506: Deluxe version of No. 1505; black or red tracks; 14.5" x 3.75". $15

Vol. 527: Bookshelf Games: black cardboard box; board 7" x 2" open. $35

Vol. 557: Bookshelf Games: *The Genuine Leather Edition*: gutta percha-style red cover; 7" x 2" open. $35

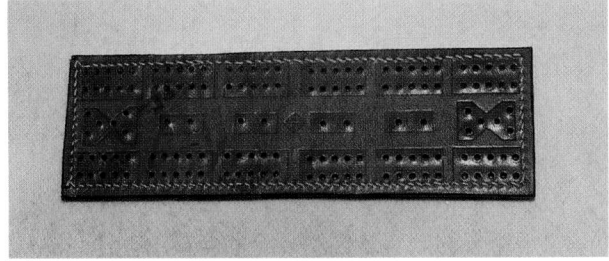

No. 637: Flat leather; WWII; 7" x 2" open. $30

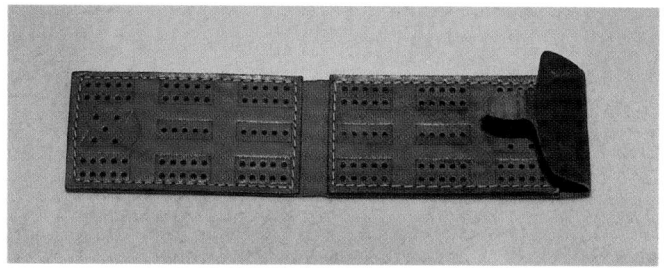

No. 651: folding leather; WWII; 12.25" x 2.25" open. $25

No. 691: 2P, T.A.; WWII folding wooden board, Burgundy leather covered box; cards included; 4.6" x 1.6" open. $25

The Marble Man: Woodbridge, Virginia: - present

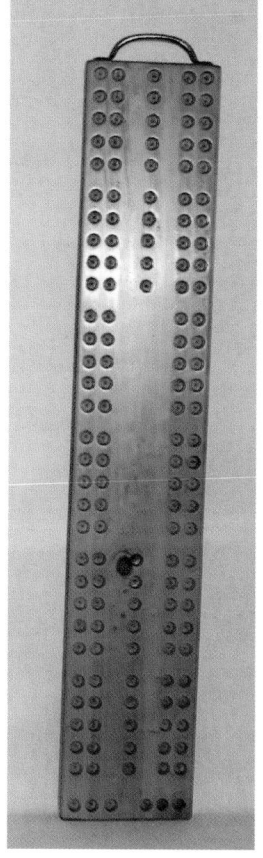

Founded by Jack and Sue Hahn, the company hand-crafts a variety of games, including cribbage boards, which are played with marbles rather than the traditionally used pieces. The marbles are also created by Jack from recycled glass.

No. CR: Various colors available; wall hanger; 30" x 5.5". CMP

Maynard: Minneapolis, Minnesota: - present

Cross Crib: cribbage variation; folding board; one player plays up and the other plays across; uses 26 cards (1/2 deck); 22" square. CMP

R.F. McCrillis, Mfr.: Norwalk, Ohio: 1930s - 1940s

McCrillis was a designer of cribbage boards and other games such as Pinochle in the 1930s for various manufacturers, including W. C. Horn, Bros. & Co. The name *McCrillis* was incorporated into the Horn stamp on the bottom of their cribbage boards, and it is assumed that Horn bought out McCrillis.

Melling, Herman W.: Jackson, Michigan

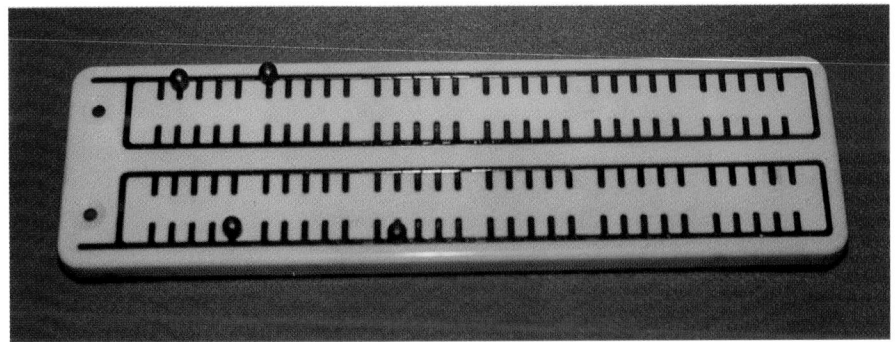

Crib-A-Matic: Bakelite channeled board; 2 brass balls each player, which slide along channel for scoring. Balls move only in one direction, and upon completing the first trip around, a street counter is triggered by the ball, moving to "2," indicating second trip around. 10.5" x 3". $60

Meriden Britannia Co.: Meriden, Connecticut: 1852 - 1898

Meriden Britannia Company manufactured silver products in the 1800s. When Rogers-Smith Co. had financial difficulties, Meriden Britannia Co. took over the business, and it was retained as a subsidiary. Both companies manufactured several nearly identical products, including a cribbage board, which were stamped with each company's mark. In 1898, Meriden Britannia Company and 16 other silver companies merged to form the International Silver Company, which is no longer in existence.

No. 30: Silver box, pull-out drawer; 11" x 3.5" x 1.75". $300

No. 34: Smaller version of No. 35. $100

No. 35: 3P, T.A.; with 6 small feet; playing area same as found on No. 30 and is surrounded by 22 small scrolls; ends are decorated with a larger single scroll. $125

No. 2851: Box with pull-out drawer at bottom. Simpson-Hall Miller catalog, 1895. $300

No. 2852: Folding box; Simpson-Hall-Miller catalog, 1895. $100

Metro Mfg. Co.: New York City, New York

Metro's logo was a 3 leaf clover with **M E T** (one letter found in each leaf).

Bookgames The Game Lovers Library, which was manufactured by Metro, consisted of a series of boxed games which were sent to servicemen during WWII.

After Baron bought Metro they continued to manufacture some of the board styles.

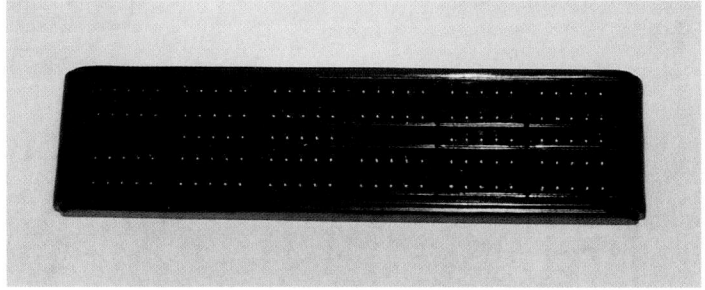

No. 17: 2P, brown Bakelite; identical to Baron 17/100; 9.75" x 2.5". $15

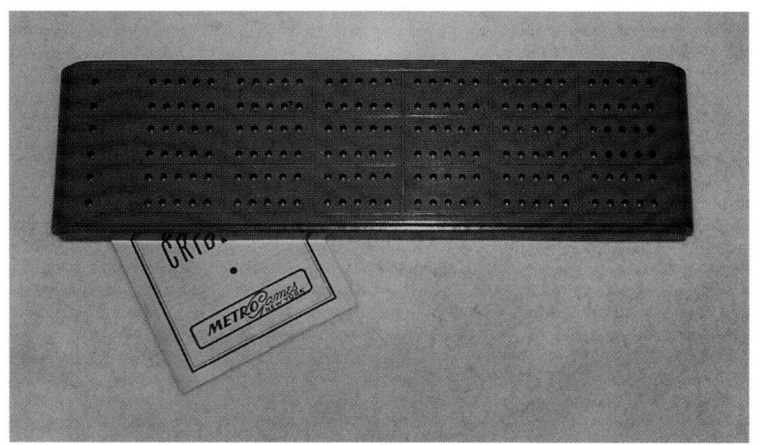

No. 18: 3P, T.A.; maroon or brown Bakelite; identical to Baron 18/100; 10.75" x 3". $20

No. 255: *Bookgames:* plain or embossed leather case; under the lid was an advertisement *-Buy War Savings Bonds and Stamps Now*; board 7" x 2" open. $35

No. 260: *Bookgames:* identical to No. 255, but included a deck of cards. $35

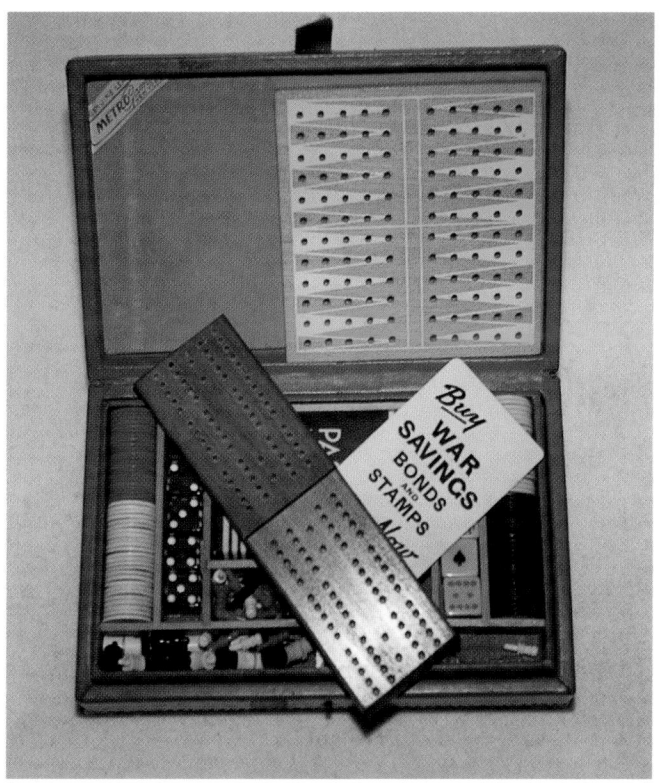

No. UNK: WWII leather game box; Metro was the first manufacturer of this style game box; box 8.5" x 5.5". $30

Miller Designs, Inc.: Franklin, New Hampshire: c. 1985 - 1990s

Manufacturer of high end quality boards; hardwood boards with full brass or ceramic plate on face, which have color-coded or plain streets.

No. 2CTB: Classic Cribbage Board: 2 or 3P, once-around "Z" shape track; 2 starter holes each player; brass plate on oak or cherry; solid brass feet; color-coded streets; rounded corners; 14" x 7.5". CMP

No. 2CTBca: Heritage Cribbage Board: 2P or 3P(3TCBca), once-around "Z" shape track; 2 starter holes each player; brass plate on oak or cherry; lid opens to reveal pegs and 2 decks of cards stored in compartment; 13.25" x 6.75". CMP

No. (Unk): 2P, T.A.; hand-painted ceramic fish cribbage board set in cherry frame; 16.5" x 6.5". CMP

Milton Bradley Co.: Springfield, Massachusetts: 1860 - present

Acquired Somerville Industries Ltd. of Canada in 1964 and E. S. Lowe, Co. in 1974. Until the company was purchased by Hasbro, Inc. in 1984, it had always been owned by the same family.

The older boards, manufactured directly by Milton Bradley, are stamped *Milton Bradley Co. Springfield, Mass.* on the underside, and the peg slot covers are stamped with the same information. In recent years, all of their boards have been manufactured in Japan or Taiwan, and the peg slot covers are stamped with the country of origin. All of their boards have a classic double-grooved side which tapers to the top. They manufactured three basic styles, No. 4624, No. 4625, and No. 4626.

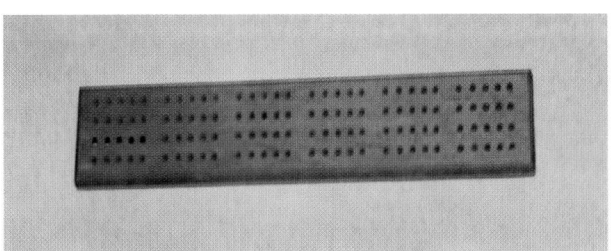

No. 4624: 9.35" x 2". $15

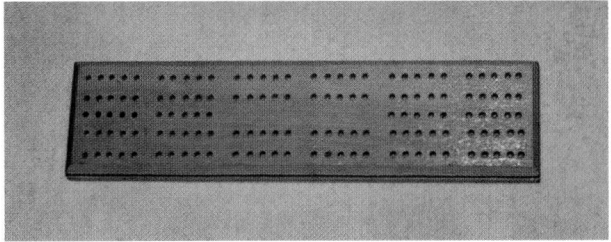

No. 4625: 9.5" x 2.25". $10

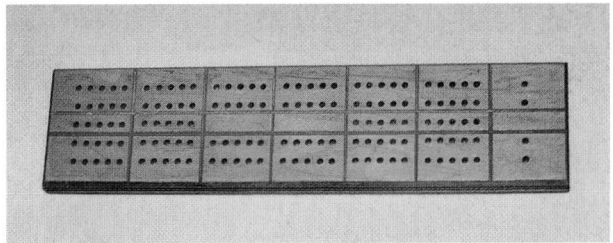

No. 4626: Milton Bradley's most common board; 11" x 2.75". CMP

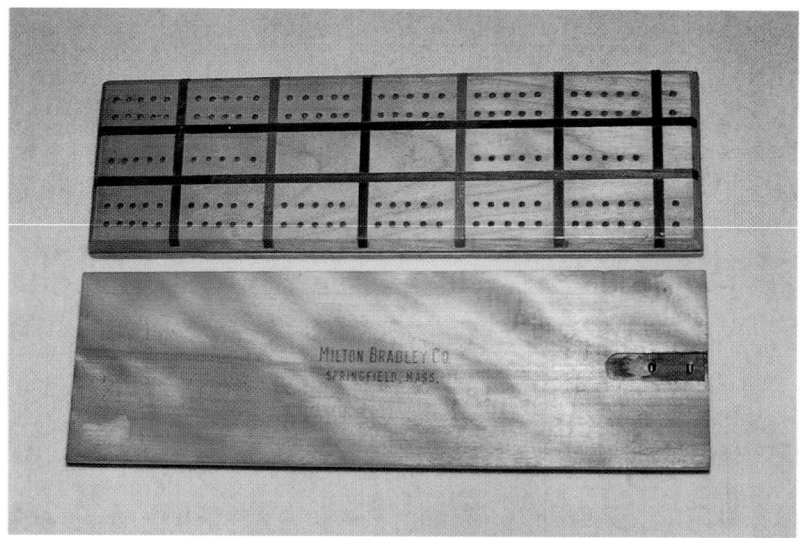

No. (Unk): Inlaid; MB stamp on bottom; 12.25" x 3.75". $30

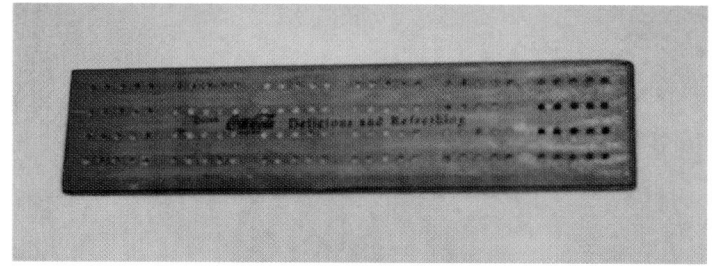

No. 4624CC: Coca-Cola Advertising Board: stenciled. Identical to No. 4624; 9.35" x 2". $40

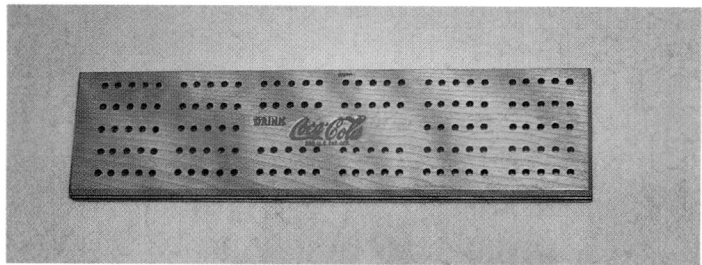

No. 4625CC: Coca-Cola Advertising Board: identical style to No. 4625. $40

No. R4535: *"Somerville by Milton Bradley"*: 2P, T.A.; plastic; 5 GW holes each end center; drawer at one end for peg storage; 7.5" x 2.12". $15

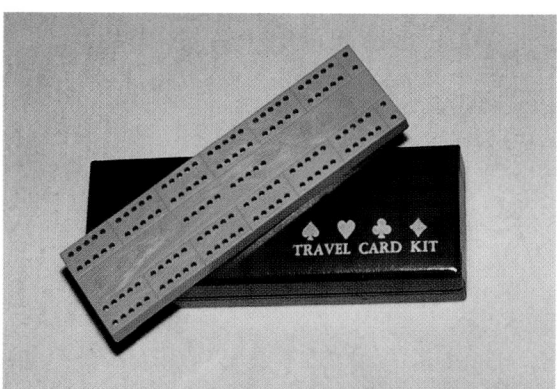

No. 5609: *Travel Card Kit:* leatherette box hinges open and stores 2 decks of cards and plastic cribbage board; card suits stenciled down center; various colors; 7.5" x 2.12". $25

Monogram Cribbage Board Co.: c. 1893

Wooden board with silver-plate scrollwork on face; stamped *Pat. Mar.8.92* (1892). Two other styles have been located, both with identical tops. One has a drawer at the end for card storage. The third one is a box with a lift-off cover. 10.5" x 3.25". $100

My Kids Toy Mfg. Co., LTD.: Encino, California

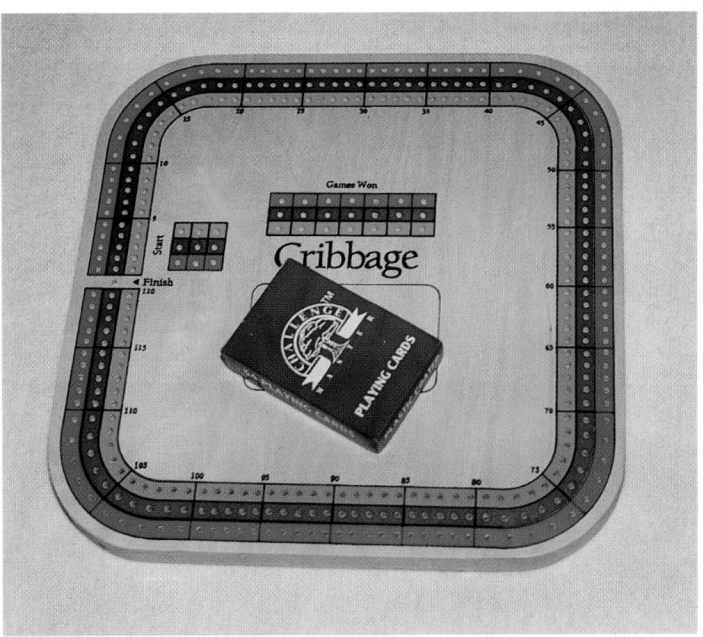

No. 19113: Hong Kong; 11.5" x 11.5". CMP

NEWMAC Co.: Minneapolis, Minnesota

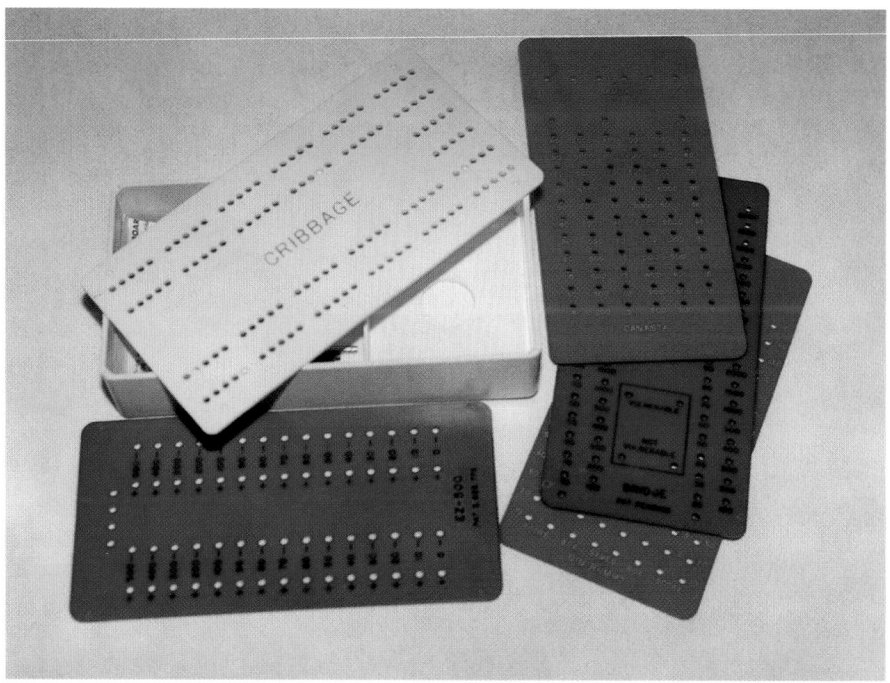

E-Z Tally Scoreboard: plastic box with 5 removable sliding tops; white top for Cribbage, green tops for 500 and Bridge, red tops for Canasta and Gin Rummy. 7.5" x 4". $25

NY Consolidated Card Co.:

2P.T.A.; embossed leather board; 2 starter holes each end; holes go through to back of board; 15" x 3.25". $30

Noble Games Co.: - present

Manufacturer of high quality cribbage boards, many with leather or metal inlays.

North Coast Trading Co., Inc.: Seattle, Washington: - present

Manufacturers of polymer hand-scrimshawed products.

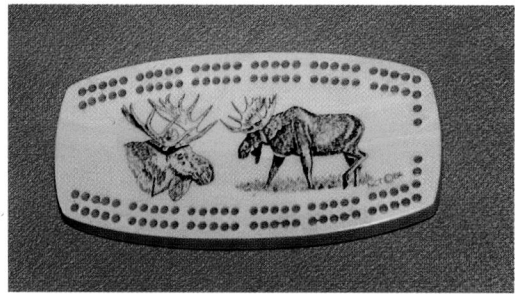

CB Series: White "marble," various designs; 7" x 3.5". CMP

CBI Series: Black or white with white insert; various designs; 7" x 3.5". CMP

OCB 300 Series: 2P, once-around; black oval board with white scrimshaw insert; 2 starter holes each player; various designs; 6.75" x 4.75". CMP

No. F201: Walrus tusk; 2P, T.A.; scrimshaw design; carved bird in relief at end; 10" long. CMP

Nypro: Clinton, Massachusetts

Parent company of Skor-Mor.

Pacific Game Co.: 12830 Raymer St., N. Hollywood, California: c. 1940 - ±1985

The Pacific Game Company manufactured a variety of games, including cribbage boards. The cribbage boards were sold under the name of Pleasantime. Some of the boards are of walnut, but two models, #750 and #755, are plastic. Many of the board tops are heavily decorated with stenciled leaves, circles, triangles, or other geometrical designs, and include the model number and their name.

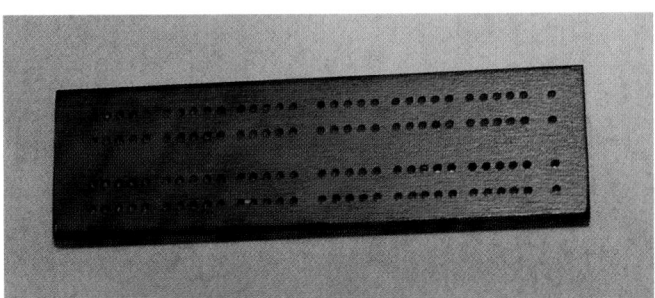

No. 702: 7.6" x 2.25". $10

No. 703: 2P, T.A.; folding board; 2 starter holes each player; 7.75" x 2.5" open. $10

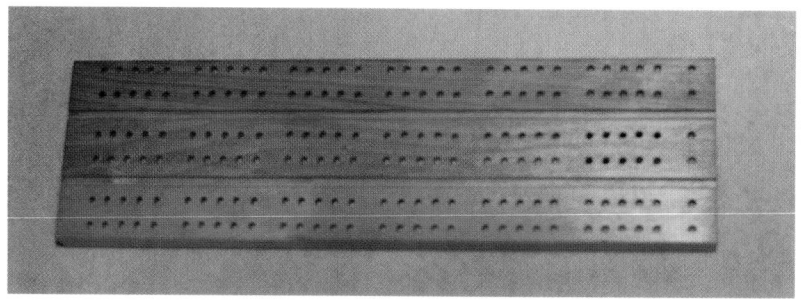

No. 705: 10" x 2.75". $15

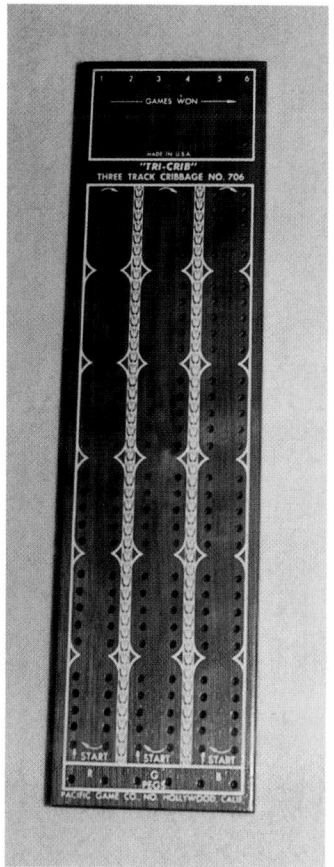

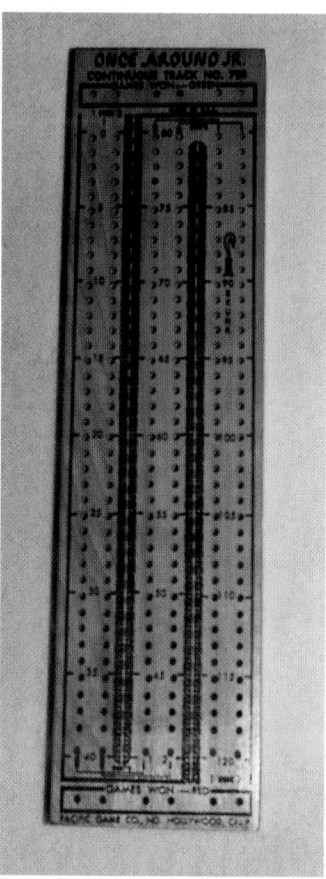

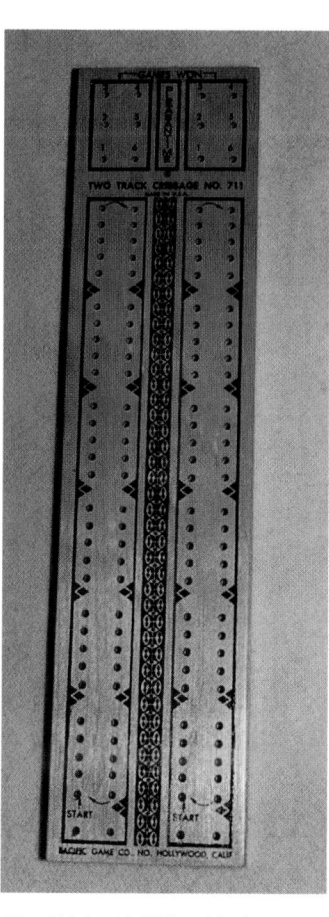

No. 706: *Tri-Crib Three Track Cribbage Board:* 11.25" x 3". $20

No. 708: 2P; *Once Around Jr.;* 11.75" x 3.12". $20

No. 711: 11.85" x 3". $15

No. 709: 2P, T.A.; inlay of light wood and diamond shaped inserts down center; 2 starter holes for each player. $15

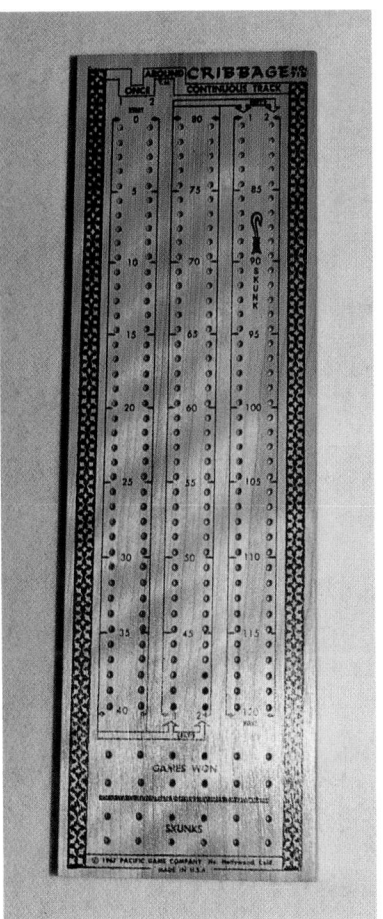

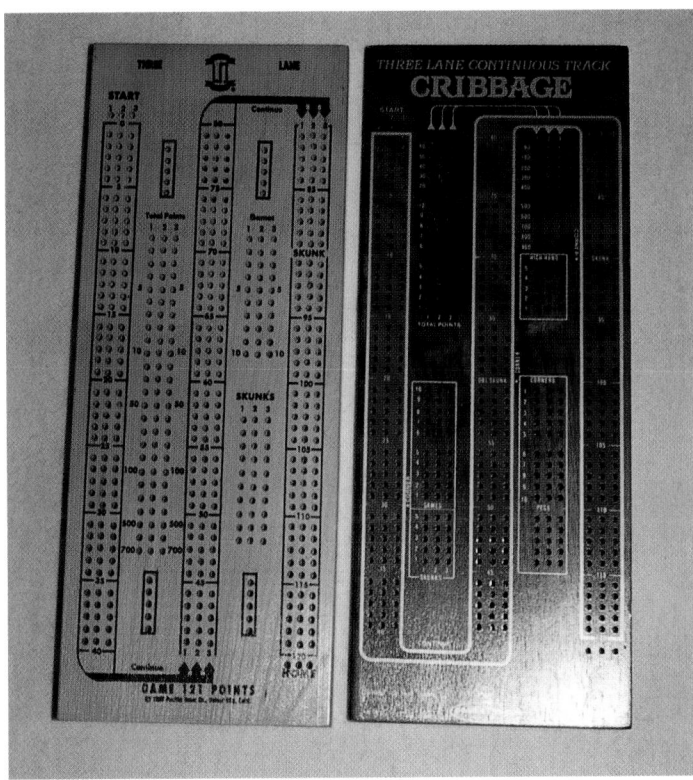

No. 715: Could be purchased with S & H Green Stamps; 13" x 4". $15

No. 720: 13" x 5.25". $20

No. 716: 2P, once-around "M" shaped track, one burgundy, all outlined in gold; 4 GW holes and 2 starter holes per player; 7" x 4". $30

No. 730: 4P, once-around wide walnut board; marked *Once Around Four Track Cribbage*, in addition to the typical decals; various scoring point holes in the center of the board. Two slot covers on underside for peg storage. 15.5" x 7.12". $20

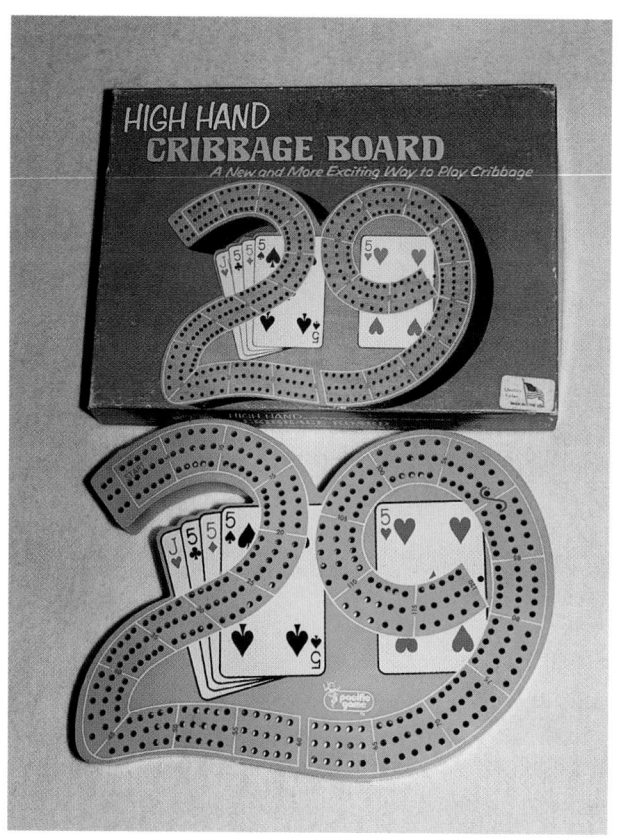

No. 750: Plastic, with compartment for card storage; 9.5" x 7". $20

No. 755: Plastic box, footed; hinged walnut board; storage for 2 decks of cards, poker chips and pegs; 15.6" x 5". $30

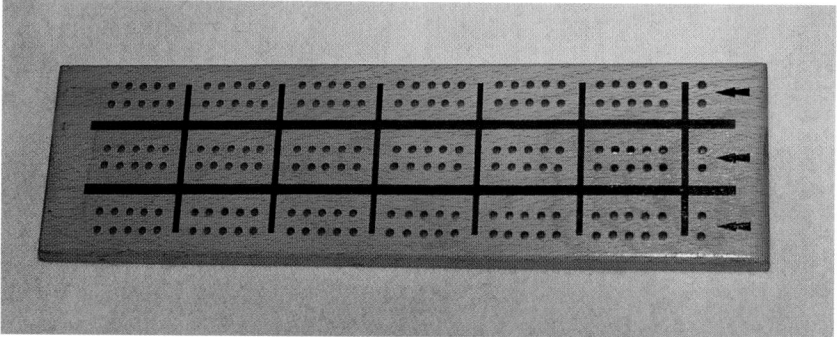

No. (UNK): 11" x 3". $20

Pattberg Novelty Corp: New York City, New York: 1859 - ?

Pattberg manufactured cribbage boards and adult games for "Jobbers," who sold them to retailers.

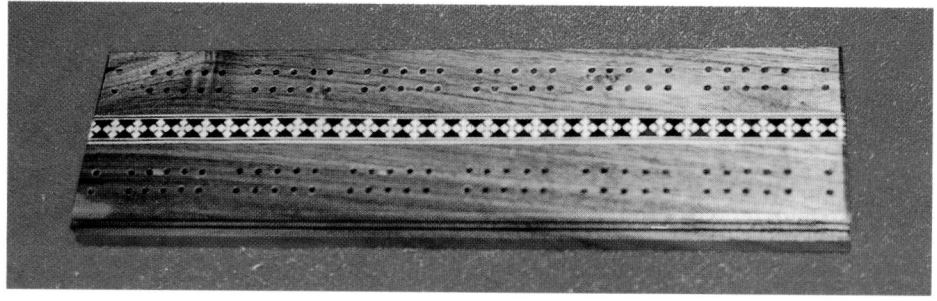

No. 56: 11.5" x 3". $15

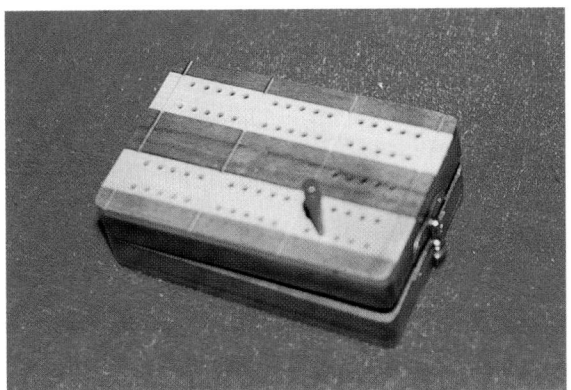

No. 628: 9.5" x 3". $20

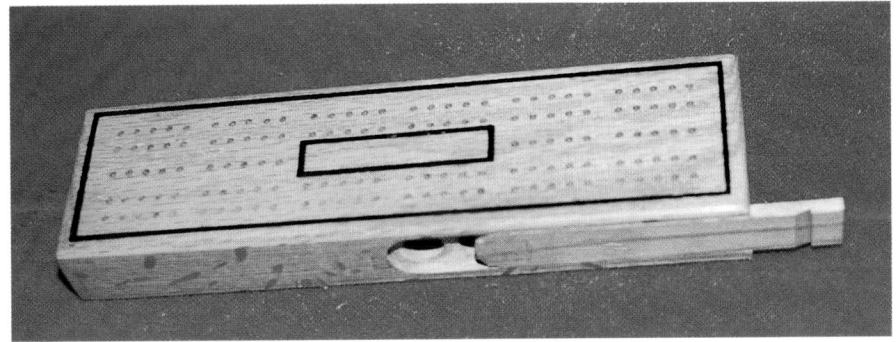

No. 694: Wooden box board with card holder on side; 10.5" x 2.75" x 1.35". $20

No. 757: 2P, T.A.; Brown celluloid board with gold line separating each set of double 5 holes; 4 white arrows show direction of play; 2 sets of 9 GW holes with *Game Tally* between; 10" x 2". $25

No. (Unk): 2P, T.A.; folding board in leather pouch; 2 GW holes, 2 starter holes each end center; 7" x 2" open. $30

Peg O' Matic, Inc.: Minneapolis, Minnesota: 1960s - c. 1975

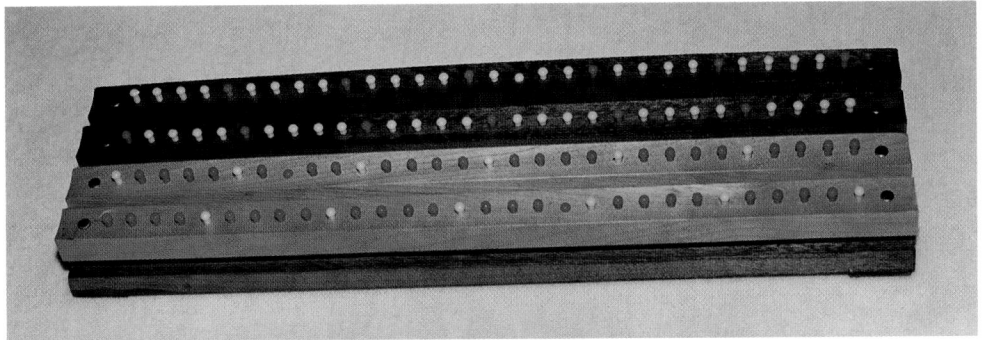

Wooden Hedgehog board with plastic pegs alternating in red for one player, yellow for other player, each 5th peg the opposite color; pegs push down, and rows are spring loaded to release them when game play ends; sold by W. T. Grant Co. around 1970 for $4.95; 14.5" x 4". $100

Pressman Toy Corp.: NYC, New York: 1947 - present

Pressman Toy Co. was founded by Jack Pressman in 1947, when he dissolved a long standing partnership in his previous business, J. Pressman & Co. The company's headquarters have been located on 5th Ave. for several decades.

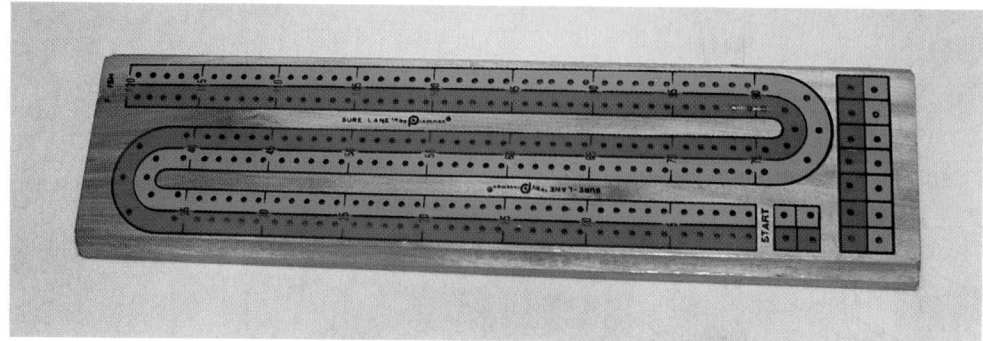

No. 1010: China; 13.5" x 3.5". CMP

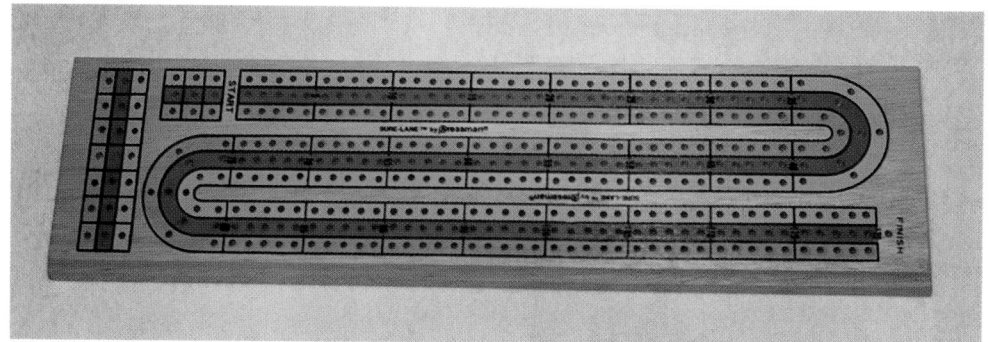

No. 1011: Taiwan; 14.25" x 3.75". CMP

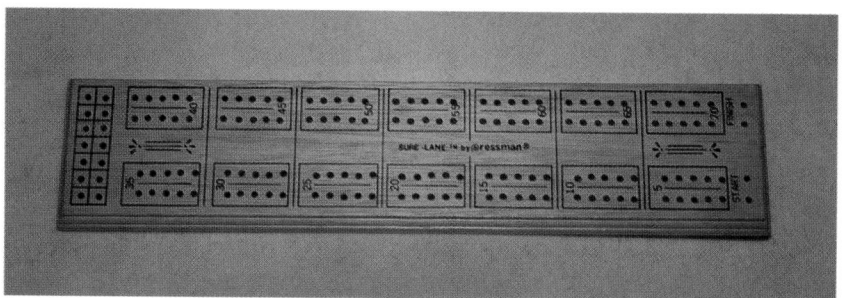

No. 1015: 7 blocks of double 5 pegging holes for a 141 point game! An **ERROR** board; Taiwan; 13" x 2.75". $25

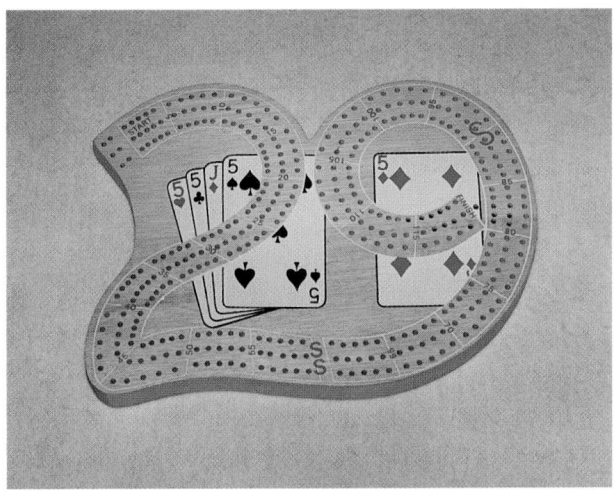

No. 1029: Taiwan; 9.5" x 7". CMP

No. 2211: *Surelane:* folding plastic; 3P, continuous "Z" tracks in green, red, blue; 7 GW holes each player at one end; 12.75" x 3.25" x .75" open. CMP

F.W. Quitman: South Norwalk, Connecticut

See C. W. Le Count.

Recreational Games: Northbrook, Illinois, Chicago, Illinois

Philadelphia Lawyer or Cracker Barrel Cribbage: An old Country Store Game Formerly Played on the Top of a Cracker Barrel: 3 sets of 16 pegging holes (total of 48), each set circling the board; pegs in 8 colors included; 16" circular. $75

Reiss Games, Inc.: New York City, New York, and Orange, California: 1970 - c. 1985

Subsidiary of National Paragon Co., *The Creative Recreation Co.*

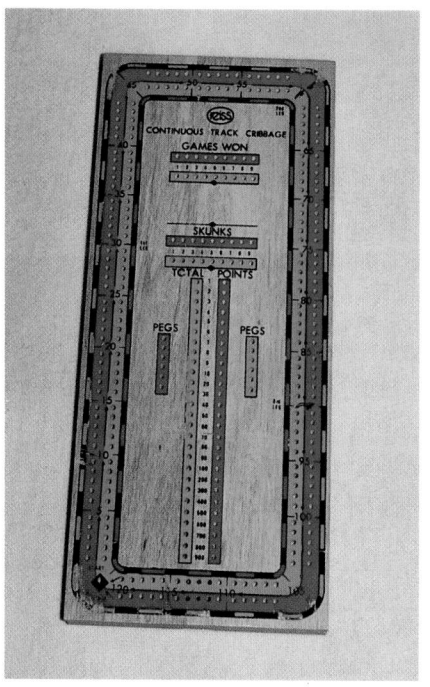

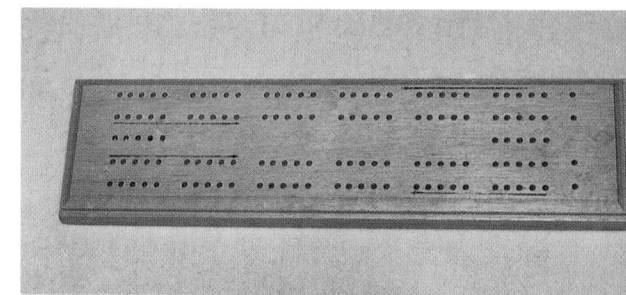

No. 237: *Traveling Cribbage Kit:* Taiwan; 11" x 3". $10

No. 235: Taiwan; © 1974;
14.25" x 6.25". $10

Ress:

2P, once around "S" shaped street; pine board with metal slider;
logo - *RESS* surrounded by oval on face; 13.5" x 3.5". $8

Rocky Mountain Cribbage Co.: Ft. Collins, Colorado: - present.

Boards are made of various hardwoods, some inlays.

Rogers-Smith Co.: Meriden, Connecticut

See Meriden Britannia Co. for history.

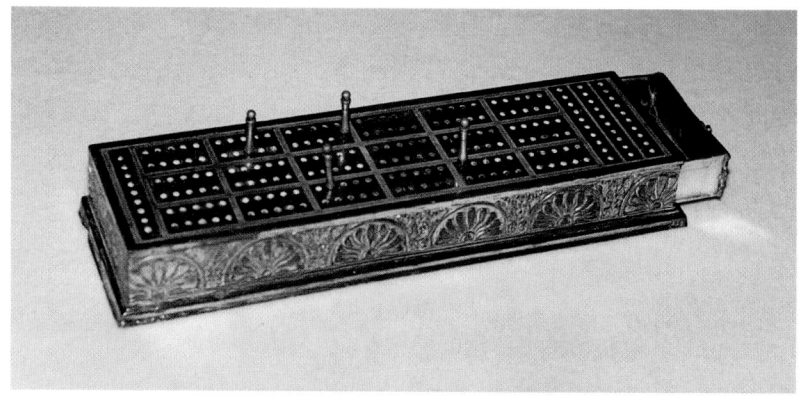

No. 15: Silver box with half circle "sun ray" scroll design along sides. Similar
board was manufactured. by Meriden Britannia Co.; 11" x 3.35" x 1.6". $300

Rottgames; New York City, New York

See H. Baron Co., Inc.

Scott:

See H. Baron Co., Inc.

Selchow & Righter Co.: New York City, New York: 1867 - present

Now owned by Hasbro.

2P, T.A.; red wooden board with 7 slim black stenciled lines crosswise, separating double 5 holes; step-down sides wooden peg slot cover; red box marked "*CRIBBAGE*"; 12" x 2.75 ". $12

R.C. Shipley Mfg. Co:

"*Roto-Score Cribbage Board*": 2P, once-around; 30 holes on either outside of the board; just inside is an oblong cube which has 5-10-15-20-25-30 down the length; push a button on either side of the board and the cube flips to 31; push the button again and the cube flips to 61-90, etc.; 5 GW holes at each end; "Pat. app. For" Similar in design to the "Saves Argument" board; 10.5" x 3" x 1.5". $60

Silver Fox Products: Poquonock, Connecticut: 1980s

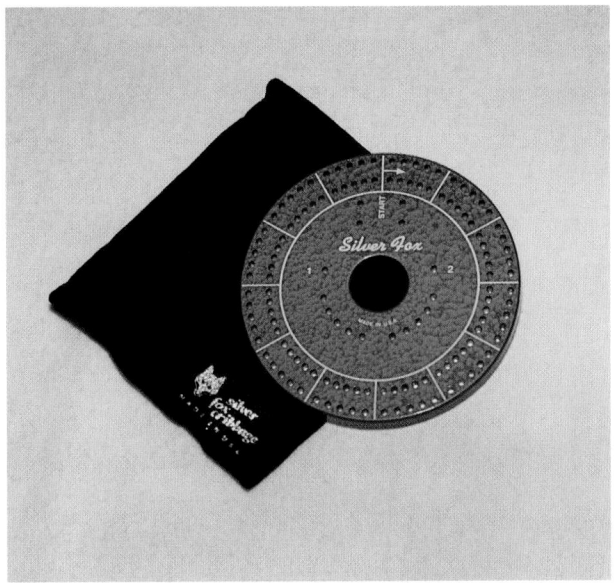

Blue metal; velvet carrying pouch; 5" diameter. $50

Skor-Mor Products, Inc.: 1970s - 1980s
Subsidiary of Nypro Co., Clinton, Massachusetts.

Logo was a target with arrow through it - *SKOR-MOR Corp.* at end. All of their boards were identified with the logo.

2P, T.A.; gold checkered center broken by 5 GW holes and 2 starter holes each end center; Gold logo; 7.5" long. $10

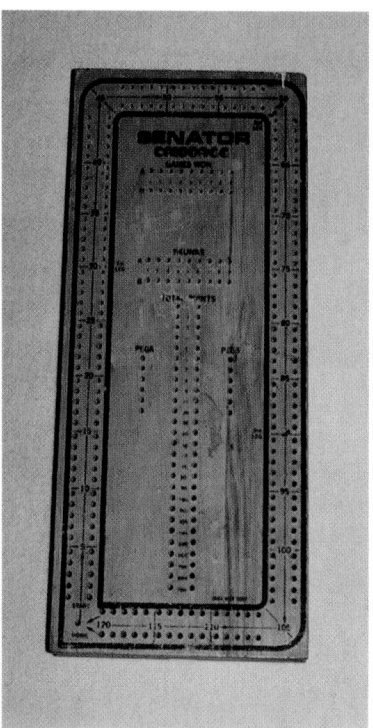

Senator: 14.5" x 6.5". $20

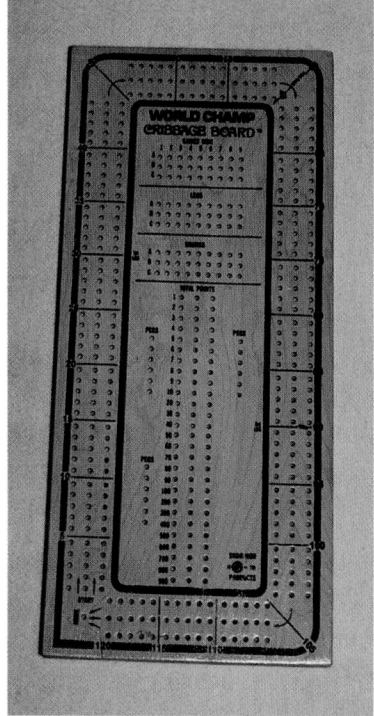

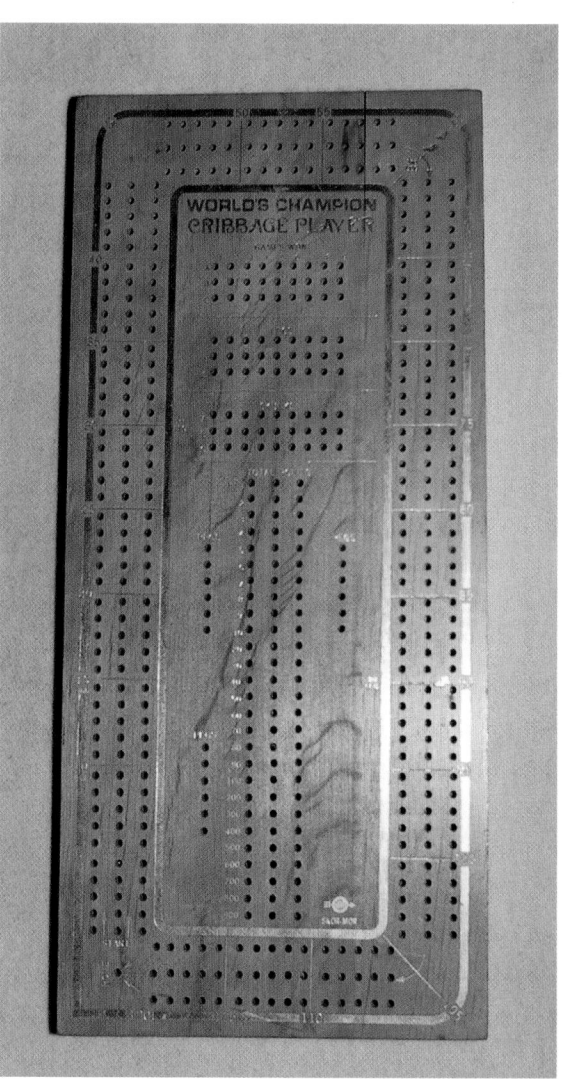

Above: World's Champion Cribbage Player: 14.5" x 6.5". $20

Left: World Champ Cribbage Board: 14.5" x 6.5". $20

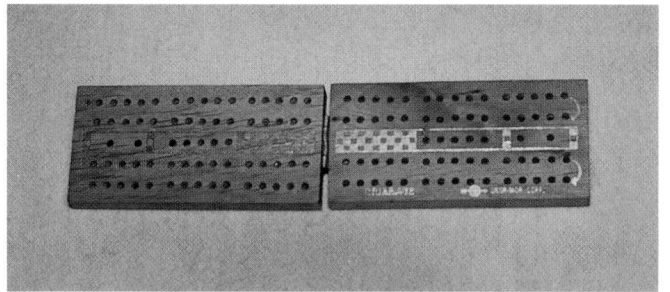

Cribbage: folding; identical to Are-Jay No. 021; 9" x 2" open. $15

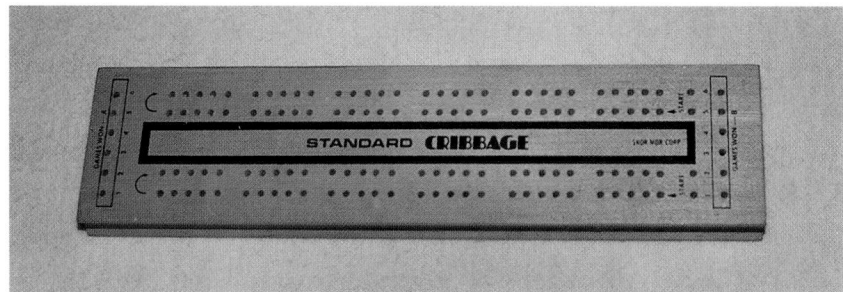

Standard Cribbage: 12" x 3". $20

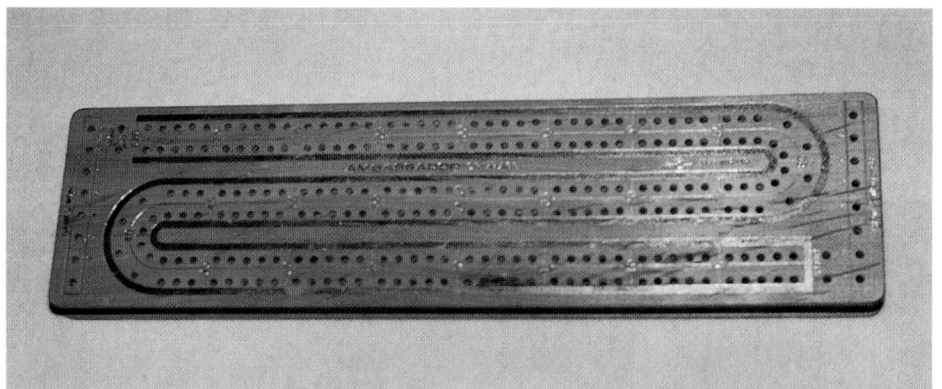

Ambassador Cribbage: 13.25" x 3.25". $15

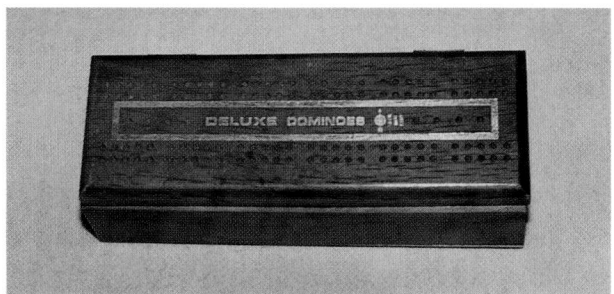

Deluxe Dominoes: box includes set of dominoes; 8" x 3" x 2.5". $20

Specialty Co.: Cortland, New York: 1900 - 1925

The Cortland Specialty Co. was founded around 1900, and it was a major source of welding and brazing compounds, as well as other types of compounds and oil products. In 1925, the entire operation, which included plants in 7 locations, was sold to Deyo Oil Company of Binghamton.

Although the history of Specialty's manufacture of cribbage boards is not recorded, the company produced 2 hedgehog boards which were identical in style, including the nickel-plated brass pull-up pegs. One board, however, also had decorative silver metal corners and a scrolled design in the center.

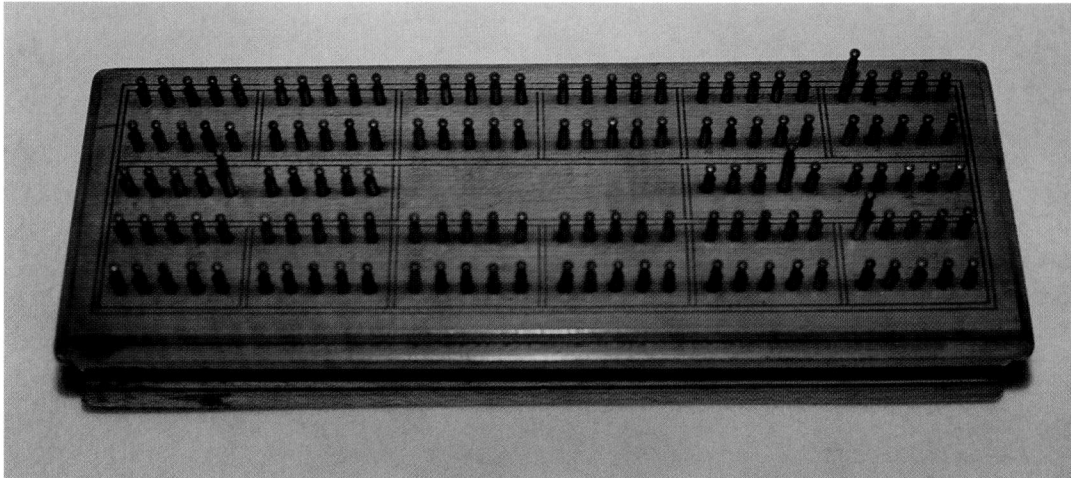

Maple; 11" x 4" x 1.5". $195

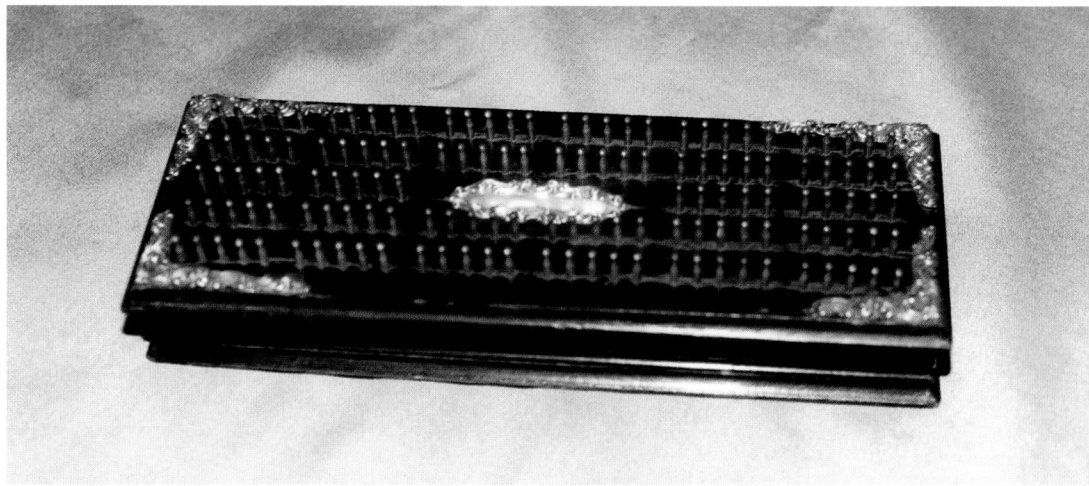

Decorated silver corners and scroll in center; 11" x 4" x 1.5". $250

Sport Boards, Inc.: Blaine, Minnesota: 1980s - 1990s

Bill Thielen, the president of Sport Boards, originally tried to make cribbage boards from bowling pins, designed after one that had been given to him. He soon found, however, that bowling pins were an expensive base product, for they did not always split right down the middle!

Ultimately, he designed, patented (Patent #D302135; 07/11/89), and manufactured the injected plastic bowling pin board — it became a smashing success. The metal pegs are shaped like bowling pins.

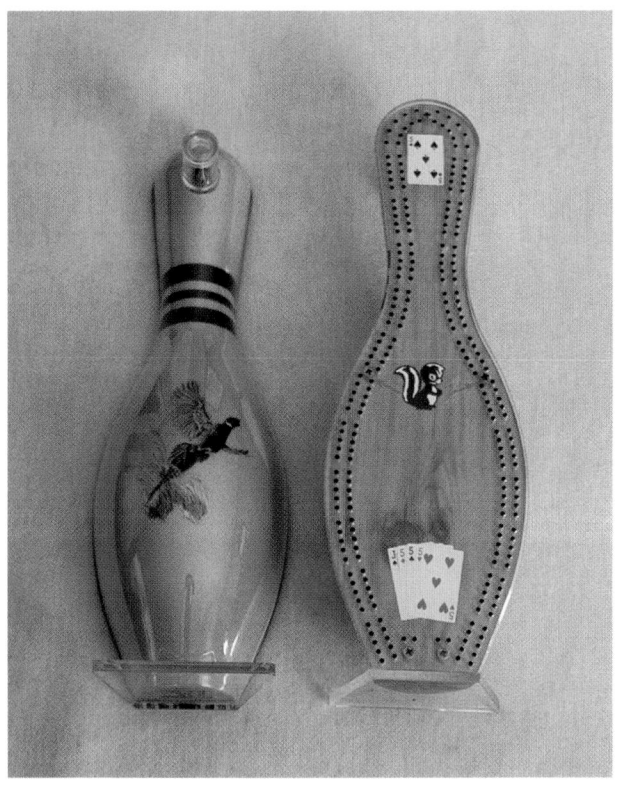

Plastic with various decals of wildlife, sports, logos; blue, tan, or white; 15.5" x 5" x 2.5". $40

Stancraft Products: St. Paul and Minneapolis, Minnesota

See Standard Packaging Co.

Standard Packaging Co.: St. Paul and Minneapolis, Minnesota: 1919 - Present

Hoyle, Kent, and Stancraft boards are all grouped under one heading in order to facilitate the identification process, as their board model numbers are in sequence. These companies have belonged to one large corporation that has merged, split, or faded out some of the subsidiaries down through the years. Brown and Bigelow was founded in 1896, and Standard Packaging Corp. was founded in 1919. The two companies merged in 1960. In 1961, Hoyle Products became a subsidiary of Brown and Bigelow. *Stancraft* and *Kent* were Brand names of Hoyle Products.

Standard Packaging and its subsidiaries identified many of their boards with removable labels, but most Hoyle boards have their name on the face.

The newer Stancraft boards had narrow slot covers, and the Kent boards had wide ones. Older Stancraft slot covers feature a flange, which is rarely seen on other boards.

No. 5002: Stancraft (Kent): 2P, T.A.; *Standard* stenciled in red; 11" x 3". $15

No. 5011: Hoyle: 2P, T.A.; 2 starter holes, 5 center holes each player; identical to Kent No. 5051; 11.75" x 3.6". $10

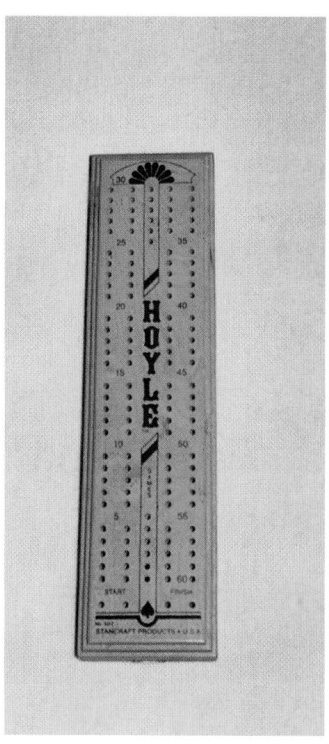

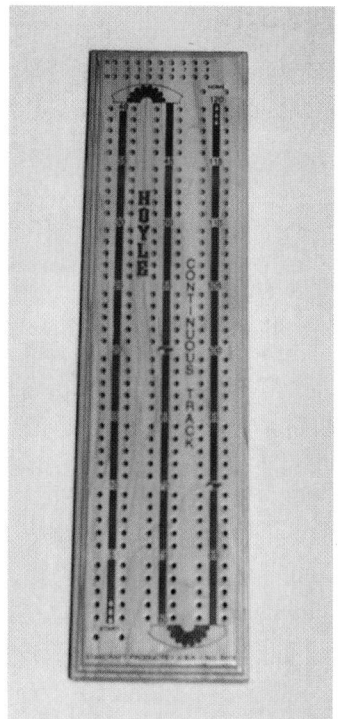

No. 5012: Stancraft (Hoyle): this board was also used as an advertising board for *Champion Spark Plugs*; 11" x 2.85". $20 - $35

No. 5013: Hoyle: 13.25" x 3.5". $10

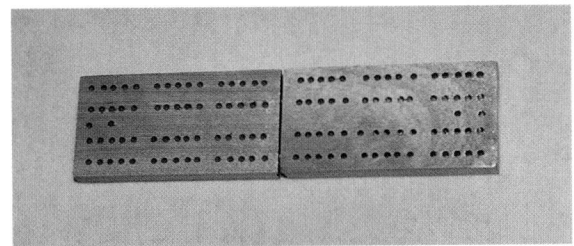

No. 5015: Hoyle: 7.25" x 2". CMP

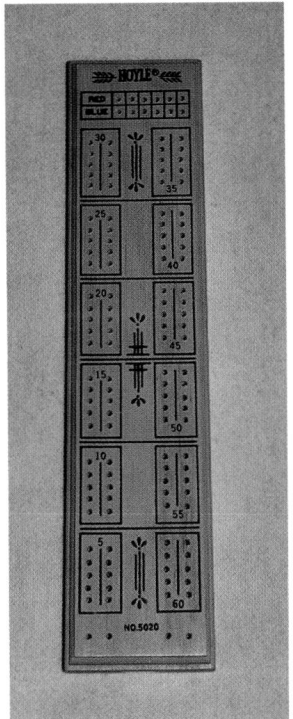

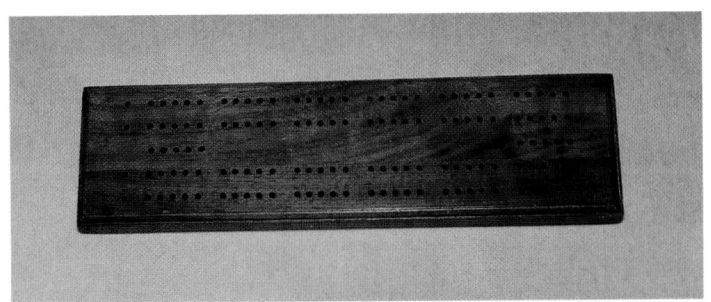

No. 5021: Stancraft (Kent): 11" x 3". $15

No. 5020: Hoyle: 1.75" x .75". CMP

No. 5022: Hoyle: 2P, continuous color tracks; 7 GW holes ea.
player; 13.5" x 3.5". CMP

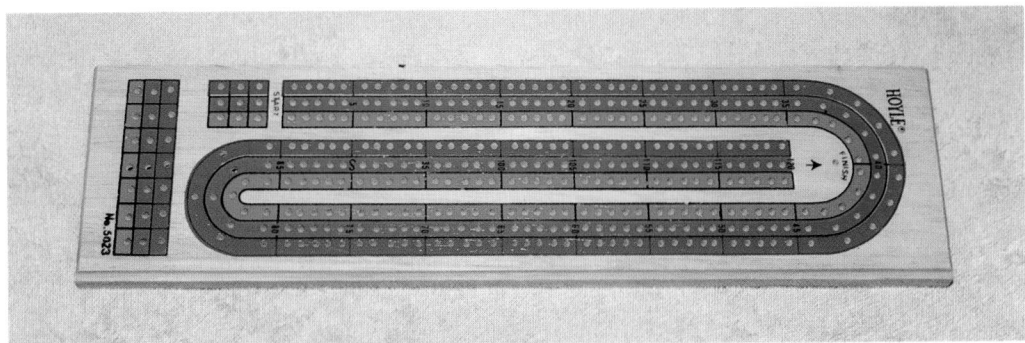

No. 5023: Hoyle: 15" x 4". CMP

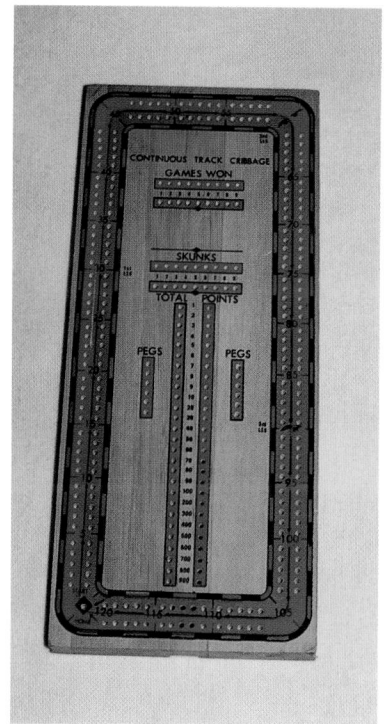

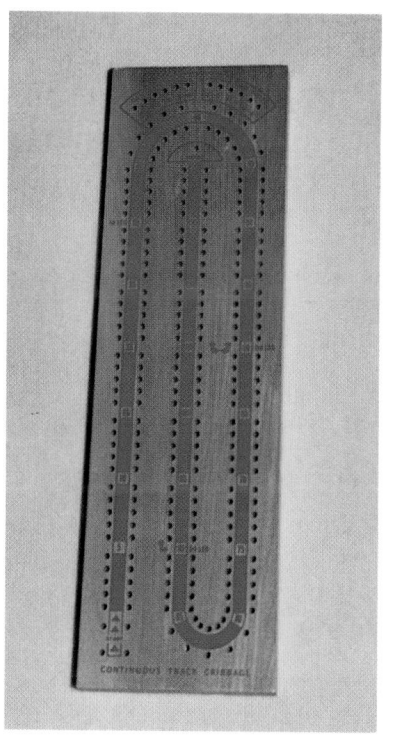

No. 5024: Hoyle: 14.5" x 6.5". CMP

No. 5053: Kent: identical to Crestline No. 114; 13.25" x 4". $20

No. 5025: Hoyle: 3P, "29" board; 5 of Diamonds; 9.5" x 7.25". CMP

No. 5051: Kent: identical to Hoyle No. 5011; 11.75" x 3.5". $10

No. 5062: Hoyle: 2P, T.A.; center inlays; 5 center GW holes ea. player; 11.75" x 3.6". $15

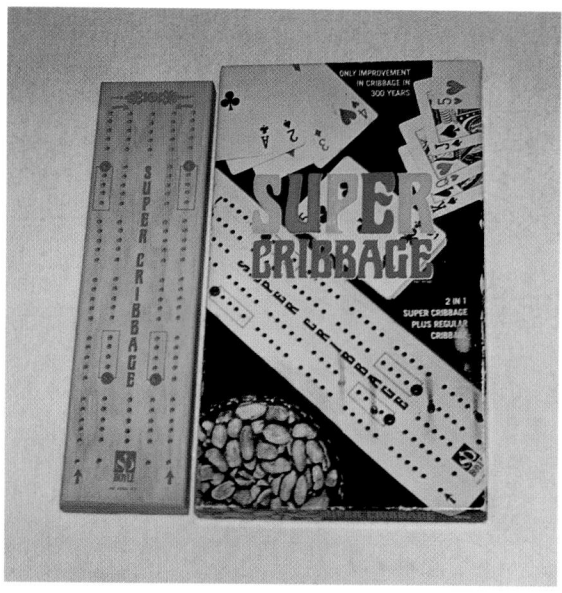

No. 5070: Hoyle: *Super Cribbage* (1972); game variation; 11" x 3". $25

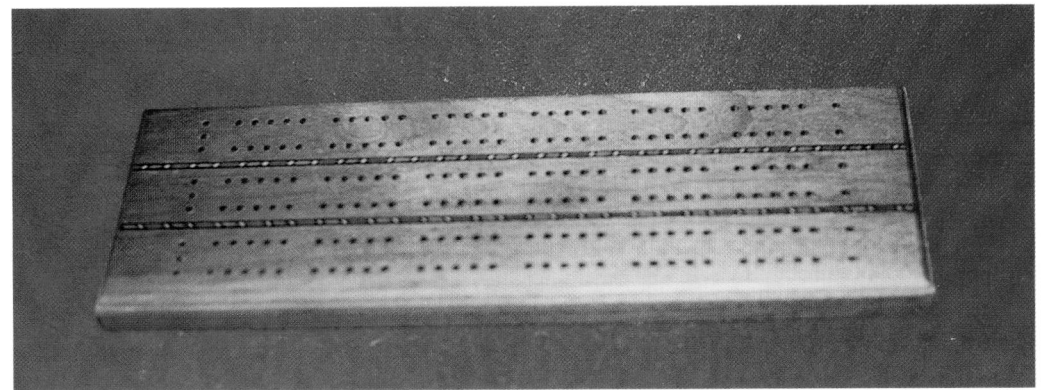

No. 5073: Kent: center inlays; 11.5" x 3.75". $15

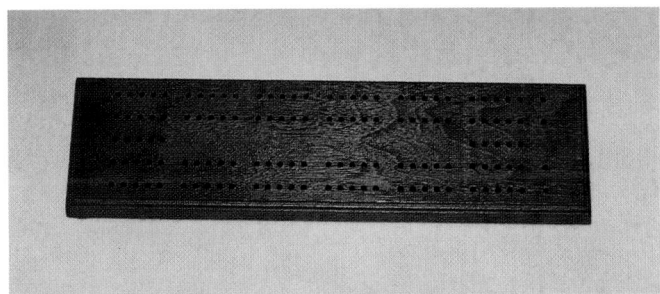

No. 5080: Hoyle: plastic; 11" x 3". $10

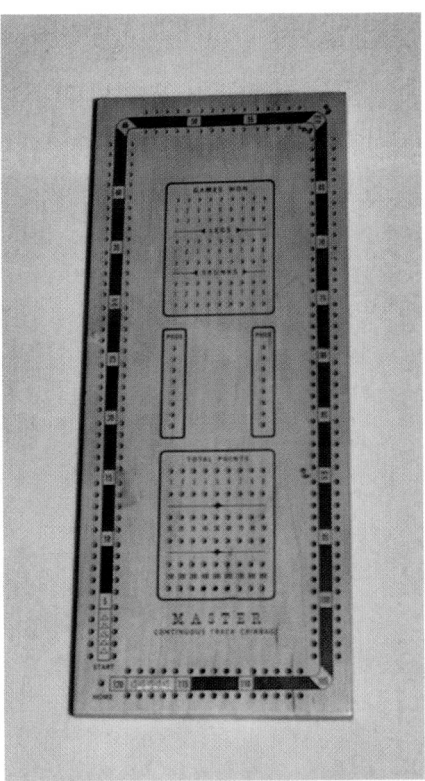

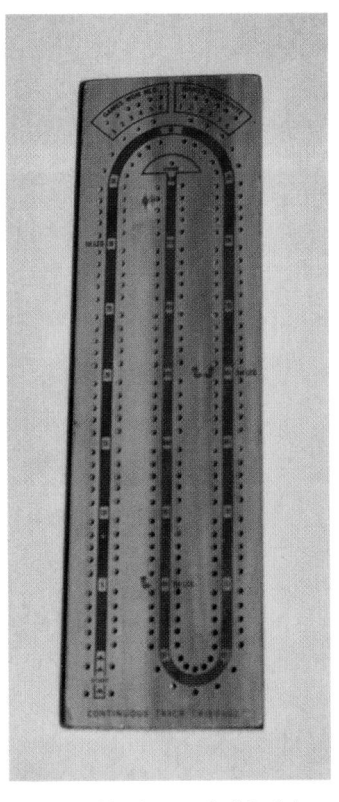

No. (Unk): Stancraft (Hoyle): stenciled; 14" x 5.75". $25

No. (Unk): Stancraft (Hoyle): 13" x 4". $15

No. (Unk): Kent: identical to above Hoyle, but has wide slot cover; 13.12" x 3.85". $15

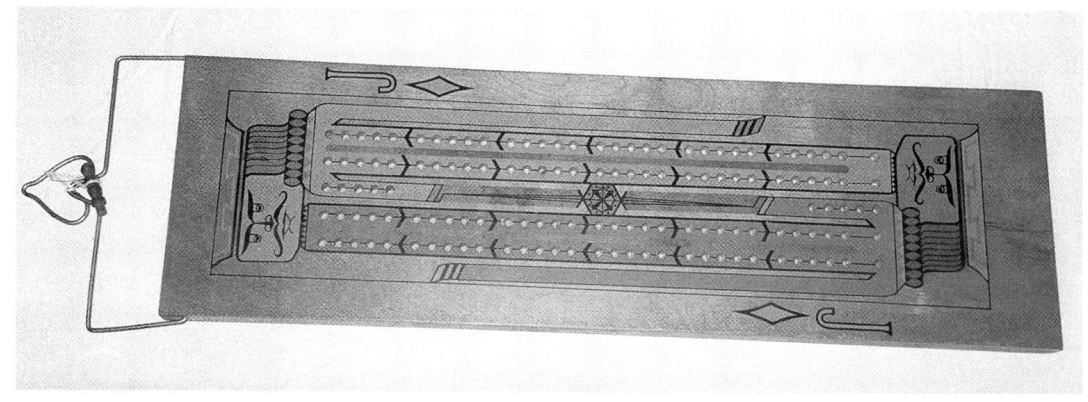

No. (Unk): Stancraft: green & red *Jack of Diamonds* figure on entire face; 24" x 7.25". $50

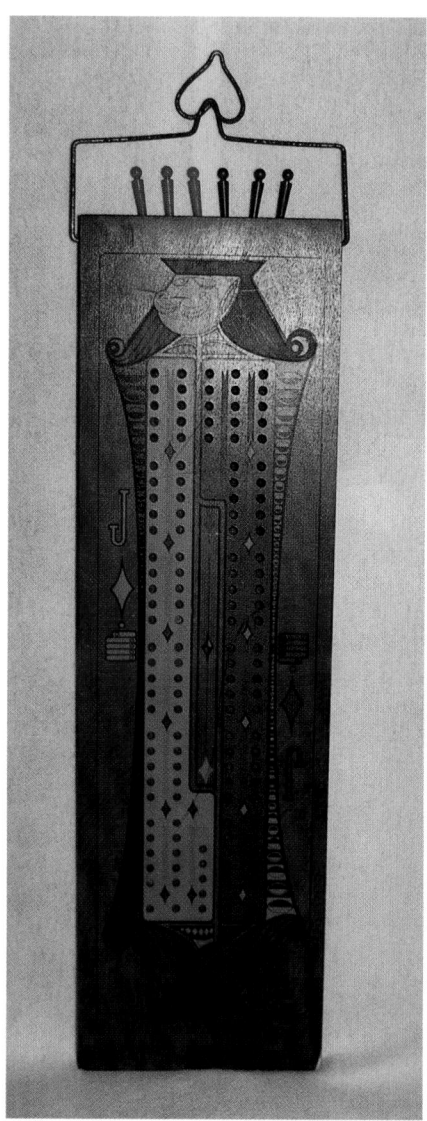

No. (UNK): Same as above,
but different faces. $50

W. C. Stevens, Jr.: Canoga Park, California: 1980s

Stevens designed and manufactured the first paper cribbage board called the *Official Cribbage Tournament Scorepad.* © 1983.

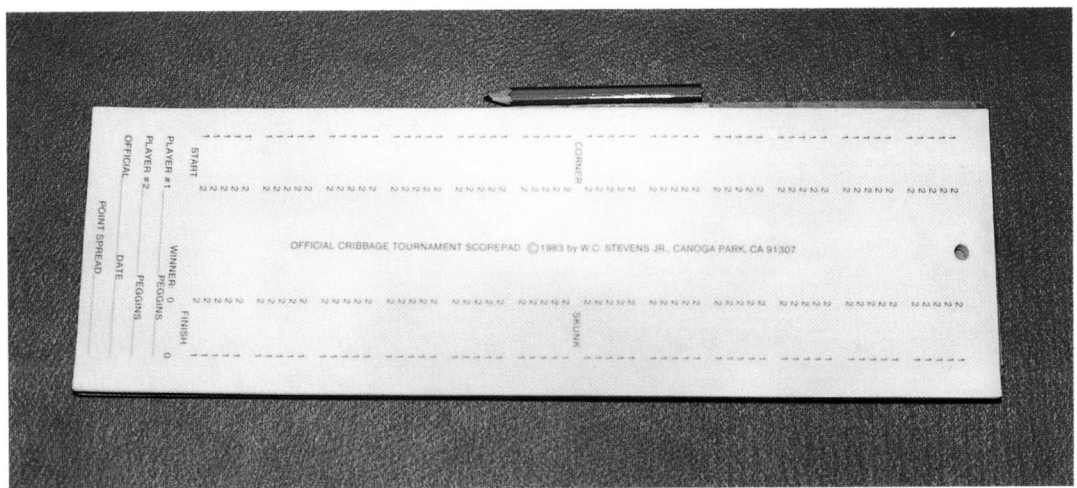

Paper board: 50 sheets to pad; 14" x 4.5". $20

Terkelsen Machine Co.: Boston, Massachusetts

The Molded Products Division manufactured a Bakelite cribbage board, (Patent No. 2017479 issued in 1935).

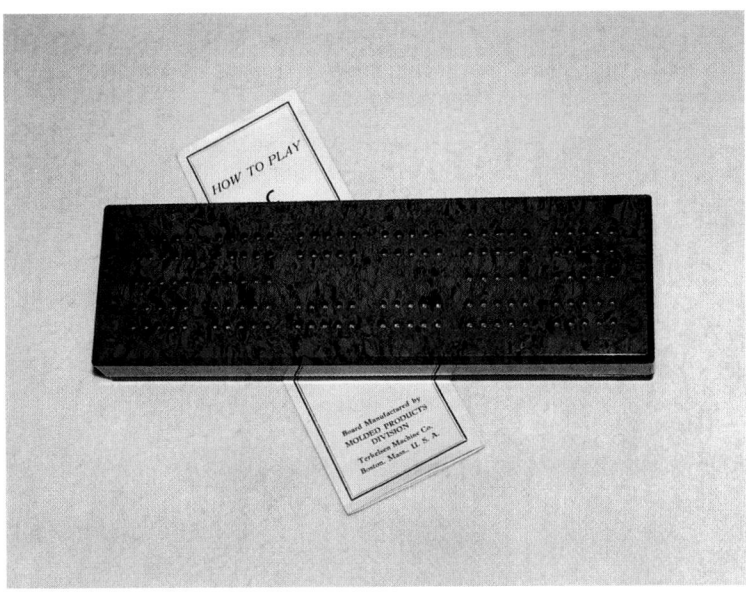

Bakelite:green lift-off cover, black base; 10.25" x 3". $30

Thermometer Corp. of America: Springfield, Ohio

No. 7704: *Traveler's Pal Game Box:* plastic box with hinged board; Poker chips, dice, pegs and cards store inside; identical sets have been found with various companies' names; 7.5" x 2.5" x 1.5". $24

T.N.M. Machine: Maplegrove, Minnesota

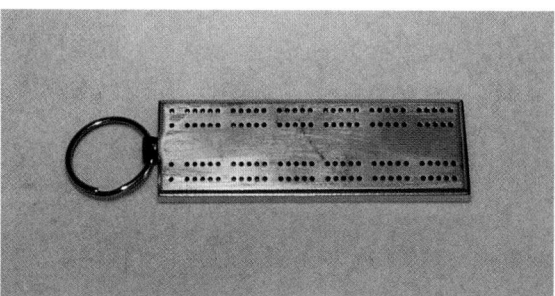

KRIBSKEY By T.N.M. Machine: metal key ring; smallest known manufactured playable board; 3.75" x 1.25". $15

Tower Manufacturing & Novelty Co.: c. 1900 - 1920

Tower manufactured several styles of boards exclusively for the Sears, Roebuck and Co. catalog. They also imported many cribbage boards, including a spring-loaded "Hedgehog" model. Some boxes are marked *Northern Cribbage Board Co. Cable WI.*

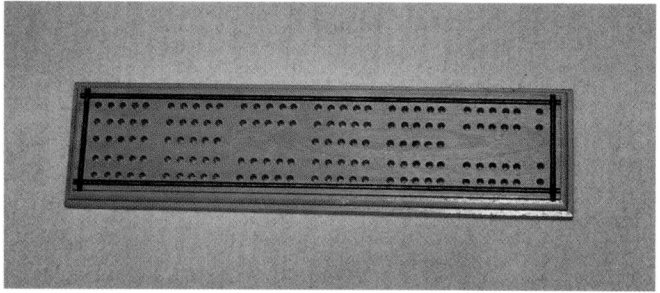

No. 35: Inlays; 11" x 2.75". $25

No. 3562: 2P, T.A.; 10 GW holes each end center; 2 starter holes; black and yellow inlays near edge criss-cross at corners; 11.5" x 3.12". $25

Towle Manufacturing Co.: Newburyport, Massachusetts; 1880 - 1980s.

Towle was a world famous manufacturer of silver products, one of which was a silver-plated cribbage board.

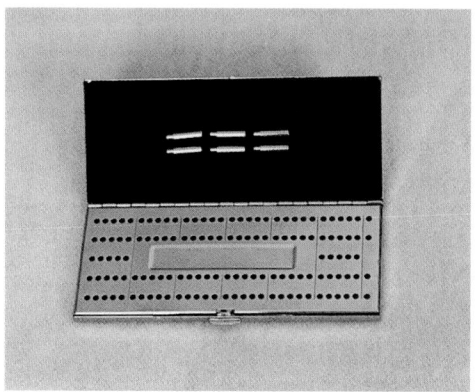

Hinged top, board inside; 5.25" x 2". $35

Trojan Games Co.: Minneapolis 15, Minnesota: 1930 - c. 1950

Their cribbage boards had long, thin brass (or wooden) slot covers. Most boxes had a light brown wood grain design with a cribbage board outlined across the entire face. The company logo was a Trojan Horse.

No. 150: 2P,T.A.; 1 groove down center; step-down sides; wooden slot cover; 10.5" x 2" x 1.5". $20

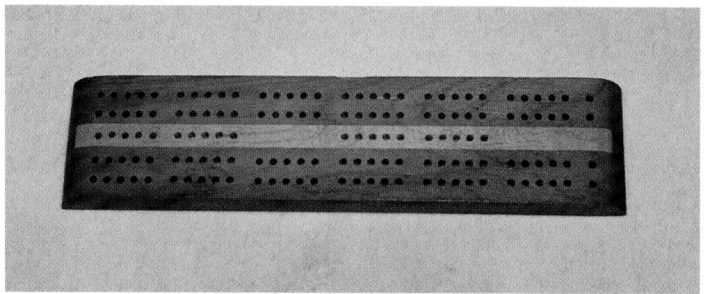

No. 152: Inlaid; 11.12" x 2.6". $20

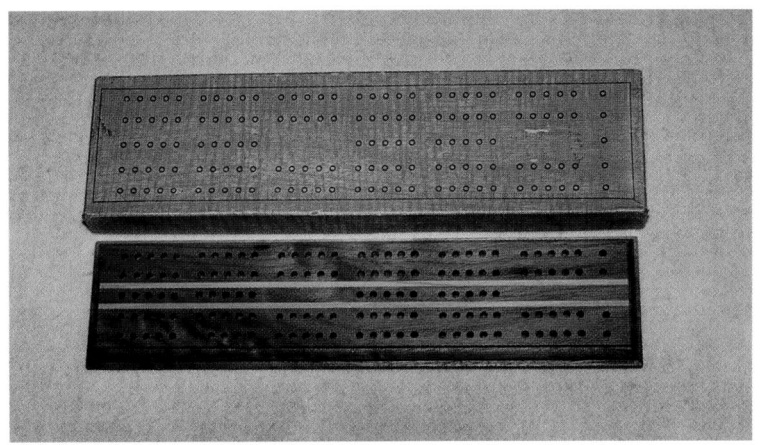

No. 154: Inlaid; 11.25" x 2.75". $20

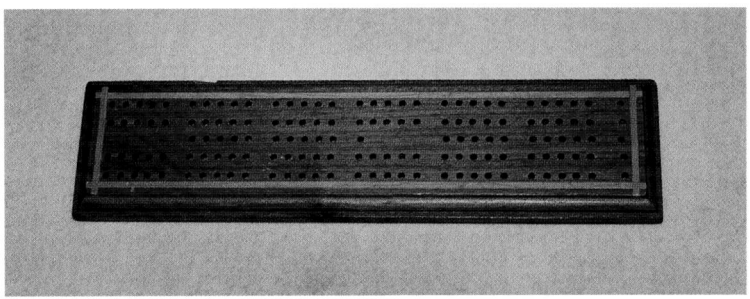

No. 156: Inlaid near edges; 11.5" x 2.75". $20

University Games:

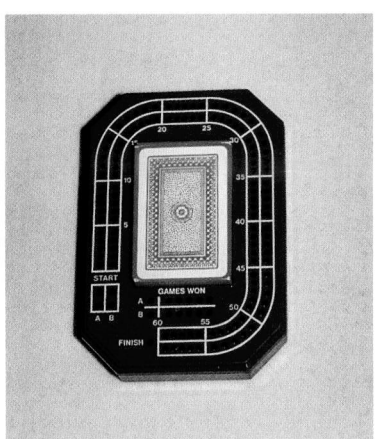

No. UG5080: 5.5" x 3.75". $10

U. S. Playing Card Co.: Cincinnati, Ohio: 1894 - present

No. (Unk): 2P, T.A.; double 5 holes surrounded by rectangular block with numbers times 5 in each block; stenciled design at one end; 6 GW holes and 2 starter holes each player; Taiwan; 14" x 3.5". CMP

BICYCLE: 3P; folding plastic, holds cards; Brooks style red, white & blue tracks; 2 starter holes each player, 1 finish hole; Taiwan; 11.75" x 3". $10

Vandercraft: Prineville, Oregon: 1979 - present

Vandercraft was founded by Joe Nelson, an avid cribbage player. Besides cribbage boards, the company has also manufactured wooden post cards. During the Gulf War, Vandercraft manufactured over 1000 cribbage boards for the American Cribbage Congress, which were distributed to the troops involved in Desert Storm.

Although Nelson died in 1996, the company is still in operation.

Hand-crafted duck decoy, various species; board pictured is a prototype; 16.5" x 7". $150

Various pictures of wildlife, figures, nautical scenes, in center; peg storage pod on side of board; 17" x 7". CMP

No. (Unk): *Desert Storm Cribbage Board.* $20

Westcraft: Berwick, Maine

The "4 in 1" cribbage board (Pat. No. 2,432,167, issued 12/09/47) received by Charles J. Manuel. A similar model manufactured at a later time was referred to as the *Liberty Board.*, and it was marketed by Marketing Services of Maine. The *Liberty Board* is shown.

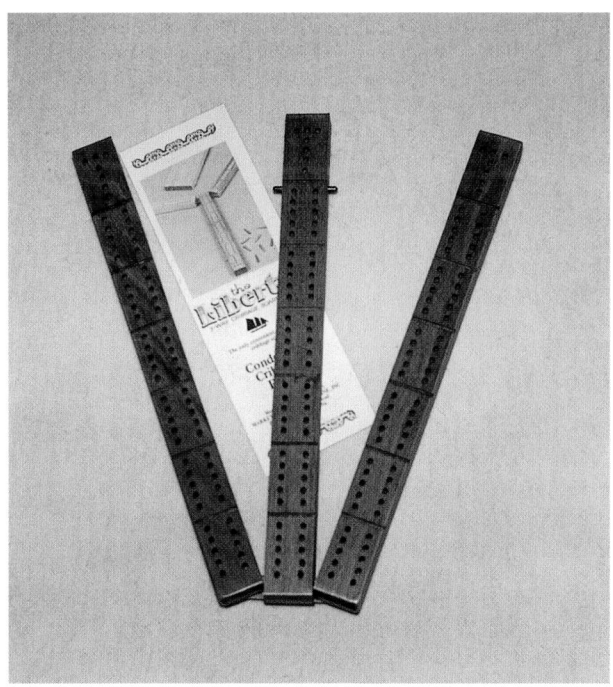

Secret hinge: when closed, the board takes on the appearance of a solid cribbage board; 11" x 3". $30

Whitman Publishing Co.: 1916 - present
Subsidiary of Western Publishing Co., Racine, Wisconsin (sold to Hasbro in 1994).

Distributed cribbage boards. Peg covers were usually marked *Whitman*.

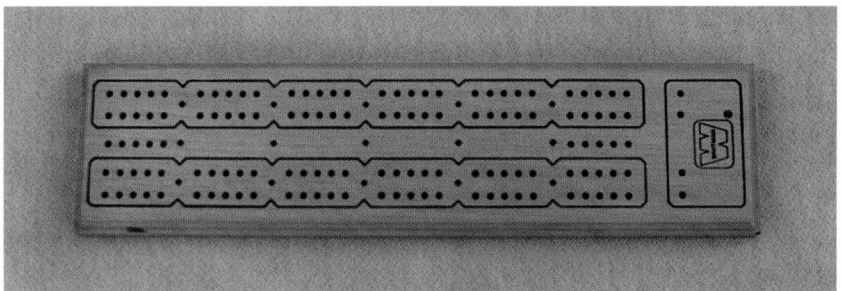

No. 4230: 11" x 2.75". $5

No. 4879: 2P, T.A.; 10 GW holes each end center, 2 starter holes each player; double grooved sides; Japan; 11" x 2.75". $5

130

Windsor Manufacturing Co.: Windsor, Wisconsin: 1945 - 1948

The business was established in 1945 by three men, Charles Doan, Ray Walker, and Earl Lindley. The men met while they were serving in the armed forces during WWII, and they formed the business after the war ended. The business closed in 1948, after 3 years of operation. The factory, a Quonset hut, is now used as a private residence.

Among the products that were manufactured by Windsor were a *Foolproof* Hedgehog-style cribbage board, a Smear and Euchre combination board, a folding cribbage board, and a bow kite.

1) 2P, T.A.; *Hedgehog;* walnut top with maple bottom; total of 122 pegs with sets of 5 pegs alternating from brown to blue; no spring load, no pegs in center; 13.5" x 2.75" x 1". $150

2) 2P, T. A.; *Hedgehog;* basically same as No. 1, but pegs alternate in sets of 5 red, green, brown, gray, and cream color; 13.25" x 2.75 "X 1". $150

3) 3P, T.A.; folding board; deck of playing cards and metal pegs stored inside; 8.5" x 3" open. $50

MANUFACTURED: MANUFACTURER UNKNOWN

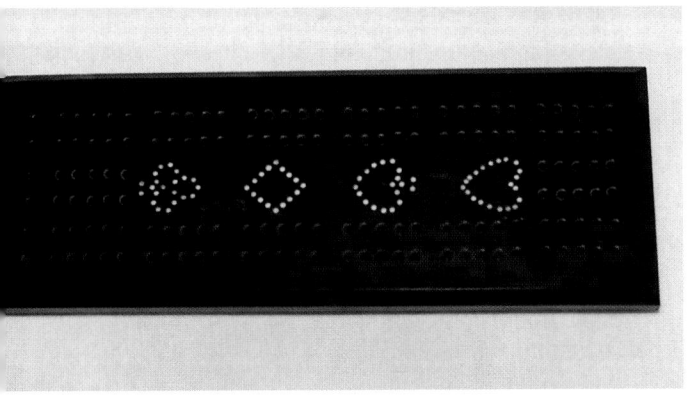

Bakelite: There are many Bakelite boards in existence whose manufacturers remain unidentified. Many are black and feature beveled top edges, grommets in all the pegging holes, or have white imprinted designs on the face. 11" x 4". $25

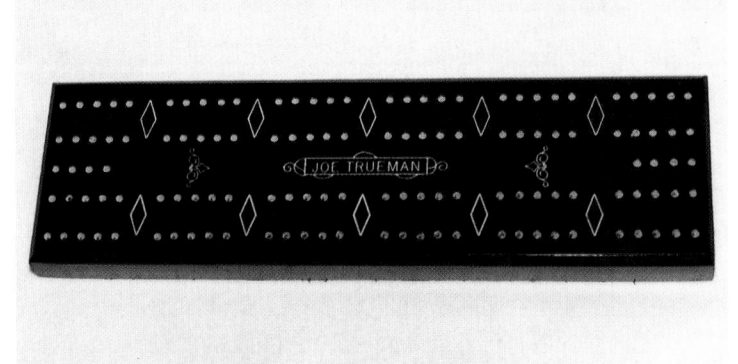

Black Plastic: The black plastic boards bear features similar to the Black Bakelite boards, and only close examination can determine which product has been used. 12" x 3.5". $25

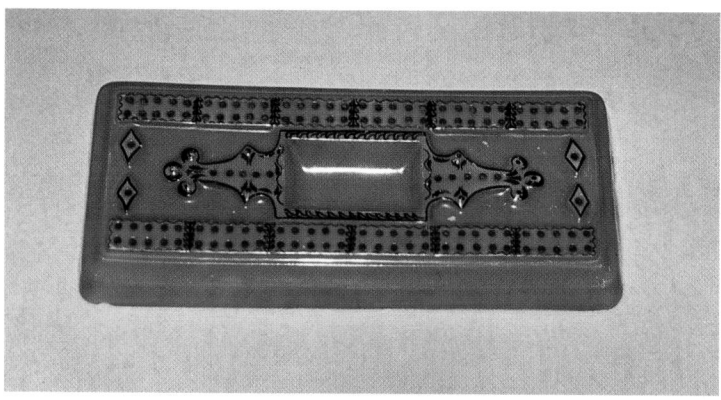

Ceramic: This board bears a striking resemblance to pottery originating from the Ohio industries. It was manufactured in orange or yellow and has a hollowed out area for peg storage in center of board. 10" x 4.5" x 1". $150

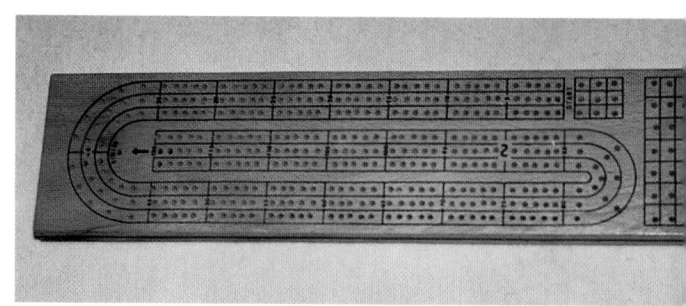

Companion Board; No. B30: Japan; 14" x 3.5". $15

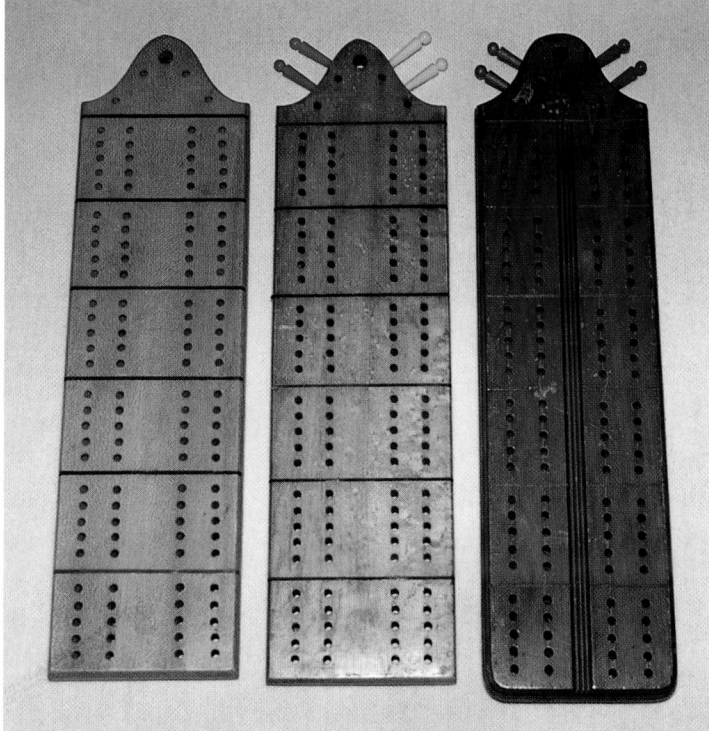

City Club Board: All holes go straight through the boards and use 2" pegs. One end is curved and includes 2 starter holes each player as well as a hole to hang the board. The 3 progressive models are shown, all having identical features unless other wise noted. Probably manufactured in the 1920s or 1930s. 16.5" x 4.5". $20 - $35

Center Diamond Design: 10" x 2.75". $5

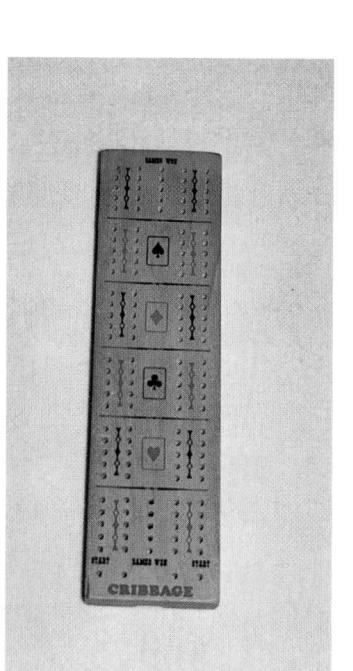

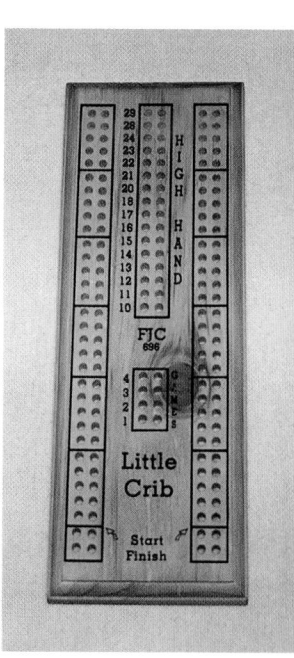

Cribbage: Stenciled with symbols of four suits in center; 10" x 2.75". $10

FJC: 696: *Little Crib;* 12" x 4". $15

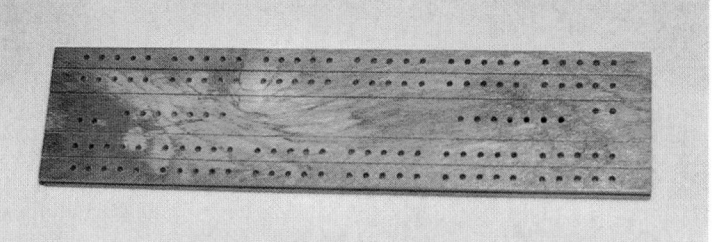

Companion Board: No. B28: Identical to Baron 28/250; Japan. 13.5" x 3.25". $15

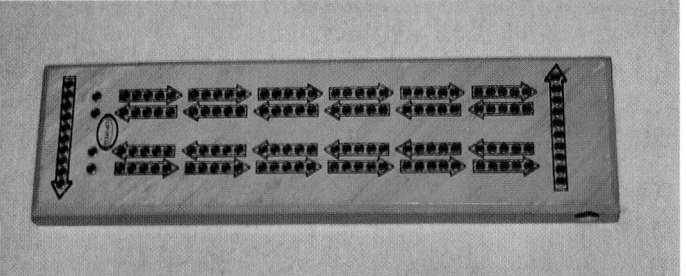

Flip-Pegs: Metal grommets in all holes: 12.25" x 3.5". $8

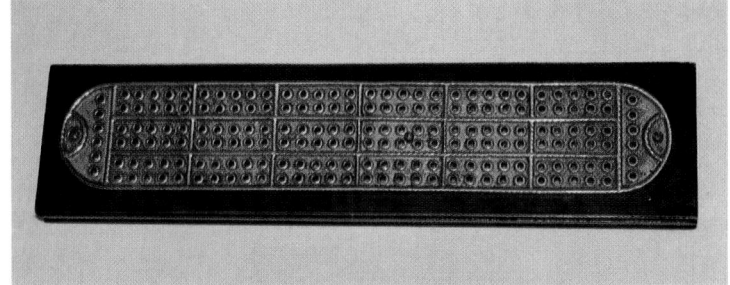

Metal Top/ Wood Base: This board probably was manufactured in the early 1900s, at the time when Le Count boards were quite popular. The outer edge of the metal top is scrolled and its edge is flush with the wooden base. 9.5" x 2.75". $40

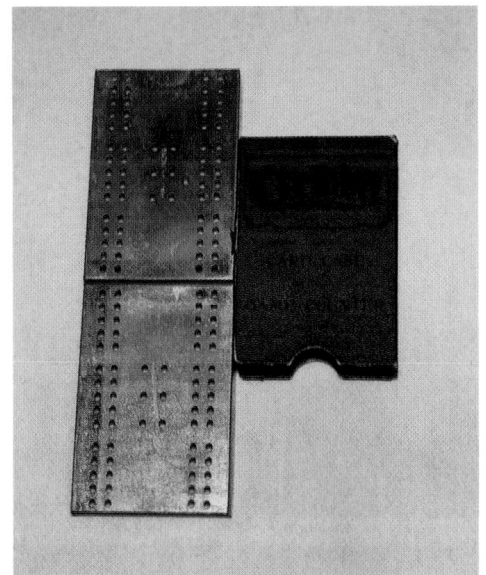

Gribbitt: A Combined Card Case and Universal Game Counter: hollow nickel metal case, which holds a deck of cards when folded. End of board is open when folded and stores in a dark green cardboard case; stamped *Pat. Pend'g*; 8" x 2.5" x .75" open. $25

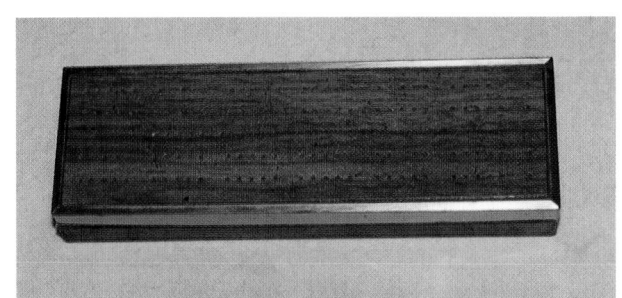

1984 Olympic Games Box: The box is simulated leather with metal edges. The hinged lid, which is the board, opens to reveal the Olympic symbol on its underside. Two decks of Olympics playing cards are stored inside. 9.5" x 3" x 1.5". $30

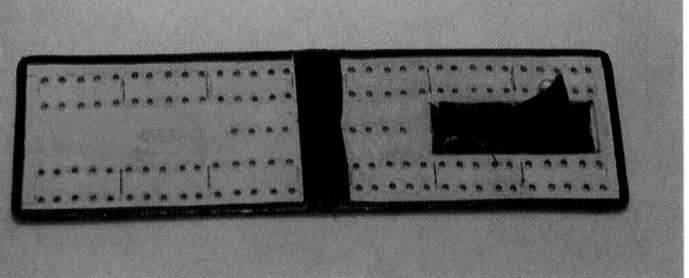

Leather Folding, with "pull out" peg pouch: There is much evidence that this board was carried by servicemen during World War I, and many of the boards are still in existence. They came in either red or green outer case with beige playing field. The "pull-out" pouch lies flat when the board is closed, and the board stores in a flat leather case. 7.12" x 2.12" open. $30

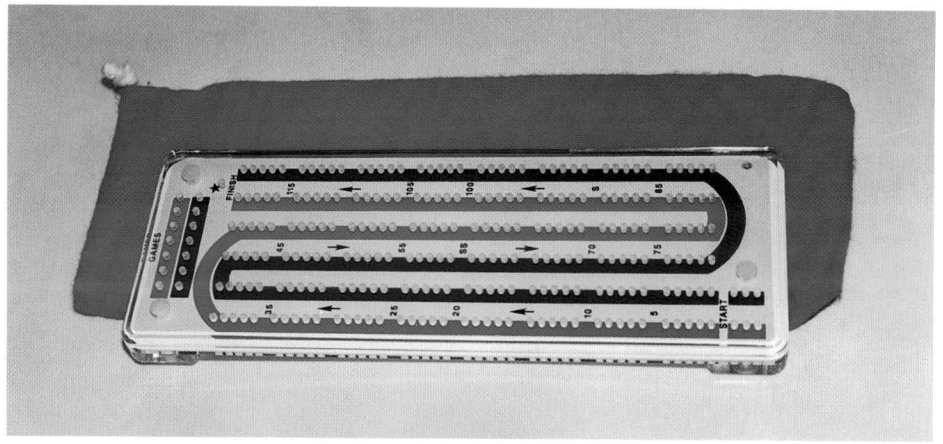

Patriotic: Clear acrylic; 13.5" x 5". $50

Polished Brass: The hinged lid opens to reveal the board. 6 brass pegs are stored on the velvet cover which is under the entire lid. Towle sold an identical style which was silver-plated. 5.25" x 2". $25

Resin: This was a poured board, possibly made from a product known as *synco resin*. 24" x 7". $50

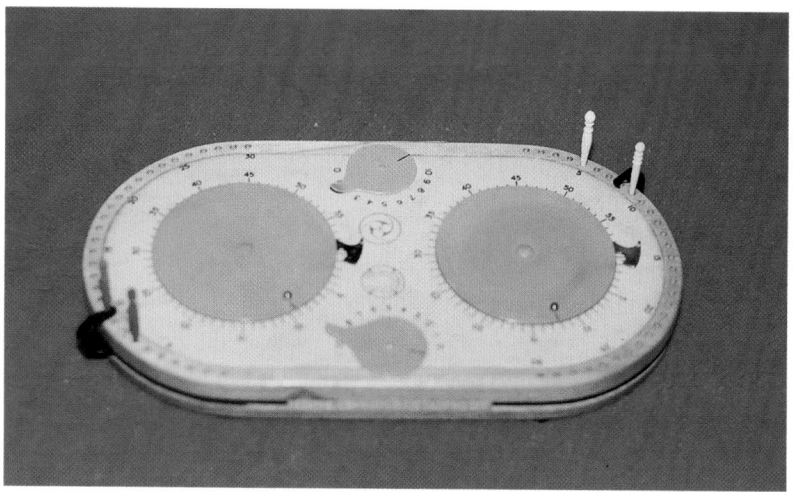

Slip Gear: Oval metal. See Chapter 2 for details. 9" x 5". $75

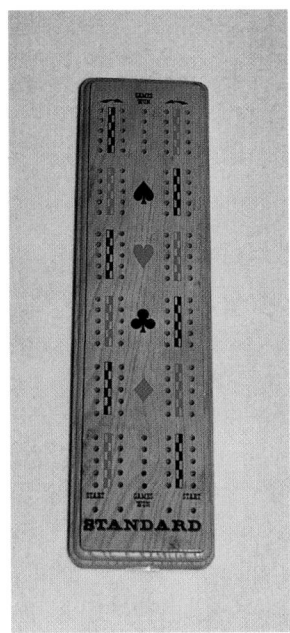

STANDARD: Stenciled *STANDARD* and symbols of four suits down the center; 11" x 3". $10

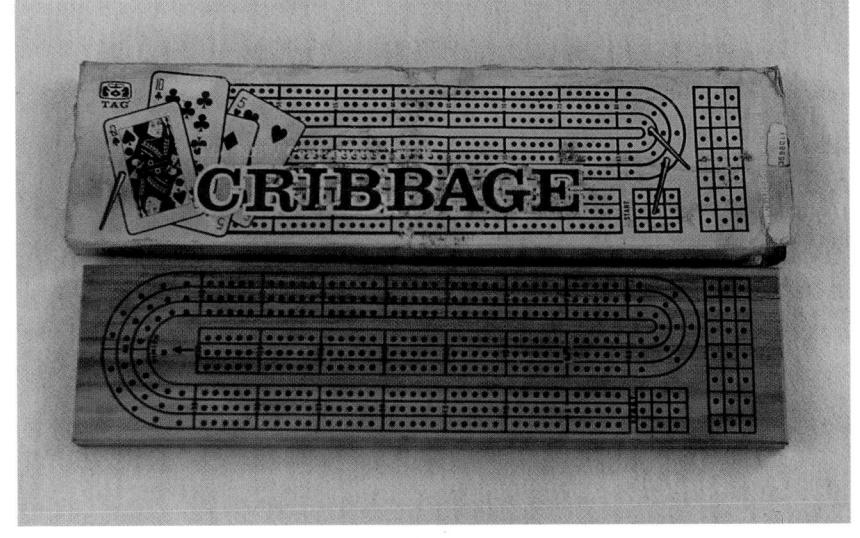

Tag: No. 9603: USA; identical to Crisloid, No. 1030. 14.5" x 3.5". $10

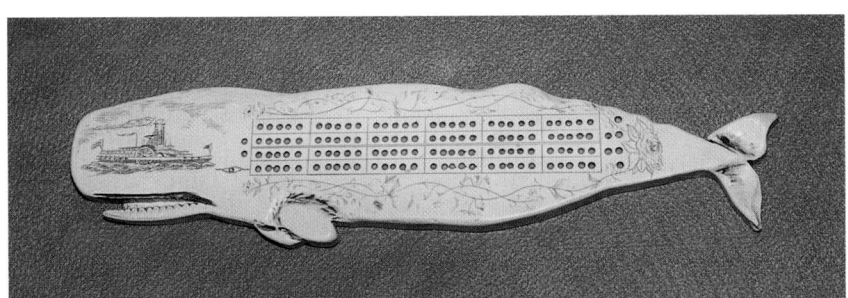

Whale: Made of a polymer; various distributors carried this board which was part of the *History Art USA* collection. Was distributed in the 1980s. 12" x 2.5". $40

White Metal Folding: No. 754: The outer case, marked *Cribbage Board*, unfolds to reveal black cardboard playing field. Taiwan. 5.5" x 1.25" open. $10

Chapter IV.
Getting Started Collecting

The Board That You Learned On

Many cribbage board collectors have the board that they learned on in their collection. For some reason, even if they have not played cribbage for many years, the board remains in their custody. Our homes are full of such items, for many of us come from the era prior to the advent of yard sales, and we had family who survived the Great Depression. We have saved nearly EVERYTHING! If you don't have the board that you learned on in your possession, just check with other family members. One of them probably has it stored in some obscure corner, if it isn't still being used.

Once a collection begins to grow, boards with this sort of history take on new meaning. I have collected many locally owned boards over the past several years, and the former owners were pleased to know that the boards were going to be preserved in my collection. Although most of them are crudely hand-crafted, they do add a certain charm to my collection, and I enjoy displaying them. They are also a constant reminder that the game of cribbage has been held in high esteem over the years by my friends and relatives.

Cataloging Your Collection

After you have been collecting for awhile, you will realize that your collection is beginning to get out of control. The boards are stored everywhere — in closets, in boxes under the piano, or stacked on top of each other. You have lost track of what you have stored, and you can't even remember if your collection houses the Horn C5 that you spotted in a store a while ago! Did you just look at it, or did you end up purchasing it? If you haven't been writing down your acquisitions, then the time has come for you to make a record of your collection.

There are many thoughts on cataloging collections. Some people believe in taking photos of all their boards and attaching them to cards describing the individual board. Although this is probably the most efficient method of verifying ownership, it can be quite tedious. Other collectors maintain a running loose-leaf notebook which is sectioned off for the individual manufacturers. The process is relatively simple and facilitates quick reference of the collection. If the collection gets out of hand, then the

system can be easily converted to something more regulated.

The method that I use for cataloging my collection utilizes index cards, with each board having its own card for storage of data. Rather than cataloging by manufacturer, I have filed by category using numbers, and the matching number is applied to the board on a label. This generic method is as follows:

001-099 Ivory, bone, man-made ivory
100-199 manufactured, not yet identified.
200-299 miscellaneous manufactured, identified
300-399 hand-crafted and odd numbered holes
400-499 divided into advertising and souvenir
500-599 divided into inlays and foreign
600-699 manufactured - metal tops and unique designs
700-799 divided into cribbage games and dual duty boards
800-899 divided into manufacturers such as Horn, Drueke
900-999 divided into prison, war, and handicap

This method of cataloging has enabled me to break down each 100 series further as my collection grows. Although this system works well for me, it may not be the best method for other collectors. I urge everyone to try several methods and to choose the one which is easiest to follow.

No matter which method is used for cataloging, there are some basic pieces of information that should be documented on all boards. The following is a sample of the data that should be included on your cataloging card:

No._____ Cribbage Board Collection Bette L. Bemis
Hndcrft:_____ Mfg:_____ By:_____
Pat:_____ No:___ Date:_____ Pat. Pend._____
Peg Storage: Y___ N___ Side___ Bottom_____
Track: 2Play___ 3Play___ T.A.___ Cont.___ Other_____
Sides: Tapered__ Step-down__ Flat__ Other_____
Board Material: Wood__ Metal__ Plas__ Other_____
GW Holes:_____ Starter Holes:_____
Size: L_____ W_____ Deep _____
Instructions: Y___ N___ Condition_____ Date_____
Box/Cover: Y___ N___ Condition_____
Date Purch:_____ Cost:_____
Source:_____
Special Features_____

Resources

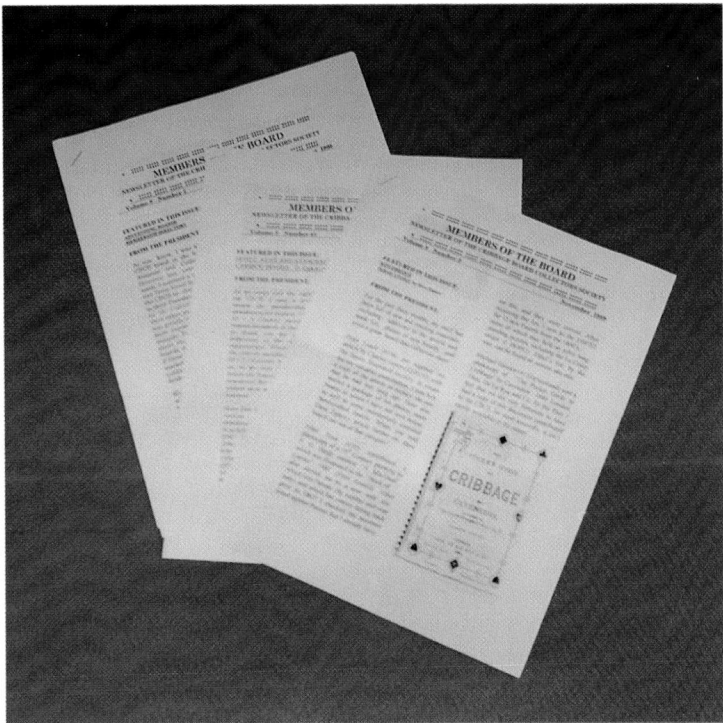

Cribbage Board Collectors Society

As I stated in my introduction, over a period of time I received many letters inquiring about old cribbage boards. Out of desperation, I began collecting on my own in order to better understand the questions asked and to be able to provide at least a basic response. Eventually, I sent out a questionnaire to everyone who had written, hoping that one of them would take the bait and request a list of other interested collectors. My ploy didn't work, but many of them wrote back indicating that they would be interested in joining an organization on cribbage board collecting, if one was formed. Now I was in deep trouble, for this was a challenge that I couldn't resist!

Armed with no more than a few very cheap cribbage boards and a list of interested people, I founded the Cribbage Board Collectors Society in 1991. The organization began with a nucleus of approximately 25 Charter members, and it has grown slowly, but steadily, ever since. As the founder, I wasn't really certain about the direction the club should take, nor were the original members. We had no archives with which to work, nor any collectors who had focused on the history or preservation of documents and manufacturers.

From the beginning, I collected all data that was sent to me, and for the longest time it appeared to be just a collage of material which didn't have specific structure. The newsletters, however, and the bits and pieces that they contained, became a learning tool for the collectors, and they began focusing on information which was pro-

ductive. The collection of photos of boards grew, enabling me to send copies to other collectors for comparison. The directions for filing the data became easier to follow, and most important of all, the archives grew. One collector, Tom O' Gara, even scoured all the yard sales in his area with a sign in front of him which read *Looking for Cribbage Boards*. His finds have enabled him to uncover information about many old time companies which manufactured boards, and he has become a powerful source of information for other members to utilize.

In spite of the general consensus that cribbage boards are a minor factor in the collectors market, there are many fine collections in existence. Collectors focus on a variety of specialties including ivories, inlays, specific manufacturers, advertising, souvenir, metal tops, and of course a general cross-section of all of the above. Some collectors will buy only boards that are in pristine condition, while others, such as me, will buy them regardless of their condition if they will provide information which is important to other collectors.

Aside from the primary purpose of permanently preserving the history of cribbage boards and their creators, the other goals of the Cribbage Board Collectors Society are to provide a network of communication between collectors and to establish values. Without all these factors in place, the history of cribbage boards and their creators would have eventually been lost.

Inquiries about the Cribbage Board Collectors Society can be directed to me at the following address: Bette L. Bemis, CBCS, Box 170, Carolina, RI 02812-0170.

Bette's Cribb

Bette's Cribb is a small mail order business founded by me, as a hobby, in 1987. One of the truly unique aspects of Bette's Cribb is that it carries only products which are directly related to the game of cribbage. As a resource center, the catalog often provides customers with cribbage boards which can't be found elsewhere.

The Internet

As new web sites appear, cribbage board information increases proportionately. If a person searches the web for *cribbage boards,* thousands of entries will be found, with the number constantly increasing. For instance, the surfer can visit catalog stores from around the world, where many types of game boards are sold. Instructions for crafting cribbage boards and sites which show one-of-a-kind cribbage boards can also be accessed. The value of the Internet in making items such as cribbage boards more available to the general public will increase ten-fold as time goes by, and this valuable tool will become as commonly used as the television set.

One of the web sites which has provided me with important data on cribbage boards is the IBM Patent Server. Listing all patents that have been assigned since 1971, the cribbage board patents also contain many reference numbers for game boards which date back to the mid-1800s. In the listing of patents granted since 1971, the complete patents are shown, including the sketches which were provided with the patent applications.

The American Cribbage Congress (ACC)

The American Cribbage Congress was founded in 1979 in Raleigh, North Carolina, by a group of ten men who were concerned about the cribbage rule variations that existed in tournament play across the country. Although its primary goals relate directly to the game play of cribbage, the ACC has proven to be a valuable resource for other subjects generally associated with the game, including cribbage boards. Its web site provides the general public with direct access to many cribbage-related topics.

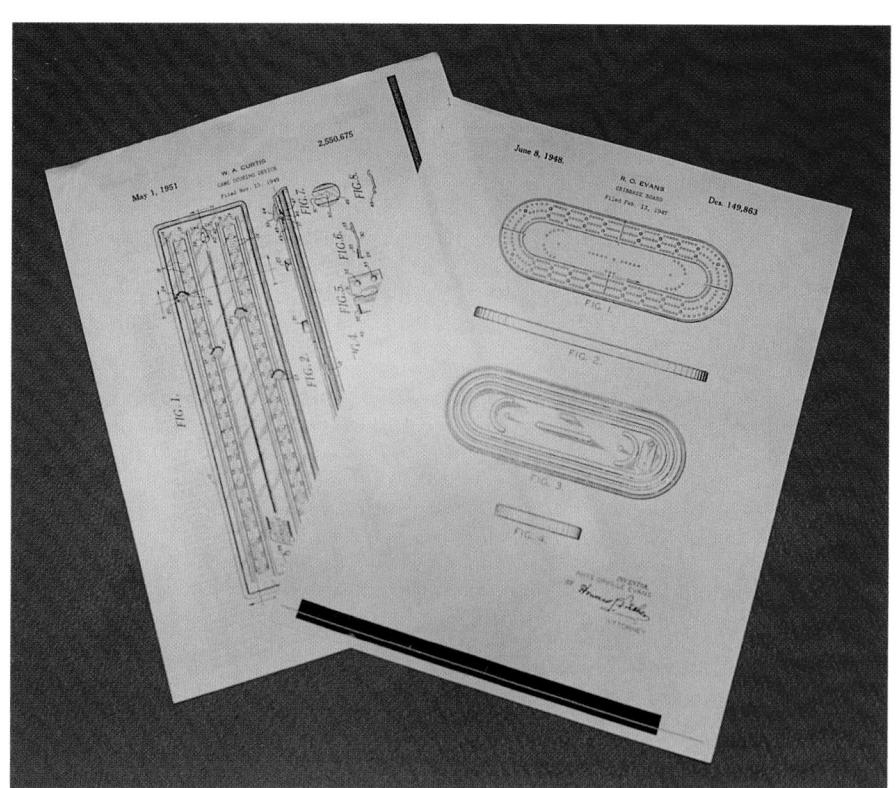

Compendia

Cribbage Board Manufacturers and Distributors (American and Foreign)

At least 150 manufacturers and distributors of cribbage boards have been identified, and the list is constantly growing as new data surfaces. The list includes some manufacturers from Canada and Great Britain in addition to all those known to exist in the United States.

A&L Mfg. Co.	NYC	sold to Crisloid 1970
Acme Ruler & Adv. Co., Ltd.	Mt. Forest Ont. Canada	1890s - present
Adco Creation		
Allan, Ltd.		
Allis Co, George C.	Derby CT	
ALPSCO	Locust Valley NY	
American Mfg. Concern	Falconer NY	
Amer. Found. For the Blind, Inc.		
Anderson Game Co.	Columbus GA	
Are-Jay Game Co., Inc.	Cleveland OH	sold to Crisloid 1973
Arrco Playing Card co.	Chicago IL	
Arrow Cribbage Co.	St. Paul MN	
Artek Reproductions	Peterborough NH	a.k.a. Artek, Inc.
Arthur Popper Games, Inc.	NY 12, NY	c. 1950
Baron, Rott & Samuels		H. Baron Co., Inc.
Baron/Scott Enterprises, Inc.	Columbia MD	
Baron Co., Inc., H.	NY 3, NY	sold to Crisloid 1972
Becton Enterprises, Inc.	Seattle WA	
BIF Mfg. Co.		
Board Room, The	Hebron ME	1993-present
BOMA	Canada	
Bonus Cribbage Co.	Minneapolis MN	c. 1959
Brewer & Sons, Charles A.	Chicago IL	c. 1925
Brooks Ltd.	Canada	
Brookstone	Peterborough NH	
C.F. Co.	Canada	
Calif. Cribb. Bd. Co.	Cupertino CA	1986-1989
Canada Games Co.	Canada	
Cape Shore Paper Prod.	Yarmouth ME	
Cardinal Ind., Inc.	Brooklyn NY	1945 - present
Carrom Co.	Ludington MI	1889 - present
Coast Craft	Canada	
Cook, Co., G.H.	Arlington WA	
Cornwall Products	South Paris ME	
Country Woods Co.	Hayward WI	
Crestline Mfg. Co.	Santa Ana CA	
Crib-Derby Co.	St. Paul MN	sold to E.S. Lowe
Crisloid, Inc.	Providence RI	1947 - present
Cristalin	Providence RI	
Curtis Products Co.	No. Woodstock NH	
Curtis Way Co.	CT	
Custom Cribbage, Inc.	Forest Lake MN	1995 - present
Dave Scott, Ltd.		
Daybranch, Inc.	Plainview NY	

Diecut	Div. Laiton-Nassit of Canada	
Drueke & Sons, Inc. Wm. F.	Grand Rapids MI	sold to Carrom 1992
Drunski, Ent.	Seattle WA	
Duncan's Woods	Portland OR	
Eaton	Taiwan	
Eddy, S. C.	Kalamazoo MI	
Euro-Amer. Mktng.,Inc.	Bellevue WA	
Evan Johnson Co.	Grand Rapids MI	1940s
Exclusive Toy Co.		
Famus Corp.	Brooklyn NY	
Field Mfg. Co., Inc.	NYC NY	
Flip-Pegs		
Fred Roberts Co.	San Francisco CA	
GerardCraft	Cape Elizabeth ME	1975 - present
Gibson, C. R.		Bought Aristocrat and Horn
Glanson Games	NYC NY	
Goodall & Son, Ltd., Chas.	London England	1800s
Goodhue, J. L.	Danville Quebec	
Gordis, Ltd.	Toronto Canada	
Gr. Amer. Trading Co.	York PA	
Grand Rapids Dowel Works	Grand Rapids MI	
Great Western Enterprises	Aberdeen WA	
Green Mountain Mfg., Inc.	Trout Creek MT	
Halsam Products Co.	Chicago 45 IL	
Hamilton Mfg.	Minneapolis MN	
Hanson Co., John N.	Millbrae CA	1947 - present
Hardwood Creations of CA	Davis CA	
Harlich Mfg. Co.	Chicago IL	
Heald Mfg. Co.	Worcester MA	
Heartwood Creations	Rockwood IL	est. 1978
Heines House TDC Co.	Minneapolis MN	
Higgins Enterprises, D.	Ellsworth ME	1970s
Home Game Co.	Chicago IL	1904 -
Horn, Bros. & Co., W.C.	Newark NJ	1846 - 1962
Hoyle Products	St. Paul MN	Standard Pkg. Corp.
J. K. Games, Inc.		
John Gill Mfg.	NYC NY	
John Samuels Co. (a.k.a. JS)	NYC NY	sold to Baron
Kencroft Assoc., Inc.	Buffalo NY	
Kent	St. Paul MN	Standard Pkg. Co.
Kingsbridge	NY	Atlantic Playing Card Co. Kingstone
Kingsway		
Kirk, C. A.		
Lamb & Co., B.	Plainville CT	
Laona	WI	
Laraia & Co.	Worcester MA	
Le Count, Co., C. W.	So. Norwalk CT	1863 - c. 1915
Life's Games Corp.	Great Neck NY	
Lion Rock Ltd.		c. 1979
Lowe Co., Inc., E. S.	NYC NY	- 1974
Maple Landmark Handcraft	VT	

Marble Man, The | Woodbridge VA
Maynard | Minneapolis MN
McCrillis Mfr., R. F. | Norwalk OH
MECO | Vancouver
Meriden Britannia Co. | Meriden CT | 1852 - 1898
Metro Mfg. Co. | NYC NY | sold to Baron
Miller Designs, Inc. | Franklin NH
Milton Bradley Co. | Springfield MA | 1860 - present
Monogram Cribbage
  Board Co. | | 1890s
My Kids Toy Mfg. Co. Ltd. | | Encino CA
N. Y. Consolidated
  Card Co. | NYC NY
NANCO (Nancy Co.) | Chelsea MA
NEWMAC Co. | Minneapolis MN
Noble Games Co.
North Coast Trading
  Co., Inc. | Seattle WA
Northern Cribbage
  Board Co. | Cable WI | Tower Products
Nypro | Clinton MA | parent Co. of Skor-Mor
Olson Co., K.A. | Owatonna MN
Pacific Game Co. | N. Hollywood CA | 1940s - 1980s
Pattberg Novelty Co. | NYC NY
Peg O' Matic, Inc. | Minneapolis MN | 1960s - 1970s
Philippine Imports | Newton MA
Pressman Toy Corp. | NYC NY
Recreational Games | Northbrook IL
Reiss Games, Inc. | NYC NY | Subsidiary of Paragon Corp.
Ress

Rocky Mt. Cribbage Co. | Ft. Collins CO
Rogers Smith & Co. | Meriden CT | c. 1890s
Roto-Score
Rottgames | NYC NY | sold to Baron
Ryco Sales Ltd. | Vancouver BC Canada
Selchow & Righter Co. | NYC NY | 1867 - present
Silver Fox Products | Poquonock CT | 1980s
Skor-Mor Products, Inc. | Clinton MA | a Nypro Co.
Somerville Ltd. | London Ont. Canada
Specialty Co. | Cortland NY | 1900 - 1925
Sport Boards, Inc. | Blaine MN | 1980s
Stancraft Products | St. Paul MN | Standard Pkg. Corp.
Standard Pkg. Co. | St. Paul MN | Hoyle, Kent, Stancraft
Stevens, Jr., W. C. | Canoga Park CA | 1980s
T.N.M. Machine | Maplegrove MN | 1980s
Thermometer Corp.
  of America | Springfield OH
Tower Mfg. & Novelty Co.
Towle Mfg. Co. | Newburyport MA | 1880 - 1980s
Trojan Games Co. | Minneapolis MN | 1930 - 1950s
Vandercraft | Prineville OR | 1979 - present
Waddington Playing
  Card Co. | Yorkshire England
Westcraft | Berwick ME
Western Import
Whitman Publishing Co.
Windsor Mfg. Co. | Windsor WI | 1945 - 1948

Logos and Trademarks

Some manufacturers printed logos or trade names on their boards without including their own name, and research has enabled us to attach most of these "orphan" names to the major manufacturers. A partial list follows:

Trade name	Manufacturer
ROYAL©	A & L MFG. CO. (continued by Crisloid)
TRIAD	ARE-JAY
CENTURY	ARE-JAY (continued by Crisloid)
TRIUMPH	ARE-JAY
CHAMPION	CRISLOID
IMPERIAL	CRISLOID (first used by Are-Jay or Baron)
STANDARD	FIELD MFG. CO.
LITTLE CRIB	FJC (unidentified company)
ARISTOCRAT:	GLANSON
BROOKS	GLANSON
TRIUMPH	GLANSON
CLASSIC	PRESSMAN
AMBASSADOR	SKOR-MOR
SENATOR	SKOR-MOR
STANDARD	SKOR-MOR
WORLD CHAMP	SKOR-MOR
MASTER	STANCRAFT
STANDARD	STANCRAFT

Glossary of Cribbage Board Technology

Abbreviations:

GW: Games Won
MBI: Mint, Box, Instructions
MIB: Mint, in Box
O.A.: once-around
T.A.: twice-around
2P: two player board. Contains 2 sets of streets.
3P: three player board. Contains 3 sets of streets.
4P: four player board. Contains 4 sets of streets.

Brooks Style: Once-around street design with 120 holes. The holes go around the curve to connect with the next street. It was originally designed and manufactured by Brooks Ltd. of Canada and was one of the first continuous track boards manufactured.

Center Holes: Also known as Games Won (GW) holes. Used for keeping track of games won. Each player has a set, if the board has them.

Concave Sides: sides of a board which curve inward toward the center, then curve outward to the bottom.

Cribbage: A card game invented by Sir John Suckling in the early 1600s which uses a board with 60 or 120 holes to keep score.

Cribbage Board: A scoring device used with pegs in the game of cribbage. The cribbage board is not an essential component for the game, but it simplifies the process.

Cribbage Score Board: Another term for a cribbage board.

Cribbidge: The original name for cribbage, as identified by Sir John Suckling when he invented the game. The earliest known documented reference on the game and its inventor is found in *The Compleat Gamester*, published in 1674 by Charles Cotton.

Double 5 Holes: Each side-by-side set of 5 pegging holes. These sets are frequently surrounded by decals, grooves, or are drilled in inlayed pieces.

Finish Hole: The winning hole. Also known as Game Hole, Home Rule, or Peg Out Hole.

Game Board: A board on which the score is kept for card games such as Cribbage, Bezique, Pinochle, Whist, Gin Rummy, and Dominos.

Games Won (GW) Holes: Also known as Center Holes.

Game Hole: The winning hole. Also known as Home Rule, Peg Out Hole or Finish Hole. It was the 61st hole in old-time cribbage, and is the 121st hole in the modern version. Not all boards have an actual Game Hole.

Grommet: An eyelet of metal or plastic surrounding a hole.

Grooves: Indents found on the face or on the sides of a board.

Hedgehog Board: Also known as a "pull-up" or "push-down" board, depending upon the method used to manipulate the pegs. Usually made of metal, there were permanent pegs in each hole. In addition to being used to keep score for cribbage, they were also used for score-keeping with the games of Bezique, Pinochle, Dominos, Gin Rummy, and Whist.

Home Rule: The winning hole. This term was most commonly used in the 19th century, and is no longer in general use. Also known as the Game Hole, Peg out Hole, or Finish Hole.

Instruction Sheet: A paper sometimes inserted with cribbage boards which provides information on how the game is played. Not necessarily considered a set of rules, as the information can vary depending on the instructor or originator of the information.

Lapout: a swing-out arm for a third player. When stored, it is flush with the side of the board. Originally featured on English boards.

Leg: Also known as Street. Refers to each consecutive 30 holes on a cribbage board.

Mint: Found in original box (if there was one) and showing no signs of use or damage.

Noddy: An English card game which is considered to be the forerunner of the game of cribbage.

Peg: Small shaped objects which fit in the holes on a cribbage board, used for keeping score. Most pegs are approximately 1 inch in length and have a tapered structure. They are made of a variety of materials, the most common being wood, plastic, or metal.

Peg Out Hole: The winning hole. Also known as Game Hole, Home Rule, or Finish Hole.

Peg-less Board: A board on which score-keeping is achieved by sliding a permanent pointer along a slot.

Peg Slot Cover: A closing device for the peg slot or pod slot, also known as a Pod Cover

Pod: Storage area on a cribbage board for placing pegs when not in use. Also known as a Slot.

Pod Cover: A closing device for the Pod, which can pivot, slide, or insert in order to secure the opening. Most Pod Covers are made of metal or wood. Also known as a Peg Slot Cover or Slot Cover.

Punchboard: Also known as a punch-out board. A pressed-paper board which had hundreds of sealed holes on its surface. Each hole had a tightly folded paper in it, which, when punched out with a key, revealed a name, number, or price to pay for the particular hole. When the cribbage punchboard was completely punched out, a seal was broken which revealed which participant had won the board.

Rules: An authoritative or specific method of play which allows for no variations.

Scorepad: A disposable sheet of paper with the numbers of play for cribbage or the picture of a cribbage board on it.

Slot: Storage area on a cribbage board for placing pegs when not in use. Also known as a Pod.

Step-down Sides: Small ridges at the top side of a board which give the appearance of tiny steps.

Streamlined Ends: The ends of the board are rounded.

Street: Refers to each consecutive set of 30 holes found on most boards, also known as a Leg. The player on fourth street is heading home to the 121st hole. Some boards, such as the race track style, have a continuous track without a break in the streets.

Street Design: The way that the pegging holes are arranged on the board. There are many styles, including the Brooks style, the "29", Racetrack, the "S", "Z", and "M" shaped tracks.

Suckling, Sir John (1609-1642): The inventor of the game of cribbage.

Tournament Long Board: A classic board with 120 holes for each player as well as a Game Hole. The board is unadorned and is used in tournament play.

Traveling Board: A small cribbage board, usually folding, which can be carried easily in a pocket or valise.

Bibliography

A Listing of books and articles written about cribbage boards and the game of cribbage is provided here in chronological order. David Zipkin, a member of the CBCS, is credited with doing the original research on this list, with listings dating back to 1647.

Anderson, Douglas. *All About Cribbage.* New York, New York: Winchester Press. 1971.

_____. "Cribbage Action Moves Clockwise." *Sunset Magazine* (June 1972), Reprint (March 1989).

author unknown. *Cribbage and Bezique Fully Described and Illustrated.* London: Fleetgate Publications, 1927.

author unknown. *The Skillful Play of Cribbage.* Heines House, 1975.

Barlow, Dan. *Crib Notes: The Comedy of Cribbage.* Dan Barlow, nd.

_____. *Cribbage for Experts (and Future Experts).* Dan Barlow, nd.

_____. *Cribbage Today.* 6 magazines issued from 12/90 to 7/92. Dan Barlow, 1990.

_____. *Fun with Cribbage.* Dan Barlow, nd.

_____. *Miracles on Fourth Street: Quiz book for Fanatics.* Dan Barlow, nd.

Bell, R. C. "Cribbage Boards and Their Predecessors." *Games & Puzzles* 23 (March/April 1974).

Bell, Robert Charles. *Board and Table Games From Many Civilizations.* 2nd edition. London & New York: Oxford Press, 1969.

Bemis, Bette L. *Cribbage Board Collecting; Introduction.* American Cribbage Congress (ACC) Web-site: http://www.cribbage.org., March 1997.

_____. *Cribbage Board Collecting; Article 2 - The Curtis Cribbage Counter.* ACC Web-site, April 1997.

_____. *Cribbage Board Collecting: Article 3 - Once-Around Cribbage Boards.* ACC Web-site, May 1997.

_____. *Cribbage Board Collecting: Article 4 - Lost and Found Part 1.* ACC Web-site, July 1997.

_____. *Cribbage Board Collecting: Article 5- Lost and Found Part 2.* ACC Web-site, August 1997.

_____. *Cribbage Board Collecting: Article 6- Handcrafted Boards.* ACC Web-site, September 1997.

_____. *Cribbage Board Collecting: Article 7- The "29" Board.* ACC Web-site, October 1997.

_____. Periodic articles on cribbage board collecting. ACC Web-site, 1998-1999.

Berkeley. *Cribbage.* London, 1901.

Berkeley. *Bezique and Cribbage.* London, 1901.

_____. *Popular Card Games.* London: Foulsham & Co., 1924.

Blom, Leo A. *The New Cribbage Games.* 1977.

Brown, Frank L. *How to Play Cribbage Well.* Columbus, Ohio: Publishing Horizons, Inc., 1985.

_____. "Cribbage Board Design." *Wood Magazine* (month unknown 1988).

Cass, Reginald B. "Table With Built-in Cribbage Board Has Two Drawers." *Workbench Magazine* (Nov/Dec. 1983): 116.

Cavendish. *The Complete Gamester.* 1925.

Cavendish. *Pocket Guide to Cribbage.* London: Thos. De La Rue & Co., 1889.

Chambers, John. *Cribbage: A New Concept.* Esmond, R.I.: J. Chambers, 1983. 2nd edition, 1984; 3rd edition, 1988; 4th edition, 1992; 5th edition, 1997.

Cluster, H. R. "Cribbage Boards Wanted, Old or Unusual." *Yankee Magazine* 56, no. 12 (December 1992): 70.

Colvert, DeLynn. *Play Winning Cribbage.* Missoula, Montana: Starr Studios, 1980. 2nd edition, 1993; 3rd Edition, 1997.

Cotton, Charles. *The Compleat Gamester.* London: Printed by A.M. for R. Cutler, 1674. Reprinted by the Imprint Society, Barre, MA: the Press of A. Colish, 1970.

Crawley, Bart, Rawdon. *Cribbage.* Camden Works, London: Goodall & Son, Ltd., 1881.

Dick, William B. *Dick's Handbook of Cribbage*. New York, New York: Dick & Fitzgerald, 1885.

_____.*Hoyle's Games*. New York, New York: Dick and Fitzgerald, 1886.

Drayna, R. "Antler Cribbage Board." *Outdoor Life* (March. 1970).

Finkel, Irving. *Ancient Board Games*. New York, New York: Welcome Rain, 1997. Hounds and Jackals, (possible forerunner of cribbage) included in book.

Fitzhugh & Kaplan. "Where Magic Ruled." (Photo of cribbage board carved by a Nunivak Eskimo.) *National Geographic* 163, no. 2 (February 1983): 200-201.

Foster, Robert F. *Foster's Complete Hoyle*. London & New York: F.A. Stokes Co., 1897.

Gilbert, Anne. "Cribbage Boards are Scoring Big With Collectors." *Today's Collector* 5, no. 1 (January 1997): 70.

Goddard, Gloria and Wood, Clement. *Games for Two*. New York, New York: Grossett & Dunlap, 1937.

Goren, Charles. "The World's Best Two-Hand Game." *Sports Illustrated* (December 2, 1957): 22.

Green, William H. *Key To Cribbage*. San Jose, California, 1882. Reprinted by the Gambler's Book Club. Las Vegas, Nevada, 1975.

Jarvis, Allen J. *Cribbage as I Think It Should Be Played*. 1948.

"Largest Cribbage Board in the World." (sketch of a 12 foot board built by Richard Massicotte, Iron Mountain, MI, published in various newspapers.) *Ripley's Believe It or Not!* (1977).

Lenz, Sidney. *Cribbage: Fundamentals and Fine Points*. 1946.

Lowder, Richard E. *Cribbage is the Name of the Game*. New York, New York: Barnes & Noble, 1974.

Lucas, Theophilus. *Memoirs of the Lives, Intrigues, and Comical Adventures of the Most Famous Gamesters and Celebrated Sharpers in the Reigns of Charles II, James II, William III and Queen Anne*. 1714.

Lunde, Otto H. "Collecting Old Cribbage Boards." *Spinning Wheel* 26, no. 2 (March 1970): 24.

Mixer, John W. *The Encyclopedia of Cribbage*. Gardena, California: Canusa Ent., 1980.

Ostrow, Albert. *The Complete Card Player*. New York: Whittlesey House/McGraw-Hill Book Co., Inc., 1945.

_____."Deluxe Cribbage Board Has Inlaid Surface." *Popular Mechanics Magazine* (1945).

Parlett, David. *A History of Card Games*. London: Oxford University Press, 1991.

_____. "Jack in the Box." *Games and Puzzles Magazine* (May n.d.); "Cribbological Postscripts" *Games and Puzzles Magazine* (July n.d.).

Pasquin, esq. (real name Williams), Anthony. *Treatise on the Gaming of Cribbage, Showing the Laws and Rules of the Game, as Now Played at St. James's Bath, and Newmarket; With the Best Method of Laying out Your Cards, etc.* London, 1807.

Rerucha, E.A. "Round Cribbage Board." *Industrial Arts and Vocational Education Magazine* (month unknown, 1957).

_____.*Cribbage Board*. Workbench Magazine 16, no. 6 (November: 16, 1960): 22.

Sellon, W. A. "Round Trip Cribbage Board." *Industrial Arts and Vocational Education Magazine* (month unknown, 1950).

Stauff, Thomas B. *Cribbage, American Style*. 1939.

_____. "Hardy Survivor, Cribbage Champ." *Time Magazine* (1940).

Walker, George. *The Cribbage Player's Text Book: Being a New and Complete Treatise on the Game in all Its Varieties: Including the Whole of Anthony Pasquin's Scientific Work on Five-Card Cribbage*. 1837.

Walker, George. *Cribbage Made Easy* (Reprint of 1837 book). New York, New York: Dick & Fitzgerald, 1866.

Wergin, Joseph Petrus. *Cribbage for Kids*. Ann Arbor, Michigan: The International Gamester, 1990.

_____. *The Cribbage Generation is Here*. Madison, Wisconsin: Huron Press, 1993.

_____. *How to Win at Cribbage*. Tulsa, Oklahoma: Winchester Press, 1980.

_____. *Win at Cribbage*. (Reissue of *How to Win at Cribbage*) Herts, England: Oldcastle Books, 1993.

Wolff, Teresa. "Bette's Cribb." *Women's Circle* 39, no. 3 (June 1996): 32.

_____. "Cribbage Boards." *Antiques and Collectibles* 100, no. 9 (November 1995): 56.